Beyond All Reason

SRHE and Open University Press Imprint
General Editor: Heather Eggins

Beyond All Reason

Living with Ideology
in the University

Ronald Barnett

The Society for Research into Higher Education
& Open University Press

Published by SRHE and
Open University Press
Celtic Court
22 Ballmoor
Buckingham
MK18 1XW

email: enquiries@openup.co.uk
world wide web: www.openup.co.uk

and
325 Chestnut Street
Philadelphia, PA 19106, USA

First Published 2003

A catalogue record of this book is available from the British Library

ISBN 0 335 20893 2 (pb)   0 335 20894 0 (hb)

Library of Congress Cataloging-in-Publication Data
Barnett, Ronald, 1947–
    Beyond all reason : living with ideology in the university / Ronald Barnett.
        p. cm.
    Includes bibliographical references (p.) and index.
    ISBN 0-335-20894-0 – ISBN 0-335-20893-2 (pbk.)
    1. Education, Higher–Aims and objectives. 2. Ideology. I. Title.

LB2322.2 .B367 2003
378′.001–dc21   2002074941

Typeset by Graphicraft Limited, Hong Kong
Printed by St Edmundsbury Press, Bury St Edmunds, Suffolk

For Elizabeth

Contents

What persuades men and women to mistake each other from time to time for gods or vermin is ideology.

(Terry Eagleton, *Ideology*, 1991: xiii)

What gives ideology its force is its passion.

(Daniel Bell, *The End of Ideology*, 2000: 400)

The best lack all conviction, while the worst are full of passionate intensity.

(W.B. Yeats, *The Second Coming*)

The history of ideological positions cannot be written properly except by those who are themselves liable to think in ideological terms, and are aware that they are doing so.

(Isaiah Berlin, in conversation with R. Jahanbegloo, 2000: 24)

Acknowledgements

I should much like to thank Colin Bundy, Rajani Naidoo, Jon Nixon, Alison Phipps, Peter Scott, Frank Webster and Richard Winter, who allowed me to disturb their (2001) Christmases by reading the entire manuscript and both offering me support for this endeavour and making many helpful points and suggestions. I know that none of them will see reflected here all they might have looked for, but I hope that each will see some movement in the direction they were intimating. The company of such generous critical friends is much in keeping with the proposals I make for ways in which the university might be realized amid the turmoil of the ideologies that beset it. I should also like to thank Nigel Blake, Gerard Delanty, Steve Fuller and two anonymous reviewers who offered, through the publisher, comments on my proposal for this book. Nick Abercrombie deserves double thanks for acting in both capacities.

As the preparation of this book was nearing its completion, I was delighted to receive in person a signed copy of *Life, Education, Discovery*, a memoir by Roy Niblett. That gift marks a friendship stretching back a quarter of a century. It has been said of my writing that it continues the tradition that Roy represents. Perhaps what was meant by that observation is that, like Roy, I continue to believe in the possibility of the university and am trying to show what that might mean in a turbulent age. If that is what was meant, I am very happy for my work to be seen in that way and to acknowledge my debt to Roy Niblett, who continues to be a mentor to me.[1]

I would wish to record my appreciation of the Institute of Education, especially the Director, Professor Geoff Whitty, for providing me with a period of sabbatical leave which gave me much needed space to complete the manuscript. My appreciation goes also to Upma Barnett, who not only extended an editor's eye over the manuscript and gave me much to think about in the process, but also gives me unfailing support for my writing efforts. Lastly, I would like to thank John Skelton, Managing Director at Open University Press, for all his support, not only for this book but also for working with me in the longer project on which we embarked back in 1990.

Such a positive collaboration between writer and publisher can mean much to the fulfilment of such a long-term project.

I take unequivocal responsibility for any errors and omissions that remain and any weaknesses, eyebrow-raising or otherwise. I would welcome any of these being pointed out to me, a process nowadays made much easier via r.barnett@ioe.ac.uk.

Introduction

Is the university possible?

Is the university possible? Nothing less than this is the issue before us in this book. I shall argue that the university is in considerable difficulty but that we may just be able to sustain it.

The Western university has not been merely a set of institutions that just happened to bear the name 'university'. The term 'university' has come to stand for a set of universal aspirations, principally turning on the sense of an institution that embodies and promotes a life of reason. We might be tempted to add to 'reason' other terms such as 'openness', 'generosity', 'grace' and 'compassion', but terms like these are a spelling out of what is meant by a life of reason.

With some justification, such a sense of reason could fairly have been presupposed to reside not just in the manifesto that the university wrote for itself but also in its practices, such as teaching and research and the conversations of the academics, *and* in the university as an institution. Reason was to be found both horizontally across the disciplines that had claimed shelter within it and vertically, from the interaction between a tutor and a student to the university's decision-making and policy-making processes.

All such presuppositions about the university as a site of reason are in difficulty. There are a number of ways in which this can be said to be so, but there is a particular form of non-rationality that will be before us here. In essence, this feature of the contemporary university is simple and stark: it is that universities have become ideological, being beset by many ideologies. Ideologies that we shall examine include those of competition, entrepreneurialism, quality, managerialism, research and even the idea of the academic community itself. These are but case studies, drawn from a longer list that might have included access, inclusivity and multiculturalism.

Ideologies have entered the university from several directions, within and beyond the university. Ideology has gained such a grip in universities that it is no longer clear that the idea of the university – as pointing to a site of reason – can be realized. In a sense, universities may not be 'Universities'. However, there is still mileage in the idea of university: with generosity, cool heads and determination, universities may yet be reclaimed *as* Universities.

Earlier chapters

This book takes forward a task on which I embarked in 1990 with *The Idea of Higher Education.* That task may be captured in the following question: Is it possible to rehabilitate the idea of the liberal university in the modern age? The challenge is that of a double undermining that the liberal university faces. On the one hand, its key concepts of knowledge, truth and reason are in difficulty in the contemporary age (the epistemological undermining) and, on the other hand, the autonomies that the university has enjoyed for 800 years are being reduced as it becomes interconnected with the wider society both nationally and globally (the sociological undermining).

Three of my subsequent books have taken up specific instances of this double undermining, namely in the field of quality, in the notion of competence and in the idea of higher education as a site of critical thinking. In each work, I have tried to develop a particular set of ideas that lend themselves to university practices that can combat the double undermining. I have seen this whole enterprise as having a certain symmetry to it: after all, if the university is faced with both a conceptual and a social undermining, then any counter effort that is going to be up to its task has, in turn, to be both conceptual and practical in character. I have, therefore, been trying to construct conceptual resources with a practical intent.[1] My last book, *Realizing the University* (2000), continued this project by turning to the university as such and developed the argument that the university is now encircled by a situation of 'supercomplexity', a situation of some fragility in which the very frameworks by which universities understand themselves are irresolvably contested.

Ideologies – the centre of our present concerns – may be seen as part of that supercomplex character of the contemporary university and, because ideologies are evident through both ideas and practices, deepen the double undermining facing universities. Their presence could, therefore, add to the gloom and despondency that has descended on many commentators. Cautionary accounts of present-day happenings will certainly be evident here, but the story I offer is ultimately optimistic. The very spaces – for ideas and practices – that open the way for ideologies to gain a presence also open the way for the university to do justice to its own ideals. The idea of the university may still be sustainable in the twenty-first century.

Hopes of reason

In the twenty-first century, universities seem to be caught up in swirls of forces beyond their control. They are required to see themselves as part of a global economy, as 'entrepreneurial' and as part of a networked international society. But the mega character of these contexts and their incessant dynamism threaten rational planning and decision making on the part of universities: planning appears impossible and decision making a matter of whim. Reclaiming reason within the development of universities seems to be a tall order.

Such a reflection is not just a matter of the strategic operation of universities; these are not just matters for the top brass. They are matters that go to the heart of universities in their central activities such as teaching and research, for these, too, are affected by the global and fast-moving currents in which universities find themselves. Courses are conducted, and research is undertaken, in response to half-felt market shifts, to murmurings from state and professional bodies and new unacknowledged changes in what it is to be an academic. University positionings and activities appear to be not so much unfathomed as unfathomable.

This apparent diminution in the scope of reason has to be a matter of concern for those who invest hopes in the university. For pretty well in any camp lies the assumption that the university is a site of reason. Internally, the academics assume that their own thinking, writings and activities are rational through and through. The managers, too, like to believe that there is some rational foundation to their decision making and to the operations that they put in place.

External 'stakeholders' *also* have a bet on reason in universities. The state, corporations and the professions all have their own hopes of universities and all those hopes to some extent implicate reason. New ideas, new forms of information processing and new symbolic products – all these and more are sought from universities. But such products are presumed to have substance; they are not to be flimsy, not part of a 'here today, gone tomorrow' society. If only tacitly, they are to have a connectedness to other ideas, information processing and symbols and *some* durability. Such interconnectedness is assumed in universities of the 'knowledge society', for they, too, are expected and even required to be enterprises of substance, engaging in matters of significance through sound procedures. Hopes of reason, accordingly, remain invested in universities.

Where's the universal in the university?

Accordingly, a loss of reason matters in so far as our understanding of the university in the twenty-first century is concerned. It matters, as we have just seen, *pragmatically*. It matters in terms of how universities go about their tasks. But it also matters *in principle* for our understanding of the university as such and for the part the university can play in bringing about a more rational world. Over the past 150 years or so, after all, the Western university has come to be synonymous with not just reason but also universal reason. Through that connection arose the possibility of a universal role for the Western university: doubts about the connection between reason and the university, therefore, place in jeopardy that larger worldly role that the university might play.

Several meanings of universal reason are apparent. *Firstly*, there is a sense that the criteria of the reason sustained by the university are universal. Its truth claims are universal; they do not reflect partial Western takes on the world. *Secondly*, universities are social institutions that are characteristically open: if any institution in the world approximates to Habermas's idea of an 'ideal speech situation', this is it.[2] Any one of its members can contest any claim by any one of its other members. Provided that decorum is maintained, the first-year student can have a go at the professor. *Thirdly*, universities are open to allcomers. No-one is to be excluded *or* admitted on irrelevant grounds, such as financial circumstances, gender, ethnicity or physical capacities. *Fourthly*, universities are universal in the sense that all forms of valid cognition are open to them: there are no *a priori* boundaries to the domains of reason that they might pursue. Universities have an interest in ideas as such. *Lastly*, universities are supposedly places of universal recognition: they are generous spaces in which individuals can expect to have their humanity recognized.

All these senses of universal reason in the university are now suspect. It is neither clear that the forms of reason upheld by universities can be said to be universal nor clear that universities are characteristically sites of openness and generosity. Consequently, the university – as an embodiment of universal reason – has itself to be suspect. In a world seemingly short on reason, the university seems condemned by the charge that its contribution to the making of a more rational, open and compassionate world is at an end.

Ideology

A crucial, although by no means the only, sign of this fall from grace is that the university has become an ideological institution. Ideology will become the dominant concept in the story to be told here and so a trailer is perhaps in order.

Ideology is one of the more slippery concepts in the academic literature. There is barely a statement that has been made about ideology where a counter-view has not also been asserted. Particularly poignantly for our story, some say that ideology is non-rational, while others say that it is a form of rationality. But other conflicting takes on ideology are also apparent. Some consider that ideology is a property of beliefs and others of practices. Some contend that ideology is a macro concept, referring to grand projects, while for others it is more properly to be observed in the interstices of institutional life. Some see ideology as a polar opposite of science and yet, for others, science is the very embodiment of ideology. Some see in ideology a reflection of partial and particular interests, while for others it is an expression of a total world-view.[3]

There is, however, an overriding and separate issue before us. Is the university ideological or not? If we are obliged to answer yes, then a further set of issues opens up. How extensively does ideology permeate the university? Is it perhaps pretty well everywhere? If it is, how do we live with ideology in the university? Is our sense of the university inevitably impugned, diminished and tarnished *or* can we put a positive spin on the matter? Is there a way out that can be felt to take our understanding of and our practices in the university forward?

The questions themselves betray a sense of the story to come, that ideology is, indeed, to be found extensively in the university and not just in its beliefs but also in its practices. Ideology abounds, but we do not have to cave in to it. Ideology does damage the university, but a positive story may still be told. It is still possible to be optimistic about the university in the twenty-first century. The university can, after all, practise what it preaches; at least, to some extent.

Several voices have tried to inter the concept of ideology: as we shall see in Chapter 4, their arguments take both an empirical and a theoretical form. In the latter camp, Foucault, for example, repudiated the idea of ideology, preferring instead to construct a framework around power-in-discourse. For Foucault, 'like it or not, [ideology] always stands in virtual opposition to something else which is supposed to count as truth' (Foucault 1984: 60).[4] But there is no need to polarize truth and ideology in this way. Discourses and practices that want to pass themselves off as truth-oriented – of the kind on offer in universities – can be seen to embody power *and* they can be seen to be ideological.

Prima facie, there is a double reason to take seriously the possibility that universities may have been infiltrated by ideology. On the one hand, universities as institutions may be especially well disposed towards giving house-room to ideologies, their separate conceptual structures turning out to be remarkably similar. In addition, there are good empirical reasons for believing that, at the present time, ideologies have taken up residence in universities. Far from ideology being dead on campus, ideologies are actually able to thrive in universities where, previously, they were largely absent. *Now*, ideology is especially alive on campus. On the other hand, if this is so, if ideologies are thick on the ground in academic life, the idea of the university as a site of reason will come in for an especially tough time.

Context

Universities are caught in webs. The strands of the webs link universities variously to economies, states, other universities, epistemologies and professions. Even students constitute, through their various internal and external markets, networks through which universities move. Universities are situated differentially in these webs, their interconnectedness – both with each other[5] and with the wider world – having unequal connections. Some nodes are more powerful than others; some strands are thicker than others. The currents flow more powerfully in some directions than others. In the network society, all are networked but some are networked more than others (Castells 1997). In turn, some are not just networked better than others but are more powerful centres of influence than others. Some states, some universities, some professions, some epistemologies and some institutions, in being better networked, are more powerful than others.

This is a shifting, fragile and uncertain world. Universities suddenly find the markets on which they depend evaporating as labour markets and economies change. As international institutions, universities are especially susceptible to world-wide changes but, at the same time, new spaces open up in this new world order. It also becomes possible for universities to make their own spaces by, for example, offering new products and services. By these means, they create new markets for themselves in engaging with the community, setting up spin-off companies, establishing consultancy services, reaching out over the Internet to new kinds of students, collaborating with companies in setting up courses *and so on and so forth*. In this milieu, universities become virtual universities not so much in the sense that they operate in cyberspace, but in the sense that they become what their imaginations allow them to become. Anything, it seems, is virtually possible.

Under these conditions, there is no given sense as to what a university is or should be. A university, any university, is in a perpetual state of becoming. But becoming what? There is no end point, no definite state of realization. There is no teleology at work, no particular path of evolution preordaining what a university might become. A university becomes what it may, given its circumstances, its positioning in its webs and its perceptions of the possibilities opening up amid those connections.

For some, this is a situation of regret. What we took a university to be, in its connections with reason, culture and nationhood, is past. This is a university 'in ruins' (Readings 1997). For others, the new openness in front of universities is a situation of excitement, of liberation and of hope. The horizon of universities' potential forever recedes, allowing new possibilities to come into view. There is not one project to be realized; the only limits are those of imagination, endeavour and leadership. University development becomes the art of imagining new possibilities and bringing them to fruition. The only limits to a university realizing itself, becoming itself, are those of the imaginations of its staff, individually and collectively, and their individual and collective wills.

In this context, the concept of ideology becomes potent. The notion of ideology suggests not so much a rupture with reason but a partiality in its deployment; that, too, the realm of collective beliefs has some influence on affairs; and that there are elements of power embedded in the exercise of those collective beliefs. All three elements – partial reason, collective belief and embedded power – come into play in contemporary systems of higher education, particularly through universities being called upon by their host states to play their part in developing their immediate economies (even if such a local project on the part of the state is suspect in a global age, the state having been weakened precisely by the emergence of global forces beyond its control). The growing systematicity of higher education – we now talk of higher education *systems* – provides new spaces for ideology to work its corrosive effects.

The concept of ideology, therefore, offers a helpful way of understanding the university, especially as we enter the twenty-first century. But this is not to say that we can hold to a concept of ideology presented to us by earlier writers on that subject. Rather, we have to open ourselves to the possibility that ideology has to be reinterpreted. If we live in a fragile, open-textured and interconnected world, if it is no longer sensible to try to draw tight boundaries between, say, the ideological and the non-ideological, then it does not follow that the idea of ideology has to be abandoned. What does follow is that the notion of ideology, if it is to do work for us, has itself to become open-textured and pliable and to allow for interconnectedness.

Argument

I offer two linked arguments in this book, a general argument and a specific argument. The *general* argument is that the place of reason in universities is doubly limited. It is impossible, in an age of 'supercomplexity',[6] totally to set all the decisions taken and beliefs entertained within universities on a rational basis. This impossibility takes both conceptual and practical form. The *specific* argument focuses on the empirical manifestations of this loss of reason. New projects and movements have found their way onto campus and have such force and power in them that they have become ideologies, which, in turn, act to reduce the scope of reason in our universities.

My specific argument runs as follows. Precisely because ideology is embedded in our networked life and, therefore, in universities, we cannot do away with it. We have to live with it. But this very consideration offers the more optimistic scenario that ideology can be deployed for positive purposes. Ideology need not be a totally malign influence. We can frame it for and to our own ends. We can identify virtuous projects that can help to sustain the idea of the Western university, even if some of its metaphysical baggage – of truth, enlightenment and Reason with a capital R – has to be abandoned. Ideology can work in our favour. We do not have to despair: ideology can be an ally. Strangely, through ideology, the university can live purposively and positively, even if its situation is beyond all reason.

Ideologies have, rightly, been held to be pernicious, corroding communities and institutions that fall foul of them. However, while ideologies contain non-rational elements, they also contain rational elements. Ideologies each contain a set of beliefs and they seek to persuade others of the rightness of those claims, by becoming projects for change. If this is the case, it is possible to turn the power of ideology onto itself. It may be just possible to develop positive ideologies that can combat the corrosive ideologies now to be found more or less universally in universities. These positive ideologies I term 'ide*a*logies': they recall the ideals within the idea of the university and can inject virtuous energies into our universities and so offer a hope of displacing the corrosive energies all too apparent in contemporary universities.

Plan

In Part 1, I develop the general argument as to the conditions that now hedge reason in universities. In Part 2, I pursue the more specific argument about ideologies on campus by examining, as case studies, the ideologies of competition, entrepreneurialism, quality and, *en passant*, 'managerialism'. *All* the ideologies on campus that I examine have a virtuous potential, that of widening the ideas that the university has of itself and the contributions that universities can make to the wider society, but they go wrong in having an *undue commitment* invested in them. A challenge, therefore, before universities is that of developing virtuous projects – or ide*a*logies, as I term them – that may counter the corrosiveness of ideologies on campus. It is the marking out of such virtuous projects that forms Part 3.

The book moves from being relatively theoretical and analytical in Part 1 to becoming more polemical, more practical and more forward-looking in Part 3, where principles for university leadership and organization are sketched out. Between Parts 2 and 3, I move from ideology to ide*a*logy. In the concluding 'Prospects' section, I offer a set of reflections on the prospects for realizing the programme set out in the book. Readers more interested in the theoretical framework may wish to start at the beginning and sample the chapters in the next two parts, while those coming at this book in a more practical frame of mind might wish to start with Part 2. Theory and practice are, though, necessarily crude descriptions: each has to be intertwined with the other.

It is, after all, part of my argument that the university can never be fully a site of reason and, in particular, can never be entirely free from ideology. But by trying doggedly to embed, in fine-grained practices, the elements implicit in the idea of the university – of tolerance, generosity and interconnectedness – at least reasonable practices may come to permeate the university. The university may just, after all, be attainable. It is still possible to be optimistic about the university.

Part 1

The End of the Matter

1

The Ends of Reason

The end of Reason?

The university seldom thinks about its reason; it just assumes that it is itself based on reason as such. It takes it for granted that its reason is ultimately susceptible to a single description. The university's reason is Reason with a capital 'R'.

Perhaps, deep down, it knows that things are not and cannot be like this. A moment's reflection would force the acknowledgement that running a spin-off biotechnology company, deciphering an Ancient Egyptian text and preparing students to be midwives are inherently a matter of engaging in alternative forms of life. Creating profit, possibly through the manipulation of genetic material; yielding oneself in a form of cultural anthropology; and engaging intimately and immediately with another human being: these are not just different forms of reason but entirely different ways of engaging with the world, representing different values and interests. They call for different kinds of human being. Competence in one sphere offers no assumption of *anything* in common with competence in one of the other spheres.

Why can't the university admit this? It dare not do so. It knows it within its bones but it does not dare to admit it openly. To do so would force the university to admit that the universality implied by the term 'university' is problematic. To bring into the open that there are profoundly different forms of life within itself would cause the university to accept that its tacit claim to provide a forum for universal reason is in question. Reason is now simultaneously put in the service of monetary profit, technological advance, cross-cultural understanding and experiential insight. These ends of reason are not just different but also produce tensions in each other's company: rarely are such tensions within the university's knowledge practices granted a hearing. To admit that the university harbours value systems that are in tension and even in conflict with each other would open the path to the question: 'And what is particular about the university?' If all life is in the university, how is it different from life itself?

One attempt to deflect this possibly disturbing line of thought might take the form of suggesting that this state of affairs has long been the case. Academics have long formed different tribes, each with its own rituals, styles of reasoning and value systems.[1] The split between the disciplines goes back far further than, for example, the Snow–Leavis debate in the UK of the 1960s: its origins were apparent even in the eighteenth century, as Kant implied in his essay on *The Conflict of the Faculties*. All this is so, but this reasoning neglects or even suppresses an important point and one that will serve as a motif to our explorations in this book. It is that the university is now interconnected with the wider world.

Over thirty years ago, J.K. Galbraith commented that universities were 'excessively accommodated' to society.[2] Now, a fair account would surely have to accept that the wider society and universities actually interpenetrate each other. This is not merely a matter of mutual exchange: it is more a matter of mutual activity and mutual frameworks of understanding. It is a 'transgressive' situation (Nowotny *et al.* 2001) in which it is impossible to say where the university ends and society begins, or vice versa. In this world, academics spawn their own private companies and form joint enterprises with companies in the wider society; correspondingly, the private sector looks to co-opt the universities. In these circumstances, commerce, profit and use intermingle with old-style academic knowledges; the latter, in turn, are a mixture of pragmatism and problem solving as much as they are a matter of grand theory. This is an interconnected land of fuzzy epistemologies,[3] fuzzy boundaries and fuzzy roles.

The slogans that attempt to capture something of the conditions of this new order are well enough known. This is a 'knowledge society' (Stehr 1994) and it is a feature of such a society that knowledge production is diffused across it.[4] It is not true to say that everyone is a knowledge producer *per se*, but what is clear is that the universities can no longer have any pretence to claiming a monopoly over the production of even high-level elaborate knowledge. Not only may large corporations have their 'knowledge officers' (Nonaka *et al.* 1998), but knowledge production – even of an elaborate kind – is also to be found in many situations. It is clear enough that professionals, small design firms, think tanks and consultants are knowledge brokers, utilizing existing knowledges for their clients; but groups such as these are often also at the sharp end of knowledge production itself. Nor are their knowledge offerings, which are often iconic and electronic, to be dismissed as low level, parasitic, or even – lowest of all jibes – untheoretical. Their offerings are increasingly set in a theoretical frame and are themselves creative.

Certainly, there are justified critiques to be mounted as to the extent that this much-vaunted knowledge justifies the epithet of knowledge, with a capital 'K'. These knowledges are rarely exposed to the kind of systematic critique in open debate that has long been heralded as the *sine qua non* of the academic life. Nevertheless, they come to constitute what are held to be valid renderings of the world.

New knowledges appear, each with its own tacit rules and values. Reason stands for no particular project, no one form of life. Reason as such dies out as a useful concept, or so it might appear. Ernest Gellner used to say that the big divide in philosophy was the 'Big Ditch', on the opposite sides of which stood the relativists and the objectivists. More recently, those battalions have been superseded by the postmodernists on the one hand and those, such as Habermas, who still run up the flag for Reason, on the other hand.[5] Even more recently still, the themes of globalization and complexity have come to undermine any sense of secure frameworks.[6] The anti-rationalists seem to be winning the day.

Diverse reason

The university is doubly implicated in all of this. It produces knowledges that spill out into the wider world and it increasingly manipulates those knowledges *in* the world.[7] It is party to the epistemological mayhem. If knowledges abound, that perhaps is a sign of the university doing its stuff. Reason now fulfils many ends: it is out of the bottle. But, and this is the second point, those forms of reason become complexes in themselves. They are not to be pinned down. Postgraduate students understandably ask to be told the rules of the game by which they are to be assessed, but the academics are put in a no-win situation. Either they come up with an answer, which cannot capture all the rules of the game in question (those rules never could be captured), or they come clean and admit as such, in which case they are suspected of hiding something. With the knowledges of the academy now intertwined with those of the wider world, with reason serving many ends, there is no straightforward story to be told of the criteria in play.

This, then, is our first observation. The university today is saturated with diverse forms of reason. Even an apparently single form of reason – such as that inherent in chemistry, say – turns out to be a complex of knowledges: performative, pragmatic, dialogic, assertive, tacit and even metaphysical, and all at the same time. The geologists talk of 'conglomerates', mixtures of quite different minerals held together. That is a plausible metaphor for contemporary knowledges. Individual forms of reason harboured by the university turn out to be sets of pluralities. University reason has no solidity, no boundaries and no absolute form. It evades capture.

Our second observation is that, despite its elusivity, we cannot seriously do without a concept of reason. It may not have the clean-cut form that the Habermassians would have us believe; that, if only we dig deep enough, a set of universal 'validity' conditions will be revealed. We do not have to buy the story of universal reason still to find the concept of reason worthwhile. We have to abandon any adherence to pinning down the conditions of reason in any straightforward way. But our vocabulary cannot yield the notion of reason easily. In a crazy world, it still does work for us, even if it comes in many shapes and sizes.[8]

Our third and (for now) final observation is that the university is not at an end. At least, it ain't necessarily so. It may be tempting for some to argue as follows. The modern university is a creature of modernity and that modernity is now falling away, being superseded by an age of postmodernity in which universal reason is put in question. In turn, the thinking continues, in such an age, any sense that the university still possesses an essential *raison d'être* (connected with universal reason, say) falls away. We should be cautious in following this line of thought. It is true that modernity has its problems: its philosophical pretentions to sustain, through reflection, a progressive enlightenment have long been shown to be suspect, not least by Nietzsche (Habermas 1990; Pippin 1999). But, having recognized the difficulties in shoring up the philosophical foundations of modernity, it does not follow that we have to abandon any hope of finding a universal role for the university still connected with reason as such. In an age when reason is doubted, it may still be possible to derive a base in reason for the university.

A full hearing

We are jumping ahead of ourselves. That there may just be something of a rational base to the affairs of the university has yet to be demonstrated. And, to demonstrate *that* with any conviction, we have first to take stock of the challenges in front of us. Our initial skirmishes must not be confused with the battle itself.

Any straightforward attempt to ground the university in reason has to acknowledge that reason in the university is dented on several sides. The charting of just some of that damage will occupy much of the first two parts of this book. I have just hinted that there is epistemological denting at work; knowledge gives way to knowledges which are impure complexes in themselves. But the story has also to be carried into the practices and collective beliefs of the university as an organization. There, too, we see everyday instances of reason failing to have its full hearing.

'Full hearing' is, admittedly, a tendentious term: what is to count as a '*full* hearing'? We can sidestep that question by saying simply that reason is unduly stifled; it falls short of the expressions of rationality that are open to the university. This is what happens, day in and day out – as a column for 'whistleblowers' in the London *Times Higher Education Supplement* testifies. In the very institution that prides itself on its reasonableness, there is a continuing falling short of what it might be. We do not have to invoke a sense of a situation of full Reason still to identify shortcomings in the expression of reason.

In the academic practices of the university and in the stories the university tells of itself, reason is *there* and perhaps even more than it was; but it is still not all that it might be. Who gets a hearing? Who does not? What stories can be told? Which ones are outlawed? In the contemporary university, some voices are given more time and space than others; some readings of the university's position are accorded more weight and respect than others. Each set of comments may be heard in the committee meeting without interruption, but some may just be written up more fully in the minutes than others. A university may consider itself to be a place in which everyone and every point of view is heard equally, but its mission may have already set it on a sure path. Critique of the university's policies or a department's priorities may turn out to be curbed.

The thwarting of a full and equal hearing is not, it should be said, a prerogative of those holding managerial or administrative positions. The academics themselves may turn on new efforts to organize and manage the university (easily branded as 'managerial*ism*') *and* on some of the new presences on campus, especially those of the state agencies in the domain of 'quality'. The accusations are understandable and, indeed, often have right on their side. The implication is that, if only the academics were left to themselves, academic life not only would be characterized by action, change, inclusivity, quality and accountability but also that it would all be achieved in a manner full of reasonableness. That the academics' seminars and conferences about university matters all too often exhibit a silence – that of the student voice – is only one indication that the academic discourse is itself characteristically skewed.[9]

Of course, to invoke the idea of a skewed discourse at work suggests a separate sense of a balanced discourse and, furthermore, suggests its feasibility. But what *could* be the grounds on which the idea of balance gains a hearing? The very invocation of balance presupposes a neutral perspective from which to view matters. Just how much weight should be accorded to the student voice? Or to that of employers? Or even to that of the academics themselves? There are, it seems, separate stories at work and no way of rationally deciding between them. A secure 'balanced' position is just not readily available. At least, that has to be a real possibility.

Sleeping dogs

Admittedly, the university doesn't have many hang-ups on this score. By and large, it just gets on with its affairs, simply making pragmatic shifts as seem to be sensible. This, surely, *is* the nature of university life, much as organizational life elsewhere. There is little systematic reflection that seeks to lay bare basic principles and value dilemmas; even less attempt to secure a coherent and unified viewpoint on underlying presuppositions; and almost certainly no attempt at all at any theorizing on what the university might be or should be doing. Such an atheoretical stance is not only understandable but also justifiable, and in several ways. The contemporary university is such a melange of interests and forms of life that systematic reflection would appear to yield little of value; indeed, for those interests that urge speed of decision making so as to secure competitive advantage in a market situation, it would appear to be a pointless exercise. Furthermore, that very range of diverse interests is connected with contrasting external networks such that the university lives in a host of separate environments. To say that the university lives in an uncertain world understates the position: it lives in uncertain *worlds*.

In those worlds, it seems that the university is beyond reason, at least in the sense of there being established general principles through which sense may be made of uncertain times. What counts is the ability simply to survive, to get by, to ensure that the balance sheet balances. Vice-chancellors don't need to be philosophers; or so it seems. If pragmatism wins the day, they had better be politicians. If solvency is what matters, then let them be accountants. And if it is noticed that much of the challenge facing universities is riding waves of unpredictability, then perhaps they should be sociologists, so as to engender a responsive culture and an appropriate set of social conditions and institutional predispositions.

Reason, then, has its limits even in the university. Organizationally, managerially and even epistemologically, there is no vantage point available from which to understand the university *tout court* which does not beg questions. In practice, the attempt at posing questions of principle or value is normally not even made; after all, it is recognized that to do so would open the way for contending positions that have no definite resolution. The claims, the perspectives, the networks, the interests would all pull against each other. There could be no unravelling of it all into a coherent pattern governed by university-wide principles. This is a 'let-sleeping-dogs-lie' philosophy. Accordingly, just getting through the year, the term or even the day is what counts.

The voices of those such as Oakeshott (1989), who looked beyond the discrete forms of life contained in the university to a unifying ideal of liberal learning embodying traditions, seem now to be of another age. The forms of life to be found within the modern university now appear to pull apart through their separate takes on reason: compare again the biotechnologist setting up a company so as to generate profit and the midwifery tutor inculcating in her students a critical reflection-in-action amid an empathic exchange of being with a mother-to-be. Reason in the university now has ends outside of itself and multiple and contending ends at that. *Qua* organization, too, reason is not exactly deserted in the university but it is put in the service of other ends such as the university's positioning and its financial well-being. Reason is no longer secluded and detached but is local and 'here and now', even within the university.[10]

Managing reason

It is as if the university managers have been listening to Richard Rorty in negotiating this state of affairs. For Rorty, no secure grounding of our hopes and values is available. All we have are our stories, our descriptions; if we differ, I cannot hope to persuade you of my reading through any appeal to independent or universal criteria. My storytelling and my persuading is just that, akin to writing a fictional story. I may feel the pain of another, but no set of principles is to hand by which I can in any secure sense seek a different world. This is a comforting philosophy for our modern university managers, intent on getting by through making pragmatic adjustments and eschewing any systematic reflection that might provide a steering framework of aims and values. Rorty's philosophy is one that would console our modern managers (if only they would read him). It lets them off the hook; it allows them to go their own way, without troubling to justify their practices and still less attempting to form a justification in the first place.[11]

It appears, then, that reason is at an end in the university, but only because it has been abandoned. The statement will be said to be absurd by some, and on two counts. Firstly, it will be said that reason is alive and kicking and is to be seen daily, in every room and in every practice. For the university's practices are built on reason. There may be no unifying reason but reason abounds. That much I implied earlier, but the lack of reason in question here is of a different order: it is a blankness towards the project of the university as such. At precisely the time when its purposes are in doubt, in which vice-chancellor's office are the questions asked: What is a university? What are the responsibilities that attach to the name 'university'?[12] Or even: what are the responsibilities that attach 'to *this* university'?

Secondly, it may be said that the questions are misguided. Vice-chancellors don't have the time to pose such apparently abstract questions, which are likely – from that vantage point – to result in no productive gain at all. Instead, however, what they are embarked on, with their senior management teams, is working out how to achieve certain ends. Ends – such as securing high scores in national evaluation exercises, procuring ever more research grants and developing new markets – are largely taken for granted. Occasionally, thought may be given to determining the relative weight attached to such ends; for example, do we, in this university, accord teaching its proper weight? From time to time, too, some collective effort may be given over to determining or refining the university's mission and, here, larger values such as a concern for equity, for inclusiveness and for service to the local community may have a hearing. So reasoning of a larger kind is not altogether vanquished: there is space for it, yet. Largely, however, the university's reasoning at its senior levels is guided in effect by 'the principle of ripe time' (Cornford 1998): When shall we do what we think is in our best interests? And how shall we do it?

This is a political and an economic reasoning at work: weighing short- to medium-term options; estimating the effort to be given to securing them; calculating their likely returns, but normally in financial terms; evaluating their respective merits; and identifying local and distant friends who might be helpful in bringing them off (in 'alliances'). Research and teaching become projects, to which a 'third leg' has now been added, essentially any other project that will secure a return on investment. Whether, how and when the university might be involved in the range of projects opening before it is a matter of calculation of return on investment in the broadest sense: Will the university's reputation be advanced?[13] Will it gain financially? Will its positioning in the global knowledge economy be strengthened? Will its academic and professional capital grow?

Two ideologies

There are two ideologies at work here and they are supportive of each other. Firstly, there is an *ideology of calculation*. For all the range of considerations that might be entertained, the assumption that matters can be calculated remains: if the university proclaims broad values in its mission statement, then, at any one time, these too can be brought into the calculations. Should it even be involved in teaching or research? These matters, too, can come into the reckoning.

Secondly, there is an ideology to the effect that fundamental matters of purpose are hardly matters for serious debate. This is an *ideology of decisionism* that amounts to an antipathy to ideation, to large stories. Some of a postmodern persuasion might say 'and that's all to the good'. On this reading, any attention to large stories – 'grand narratives' – is so much hot air.[14] This, I shall contend, is an error but, here, the university's antipathy to ideation about itself has nothing to do with an enthusiasm for postmodernism: vice-chancellors have not suddenly stumbled *en masse* over Lyotard and other continental theorists.

Amid globalization, changing state–higher education relationships, the e-revolution, the proliferation of knowledges in the new knowledge society and the arrival of markets (plural), the idea of universities playing an unequivocal role in uncovering and disseminating 'the truth' has to be jettisoned. Just as modernity gives way to late modernity, to the ushering in of a much more complex world, so too the university has to be understood now as an institution of late modernity. Universities now look to sell their knowledge products of whatever kind (without a capital 'K') to whoever will buy them. Under these conditions, an antipathy towards ideation on the part of universities is understandable even if it is neither warranted nor necessary.

We can observe, therefore, that the university is now virtually beyond reason but that this situation is partly – admittedly only partly – of its own making. The two ideologies that box it in are ideologies to which the university willingly subscribes. *Calculation* on the one hand and *decisionism* – an orientation in favour of decision making shorn of a base in principles and ideas – on the other hand: these two banners wave vigorously in the winds over the university. It may, however, just be possible for the university to run up other banners in their place.

Only reflect

Does the interconnectedness of the university with the wider society spell the strengthening of reason or its decline? The story yields contrasting readings. The pessimistic reading is that, paradoxical as it may seem, we are – in the knowledge society – in the grip of spreading unreason. The proliferating holds on the world, for all the contemporary talk about 'reflexivity',[15] are accompanied by an insistent *blankness* (to use a term favoured by Leavis). The optimistic reading is obvious enough, that we are witnessing the continuing growth of understanding and even enlightenment. The new media offer new forms of human exchange and, by extension, of human becoming.[16] As a key institution of the knowledge society, the university has a stake in these readings and plays its part in influencing the outcome between these rival viewpoints.

The pivot around which these contrary readings turn *is* the concept of reflexivity. Does the proliferation of knowledges – to which the university is necessarily party – contribute to the increase in societal reflexivity or to its diminution? The pessimists argue for its diminution. Their claim is that knowledges, especially the newer knowledge claimants, lack reflexive dimensions. These knowledges just get on imposing their will upon the world. Nietzsche, Foucault and Lyotard are among the arch-priests of this forlorn way of looking at the world. Knowledges are to be understood as vehicles of a will to power (Nietzsche and Foucault) and as discrete discourses extracting performative value from the world (Lyotard). The optimists, in contrast, argue for an increase in reflexivity. For them, knowledges are precisely sites of interpersonal and rational dialogue, not in the sense that they always live up to the ideals of reason but in the sense that they contain within themselves a drive towards reason. We do not yet live in a runaway world.[17] In their quite different ways, Habermas, Giddens and Steiner are upholders of this faith.

Where is the university placed in this contested ground? The pessimists would argue in two ways. Firstly, the university simply carries its expanding knowledges. The academics in management studies (who double up as management consultants), in computer science (who are producing computer software) or in midwifery education (recently arrived in higher education from the training school) simply get on with their knowledge practices, or so it will be alleged. Their identities are *in* their practices; and these are practices through and through. In each case, their knowledge gains its spurs through its performance in particular domains. That they find a setting for their display, *that* is the test of their worth. These are forms of life that do not bear the title 'forms of reason'; if they did, that second phrase would add nothing to the description.[18]

Secondly, the pessimists might say that the university's knowledges are themselves increasingly ideological. This, too, so the argument might run, is inevitable. The modern insertion of the university into the world isn't a chance occurrence. The university's increasing interpenetration with the world of work, and its acknowledgement of multiple stakeholders as having claims upon it, reflect large societal interests. The demand side of higher education becomes more influential in shaping its character than the producer side: the academics are increasingly listening to voices around them, inchoate as they often are.[19] Even the historians assist their students in their positioning in the labour market through explicit injections of 'transferable skills' into the curriculum.[20] The pessimists' view is that, in acceding to the external voices, higher education is abandoning its own traditional calling, allowing its purity to be corrupted by ideological forces.

The optimists argue to the contrary. They say that the university has for far too long been introverted and concerned only for itself, with its knowledge services shaped purely by the interests of the academics; in short, it has been shaped by an ideology but the ideology in question is an academic ideology. The cry of 'learning, or knowledge, or research for its own sake' was – and is – simply the cry of those who can see that they are being dispossessed. That the university is now being urged to widen its epistemologies so as to take on more overtly societal configurations is, for the optimists, all to the good. If the new epistemologies are not just social but are also ideological then the university is becoming a site of multiple ideologies, and that must be better than its being under the sway of the dominant ideology of the academics. A plurality of ideologies heralds choice and even some kind of freedom. The new knowledges might be branded as 'performativities' but, if they represent contrasting sets of interests, then they must be offering new spaces for understanding the world.

The optimists have a further card up their sleeve. They argue that the university's knowledges do live out their reflexive promise, at least to some extent. Science is much attributed to be blind to its own character and interest structure, but the charge can be overdone. Science itself has its own internal debates, some of which spill out, raising questions as to the scope of scientific theories. Science is also being picked up in the public domain, such that science finds itself being publicly accountable. The contemporary debates as to the scope of Darwinism (to what extent is it applicable to psychological and sociological phenomena?) exemplify the former; the debates over medical genetics exemplify the latter. Science, accordingly, has its own reflexive moments.

More broadly still, many of the professional knowledges do not need to be encouraged to be reflexive: they have reflexivity built into their bones. Social work, the health professions and even – if to a lesser extent – business and management studies: these practical fields continually interrogate their own epistemologies. Admittedly, their self-interrogation is witness to their nervousness as to their own status: Are they sciences? Are they critical? Are they knowledges *for* their practices or studies *about* those practices? How do they legitimate their more interpersonal dimensions? Do they orient themselves to their professional fields or to the academic world? In a pecking order in which both science and purity receive the highest marks, their preparedness to interrogate their own knowledge offerings is explicable as being born out of a collective self-doubt. Nevertheless, their reflexivity is apparent.

It emerges, therefore, that – as with other issues in our opening explorations – the story of reflexivity can be read both pessimistically and optimistically. The proliferation of knowledges and their take-up by higher education can be seen *both* as the spreading of unreason and as the growth of reflexivity. The pessimists have much on their side and their claims should be taken seriously, but the optimists show that not all needs to be seen in a negative way. There may be a way through, theoretically and practically, that will assist the spread of reason and sustain the place of the university as a key site of reason.

Reasonable hypotheses

Reason is a multidimensional concept even or especially in the context of the university. The dimensions that we have so far alighted on here are three-fold. Firstly, reason implies the seeking and rendering of accounts. In the life of reason, propositions and actions can be called to account and those accounts shall be rendered. There is an *axiom* at work that propositions and actions are based on reasons and an associated *principle* that those reasons should be made transparent to *any* questioner. It is the combination of both axiom and principle that enables the university to understand itself as a site of critical reason. The life of reason implies the possibility of working towards shared understandings *and* an injunction to do so. Secondly, it is a necessary condition of such account giving that there be present an open process of communication undistorted by power or inequality. Thirdly, reasons proffered in support of propositions or actions shall be universal in that they do not rely on particular interests.

The life of reason on campus, as represented by these three conditions of transparent account giving, undistorted communication and universality, is potentially present both in the practices of academics and in the university *qua* organization. We have, therefore, the typification of the life of reason as represented in Table 1.1 of six box spaces.

My key claim of this opening chapter is simply that, under the contemporary conditions in which the university is placed, doubt can plausibly be lodged as to whether the life of reason is being fully maintained in any of the six box spaces. That is all I wish to do at this juncture: to raise as a plausible hypothesis that reason, as understood in the university's self manifesto, is being impaired in each of its potential sites.

To call attention to the attenuated rationality of the university is to point to the conditions of the networked university. *Firstly*, those knowledges that it has seen as its own themselves widen to embrace other interests: the theories and concepts of a knowledge field, such as chemistry, reflect societal and even global interests. Happenings in the Pacific Rim, news stories and even public health scares, and economic changes in the agrochemical

Table 1.1   The life of reason in universities

	(a) *Transparency of reasoning processes*	(b) *Open communication process*	(c) *Universality of judgements*
University as organization	Clarity over decision making	Decisions having collective backing	Reflects a sense of the university's responsibilities as such
Academic practices within disciplines	Knowledge claims put into and legitimated in public domain	Processes of academic debate undistorted (e.g. by gender, power, ethnicity)	Judgements driven by interest in 'truth' (not by any more local or instrumental reason)

business: such contextual features influence the actual substantive character of a knowledge field itself. There is no boundary between a knowledge field and its wider hinterland.

Secondly, new knowledges enter academe that wear their practical interests on their sleeve. Transport studies, business and management studies, computer sciences, food technology and nursing studies are just examples of this development. The practical fields shape the reflexive endeavours. The academics are necessarily consultants to their respective practical fields.

Reason – its criteria, its character and even the shape of its 'findings' – is now influenced by the consumer. The days of producer capture, when the academics could say that those conditions of knowledge production were their business alone, are over. Not that the academics mind too much having to accommodate to extramural interests, for their identities are now much more formed in those practical worlds. Medicine and engineering were long held to be exemplars of such productive partnerships, but that interpenetration is now widespread. There is no reason to think that there are any pure sites of academic reason these days.

Conclusion: the pessimists have it for now

In themselves, the developments that we have just surveyed could be welcomed. They herald the widening of reason both in society and in higher education. The knowledges in higher education widen *and* society is enabled to become more reflexive as its knowledges are produced and disseminated in a culture of critical inquiry. But this hopeful reading is assailed from several directions. Sociologically, suspicions arise that these knowledges harbour unacknowledged interests or that their practical interests are the driver such that truth becomes that which works in practice. Newman's sense of knowledge being 'its own end' – as the foundation of the university – is passé.[21] The very complexity of the new knowledges, too, forbids their becoming fully transparent, even to their practitioners. What are the truths inherent in 'golf studies'?

Philosophically, too, the many ends of reason that knowledge and the university now serve pose difficulties. The fragmentation of Knowledge into so many knowledge projects can be seen as a societal vindication of the sense that we are philosophically into an age without foundations. Knowledge no longer has to conform to certain criteria: anything seems to go. Sociology is just catching up with philosophy, which reached this point over a century ago with Nietzsche. Nietzsche's contemporary heir, Rorty, is simply underwriting the current open-ended state of affairs. Pragmatism is the name of this game, a term to which Rorty is happy to subscribe.[22] There is no universal rule that knowledges have to obey, if only because any such rule would have no foundations: our knowledges can only be – as Lyotard saw it, at least – a matter of discrete language games. When we look at higher education and see its profusion of new knowledge fields, we are simply seeing discursive practices seeking to yield a return of some kind; we should not assume that we are in the presence of a new kind of Knowledge University.

The implications of the pessimists are either that we should give up terms such as knowledge and truth in describing the university or that, if we hang onto them, we should see them as metaphors for all kinds of discursive practice that may have nothing in common. Related ideas such as reason, reflexivity, critical dialogue and enlightenment also stand under suspicion, if not yet in the dock. For the most part, those who work in universities, especially those responsible for their management and leadership, ignore such matters and eschew any such vocabulary. They just get on with leading and managing, thereby endorsing the critics as to the reflexive impotence of universities. The very institutions that might have been expected collectively to address such challenges – *universities* – seem to find it either unpalatable or beyond their resources to do so.

There may be a way forward, both conceptually and practically, for universities. The optimists may yet have some practical and conceptual ammunition up their sleeve. Universities just may be able to constitute themselves as sites of reason. For the moment, however, the pessimists appear to be winning the day.

2

A Complex World

Introduction

Our contemporary world grows ever more complex and so it is for higher
education. Complexity is itself a diffuse concept and we shall unravel some
of its own complexities in this chapter. To get us going, all we need to take
'complexity' to refer to here is a situation in which the relevant entities and
forces that affect one exceed one's capacities to understand them. The
university, for instance, cannot fully comprehend all the entities and forces
that affect it. It is dimly aware of markets developing, with new competitors;
of changes in the pattern of student demands; of changing state and higher
education relationships; and, more widely, of the development of global
contours of higher education. But it cannot get on top of all of these and
many other developments: their own complexity eludes attempts of universities simply to comprehend what is going on. The university cannot even
understand its own situation.

This is a situation of complexity, with the sense of complexity here being
that of a multiplication of relevant features such that they escape anything approaching a complete understanding. We shall come on to further
observations about complexity in a moment, but noting this dual character
of complexity – multiplication *and* incomprehensibility of relevant entities
– will suffice for now. If this is the situation of universities in the contemporary world, and I believe that it is, the university as an institution
built on reason is in difficulty. If the world is such that it exceeds our
capacities to understand it, reason – at best – seems to have its limits. The
idea, present in the university more than any other institution, that reason
can see us through our challenges and it will all come right in the end, that
given enough intellectual effort we can at least come to a fair understanding of our situation, that idea *as an idea for legitimating the university* has
now to be ditched. In that case, does the idea of the university as an institution founded on reason have *any* applicability? If so, how far does that idea
carry us?

Forms of complexity

Let us delineate forms of complexity facing universities. I want to make five basic distinctions:

1. Between comprehension and control

In principle, it could be the case that a university understands pretty well the features of the environment within which it finds itself but is unable to do much about those features. A university with a weak research record may judge that the cards are stacked against it such that it is unable dramatically to turn round that situation. It *comprehends* much of the situation but is unable *to control* it. Simply, it is relatively powerless. The complex of relationships and forces through which this university moves is such that it has to recognize that it is hardly in control of its own destiny. Its mission is partly defined for it; it could not, even if it wished, transform itself into a world-leading research-based university, at least not in the foreseeable future. Understanding the complex of patterns and webs in which it is emmeshed does not, in itself, provide a *sufficient* condition of its breaking free of that complexity, even if it wished to do so. Nevertheless, such a corporate understanding would be a *necessary* condition of the university realizing itself and even making its own autonomy.

2. Between formal and informal systems

Although, in most advanced countries, we have become able to speak of a higher education system, strictly we should talk of higher education systems since each university features in a plurality of systems. Characteristically, each university is an institution in a state-orchestrated formal system of higher education, captured by flow diagrams showing the distribution of public funds from the government of the day to the institutions that constitute the system. There might be sub-systems, for instance, as between institutions that are titled 'universities' and those that have other titles, or between institutions that are permitted to offer doctoral levels of study and those that are not. Nevertheless, for some time in many countries, the sense has emerged of a unified set of institutions of higher education falling within a state-sponsored system.

Alongside a formal system such as this, we can always observe a plurality of more informal systems; for example, in relation to the resources that institutions can command beyond the state revenues, their networks, the esteem that they enjoy within various communities or the attraction that they have in different student markets. Each of these systems is itself a complex, in which there are sub-systems such that an institution may be strong in one system but weak in another. A university may be strongly placed in relation to the entry qualifications of its younger students but weakly placed in relation to the 'mature student' market. These are informal systems in that they are not formally orchestrated by any one body, still less controlled as such, but they are real.

These systems – formal and informal – form dynamic complexes of relationships and networks, in which institutions are differentially placed. Movement is possible and does occur; it may take a generation for a new university radically to transform its position in any one of these systems but it can be achieved. The challenges of bringing off such movement are, however, considerable, not least because these formal and informal systems are themselves in a dynamic set of interrelationships, the workings of which resist calculation. National funding and evaluative systems and universities becoming enmeshed with global markets and global alliances are all interconnected with the domains of work, the legal system and the life-world (through staff's and students' private and family lives). Formal and informal systems and personal dimensions: all are locked together in ways that outwit calculation and control.

3. Between systems and concepts

Systems, whether formal or informal, are intertwined with concepts. Markets, accountability, life chances and standards: all these concepts and several more come into play in the systems that we have just noted. At the same time, concepts are themselves complexes, each enmeshed in a constellation of cognate concepts and taking its meaning partly from contrasting concepts.[1] The concept of life chances is connected with concepts of access, participation, rights and democracy, and this constellation of justice (as we may term it) is set off from other concepts such as standards, free markets and institutional autonomy. Concepts and systems are, therefore, sets of intertwined complexes. Nevertheless, it makes sense to distinguish the two complexes of systems and concepts – even though they take in each other's washing. In the contemporary literature on complexity, the term 'complexity' has tended to be understood as systems complexity;[2] an understanding of complexity as conceptual complexity has been underplayed. This is unfortunate, especially in so far as higher education is concerned.

4. Between relationships in space and relationships in time

Universities have been with us in the Western world for 800 years. Their longevity is testimony, in part, to their powers of adaptation. In the contemporary world, such evolutionary capacities gain added dimensions. Terms such as 'complexity', 'globalization' and 'networks' point to enhanced relationships both in space and in time.[3] Universities become networked both intentionally and unintentionally. Intentional networks occur between individual academics but increasingly as a matter of institutional policy. Unintentionally, universities are drawn into informal global networks of prestige and knowledge relationships.[4] These relationships occur in space, across societies and across the world; and they occur in time, for the relationships unfold over time. This is no zero sum game; one university's evolving relationships rarely spell a diminution in another's. On the contrary, they can and do all expand at once. It is an expanding universe of relationships.

Space and time interact here.[5] The global spaces opening out for individual universities have time horizons but these are uncertain. Does a university attempt to be part of an international network? How long should it give such an enterprise to produce some pay-off? How much effort should it expend in the process? The spaces and the global alliances take up different shapes over time.

Universities are implicated in these time–space relationships both substantively and procedurally. Substantively, for example, universities are implicated in the developing global knowledge economy, while procedurally, universities are big players in the unfolding of the electronic revolution. Again, there is interplay between these two dimensions; for example, the electronic revolution is part of the new knowledge economy both as a *supra* product offering large economic returns and as a key feature in new patterns of consumerism. Universities buy into these new developments at several levels: they package their courses into e-universities, their academics spontaneously generate new knowledge networks, and they assist in the development of new global electronic communications.[6]

As much as they are implicated in these developments and, indeed, attempt to extract new positioning from them, universities sense that they are caught up in situations that are beyond their comprehension. Space and time may be conceptually distinct, but their interleaving adds to the complexities confronting universities.

5. Between institutional and personal identities

In a complex world, institutional boundaries become less tight as interrelationships with the wider society grow. Terms such as 'accountability', 'interprofessionalism' and even 'communication' doubtless speak to many aspects of university life, but they also speak to the university's general situation of fuzzy boundaries. In turn, vocabularies arise that carry the inner hope of doing some justice to diverse value systems.

For example, 'skills' and 'quality' appear to offer the prospect of a unifying discourse around which differing and even contending discourses can consolidate. Of course, there are critical voices from within the academy directed at this discourse but the discourse persists. The persistence of such a discourse amid such contending voices is symptomatic, yes, of power structures at work but also, it can be said, of a widespread hope born of differences, of differences calling for some resolution. Is there *any* connecting tissue in working out what 'skills' and 'quality' might mean for engineers and historians or are their professional practices entirely separate, calling for distinct answers and educational practices? Conceptual boundaries are present but are permeable: some distinctiveness *and* some commonality are called for. This is a messy situation.

In all of this, the university is faced with identity crises at both the personal and the institutional level. Does an academic have an inner life any longer or is every part of it in the public domain? Are the epistemologies with which she identifies and around which she forms her professional identity purely academic in character any longer or are they not also social in character? Ernest Gellner insisted that epistemologies were never the sole province of the academics but were always *social* epistemologies: they reflected social values both in their form and in the status attaching to their adherents. (Oxford philosophy came in for robust scrutiny from Gellner's gaze on this account.[7]) But now it seems that that *social* dimension of epistemologies is ever more insistent. In the knowledge society, the universities' collective knowledge offerings are taken up in any way possible and put to work; in the process, academic identities become societal in character. Academics come willy-nilly to take account of 'the real world'.

Epistemologies thus become ever more complex, straddling different spheres of interest. The academy's older interest in understanding *per se* is not, as some would have us believe, extinguished but it is supplemented by these new practical interests. In turn, the identity of universities and academics as such loosens. The questions, What is it to be a university? and What is it to be an academic?, yield no straightforward answers. They cannot. The conditions of our time, the arrival of new forms of complexity, both generate such questions of identity and render them unanswerable in any straightforward sense.

We're all networked (*but what are the risks and what are the benefits?*)

Through his three-volume magnum opus *The Network Society*, Castells has given us a new metaphor for understanding the modern world. For several hundred years and especially the last hundred or so years, society has become increasingly networked: systems, alliances, the spread of languages and of English in particular, institutions, concepts (such as rights and justice), persons and practices have all become progressively interlinked. What Castells brings out convincingly, I believe, is at once the global and the uneven nature of this networking. Although universities as such do not figure significantly in his story so far, we should note that universities are nevertheless a key player in the development of this networked society.

In the networked society, all are networked but some are more networked than others. Mega cities arise in this networked society that are conglomerates of interacting economic centres and knowledge and cultural production (which amount increasingly to the same thing). As a result, certain cities or regions emerge as nodal points in this global networking, exerting influence disproportionate to their location as cities or regions within particular countries. Key to these transformations are the links between knowledge production and the economy; in turn, questions arise as to the networking of universities. Paradoxically, we can observe, universities' very internationalism, and their capacities to become global players in their own knowledge networks, may reduce their effectiveness in supporting the development of their regions as centres of knowledge production linked to the economy. They may have their eye on more distant prizes.

In any event, the general story that Castells unravels for the networked society as a whole can be read for its implications for universities. Universities are in uncertain times: do they expand the risks that they face by becoming an explicit part of the global knowledge economy and, if so, do they do it by becoming 'entrepreneurial universities' in their own right, perhaps in global alliances of like-minded universities? *Or* do they share the entrepreneurial risk by becoming seen, within their immediate knowledge production region, as supplying a good proportion of the necessary intellectual capital for ventures largely underwritten by the local outposts of transnational organizations in the private sector? The different opportunities that the network society is opening up to universities, in other words, bring their own orders of risks and benefits.

The difficulty is that the very language of risks and benefits implies that matters are susceptible to some kind of rational and near-complete set of calculations, in which the full story in relation to the available options *could* be laid out. Such optimism should be avoided.

Such optimism should be avoided because the working through of those opportunities could never be exhausted and for three reasons. Firstly, as we have noted, the university is implicated in the space–time dynamic of its environment; it is already a player whether it wishes to be or not. The independent position that any kind of rational calculation of risks and benefits implies is simply not available to it. This is not to say that the attempt to evaluate its options is not worthwhile, but it is to say that there are limits to the attempt.

The second source of this particular instance of the limits of reason is that of complexity itself. Complexity, I have suggested, is a condition in which the relevant elements exceed the capacities of systems – institutional or personal – to handle them. This condition is brought about by a combination of circumstances, in which the elements themselves (i) are particularly numerous, (ii) are expanding, (iii) and are interrelated to each other; and (iv) one's own situation is implicated in that set of conditions. This fourfold set of conditions is the situation of academic life. The relationships between the units – universities and their components – are interwoven, criss-crossing and overlapping through complexes of both intended and latent relationships. Some of those relationships are stronger than others, with some universities serving as nodal points in receiving and sending more than their proportionate share of messages. There can be no algorithm with which to gain a fix on the workings of any one of these relationships, for they each work according to an idiosyncratic logic.

The idea, implicit in the concept of risk–benefit analysis, that the effects of particular strategies – such as a decision by a university to collaborate in an e-university network or, instead, to form stronger ties with organizations in its local region – could ever be identified and calculated has, therefore, to be rejected. It implies an unravelling of all the entities. It implies a separation of complex interactions that are part of the landscape in which universities find themselves. If the dimensions at work could be unravelled, then we would not be in the company of complexity.

The idea of risk–benefit analysis, it is clear, is misconceived from the start, but it is also misconceived in a quite different sense. While complexity spells the limits of reason, it also brings new opportunities by opening new spaces in which universities can develop as such. Amidst complexity, organizational and personal identities are not so much constructed as forged through effort. The very unevenness in the relationships within the networked society points to an unevenness of influence: in this globalized knowledge economy, some universities are bigger hitters than others (and literally so – their websites receive more hits than others). But this unevenness brings network strength and new spaces to do new things. It is an economy of its own, in which size is not everything. The morass of this knowledge economy, with its growing myriad of units, forms of knowledge endeavour and competing and cooperating research teams, at the same time generates more spaces for new endeavours. That the risk of particular strategies could never be computed in this milieu is only a downside, in which there are ever more new possibilities for realizing and reframing academic life.

Concepts before systems

Let us revisit just one of the five distinctions we made earlier, that between systems complexity and conceptual complexity for this distinction is crucial in the story to come.

Systems complexity itself consists of separate forms of complexity. Organizational complexity, institutional complexity and societal complexity: all come into the reckoning but there are three axes around which systems complexity turns.

Firstly, we may distinguish between forms of systems complexity that derive from *intentional* systems and those that derive from *non-intentional* systems. Formal systems, such as national funding and evaluative systems, global alliances among universities, and legal systems that bear on higher education would be examples of intentional systems; less formal systems constituted by, say, a university's disciplinary range and the kinds of academic

Table 2.1 Forms of complexity in higher education

	Intentional	Non-intentional
Natural	(a) –	(b) • Neural networks in the brain • Geo-political networks across space
Invented	(c) • Evaluation systems • Global alliances among universities • Funding systems	(d) • Disciplines • Academic identity • Social capital

identity to which it gives houseroom and the value systems that jostle within it would be examples of non-intentional systems.

Secondly, among complex systems, we may distinguish those that are *natural* and those that are *invented*. The brain is a *natural complex* system and the university – as an educational system intent on providing opportunities for minds to expand – is implicated in such natural systems. But, given that higher education cannot be understood today outside the man-made systems of institutions, it is characterized, too, by *invented complexes*.

These two sets of distinctions – intentional/non-intentional and natural/ invented – may appear to overlap, but they are analytically separate, a separateness that is immediately apparent if we superimpose them on each other. In Table 2.1, one box has to remain empty since natural systems cannot be intentional; examples, however, can be identified for the other three box spaces, even if the categorizations raise interesting questions on occasions. Entities in box (d), such as disciplines and academic identity, spread to some extent across much of the entire box space, having elements of intentionality in them and even, arguably, of naturalness. Fortunately, we do not have to delve into those matters here.

Thirdly, complex systems that bear on universities may also be *macro* or *micro* in character: international agreements on credit accumulation exemplify the former; the complexes in the brain that give rise to consciousness and self-awareness exemplify the latter.

Systems complexity, therefore, has both range and intricateness and it presents increasing challenges to university leadership and management. (I list some twenty-seven forms of systems complexity in Appendix 2.) Nonetheless, in understanding the limits to reason that characterize the contemporary university, *conceptual complexity is more significant than systems complexity*.

It is true that a university cannot, at any one time, fully comprehend the web of relationships in which it stands globally; it cannot, for instance, predict the impact of increasing its fees for overseas students within that global market. This systems complexity is beyond any full understanding: its perturbations are unpredictable. But conceptual complexity, so much over-looked, is a different order of complexity. For conceptual complexity allows the university to pose the question: *Should* those fees be raised? More than that, however, in conceptual complexity we hear the contending responses that, in their turn, reflect different conceptions of the university itself. Whose interests are served in any such raising of the fees? Does the university have a global responsibility? Is it to be a corporate global citizen? Or is it to be a free-wheeling corporate entrepreneur, taking its chances in global know-ledge markets?

Compared with systems complexity, conceptual complexity is of a higher order. For all kinds of systems complexity, it is through our concepts that we understand them and it is, *in the first place*, through our concepts that we develop even the practical resources with which to address the challenges of complex systems.

More than that, the dilemmas that present themselves as features of systems complexity are built upon conceptual complexity. A university may ask itself, as it undergoes a process of academic restructuring, how are its professors to be located in structural terms? How are they to fulfil their responsibility towards their 'academic leadership' role? Or even, how is the title of 'professor' to be conferred? What, if any, is the role of the Vice-Chancellor in that process? Is it as the most senior academic or is it as 'Chief Executive'? These questions can be addressed in purely structural terms but, in that case, the more important question will have been missed. That question is simply, 'What is a professor?',[8] and it is ultimately a concep-tual question, even if any serious answer would attempt to place it in a particular historical context. What we take a professor to be in the twenty-first century is not that which we would have taken a professor to be in the mid-twentieth century and is still less our sense of a professor in Kant's eighteenth-century Germany or Newman's nineteenth-century England.

Conceptual matters may be complicated but that doesn't necessarily make them complex. If the rules of a conceptual inquiry are clear, if the ways of moving forward are held within tight boundaries, the matter is at most complicated but it isn't complex. If we ask what is the difference between a university and a polytechnic, we can look at the conditions attaching to each kind of institution within a particular system of higher education. We can look at their differing conditions of governance and their separate sets of powers. Quickly, we can come to a sense that, say, the two kinds of institution are subject to differing regimes of control, inhabit contrasting policy spaces and have separate educational functions. But to ask the ques-tion, 'What is a university?', and to allow into that inquiry all manner of possible frames of reference, acknowledging that the frames of reference are many if not infinite in character, *and* are contested, is to turn the inquiry into a matter of some conceptual complexity.

While both are important, therefore, conceptual complexity is more significant than systems complexity. Conceptual issues can be evaded in the short term but, ultimately, they will catch up with any university or, indeed, nation. Gaining some bearing on conceptual issues, intractable as they may be, gives point and direction to getting to grips with issues of systems complexity.

Supercomplexity

I said that there are three reasons that a risk–benefit notion must founder and we have looked at just two. Firstly, the real-time implicatedness of each university's position: it cannot evade its own positioning. Complexity just is a situation where things can never be fully unravelled. Secondly, risk–benefit analysis can never hope to identify the *opportunity regime* that opens out precisely in a situation of complexity. The limits on those opportunities are posed, in the first place, by the imagination and the will of those in universities, from the course leader to the rector, and those factors must presumably remain beyond all calculation. For our third reason on the limitations of a risk–benefit analysis, we may build on our notion of conceptual complexity through the idea of supercomplexity.[9]

Under conditions of *complexity*, we are faced with elements whose mutual relationships exceed our capacities to handle them. In the medical setting, a doctor is faced with an excess of new drugs, of patients to be seen, of new bureaucratic systems to be mastered, of new performance measures by which to monitor her performance and of quasi-entrepreneurial options for developing the local practice. This situation is one in which both the personal and the immediate systems available to the doctor are threatened with overload. Many of these features, too, are interacting: placing a patient in one hospital or another presents both an opportunity and a challenge made possible by new technological systems and in which both patient responsiveness and widening performance indicators (here, the elapse of time taken to see a consultant) come into play. The doctor, in short, is a nodal point in a *complex* of intersecting webs of systems.

Supercomplexity, in contrast, points to a still further order of complexity. Behind many of the decisions that systems complexity brings stand fundamental questions, the crucial one of which – in our example – is what is a doctor? In the first place, this is the kind of conceptual matter that we have just looked at, but it goes beyond being conceptual. Within supercomplexity, the apparently simple question (what is a doctor?) brings in its train dimensions of rights, roles, responsibilities, ideologies, interests and power. Such questions are not just matters for professional seminars but are also intensely practical matters worked at daily by doctors.

How, then, might we understand the differences between systems complexity and supercomplexity? It might be tempting to say that the challenges of complexity are resolvable in a way that those of supercomplexity are not. If only the doctor had more resources, fewer patients, better systems or more time, many if not all of the challenges of complexity would disappear. It is precisely because systems complexity brings with it a bunching-up phenomenon, in which entities are compressed together, that the doctor cannot get on top of her situation; but, in principle, it would be possible. On the other hand, the dilemmas of values, responsibilities and engagement thrown up by supercomplexity do not *and cannot* yield any definite solution.

This is the start of an answer but it cannot be a full answer, if only because complexities of systems, relationships and networks that are in a state of dynamic mutual evolution do not lend themselves to resolution in any straightforward sense either. There is a difference between systems complexity and supercomplexity, but it is not that difference. What is immediately clear, however, is that the dilemmas of complexity are *technical* complexities, while the dilemmas of supercomplexity are much less pin-downable in character.

The *technical complexities* of getting through the day faced by our doctor are dissolved, *if at all*, by technical strategies (of more resources, better time management and improved systems). Any failure to effect changes in this sphere will leave at least a residue of stress: too many emails, too many patients to see and too much material to read is a recipe for personal stress and even disintegration. The systems failures that they point to can result in a patient's death. In contrast, the challenges of supercomplexity may seem to be less pressing and less stark and, therefore, the less innocuous of the two forms of complexity. The problems of engagement that supercomplexity presents can be put off, at least for the moment; those patients or even those emails cannot. This reading, though, would be mistaken.

Supercomplexity is a melange of challenges. It is, as we might say, *multi-textual*. This may sound abstract but it is, in fact, severely practical in nature. Supercomplexity is theory and practice all wrapped up: conceptual and value issues are there; so too are matters of ideology, of engagement and of practical implementation. The key challenge of supercomplexity is simple: How do we make progress in this crazy world? The question raises itself over and over, especially with professional life these days presenting, as it does, competing interest groups with their multiple ideologies and holds on professional life itself. Daily, professional life calls for the skills of the anthropologist, the diplomat and the counsellor. The challenges of supercomplexity, to repeat, are severely practical in nature.

The nature of academic life, *ipso facto*, brings all of these challenges – multi-modal, multi-layered and multi-dimensional as they are – together in a particularly heightened way. In these circumstances, the term 'super-complexity' justifies itself. Living effectively amid supercomplexity calls for *super*human qualities and yet is now a commonplace undertaking.

To pick up on one of our earlier examples, clarifying the role of 'professor' can give rise to problems. Should all professors teach? Should departments always be led by professors? Should professors have a particular responsibility for implementing a university's learning and teaching strategy? How should a university handle a situation in which some professors are able to generate earnings for themselves – especially through the production of so-called spin-off companies – several times those of other professors? Within a mass higher education system, should there be any particular limit placed on the proportion of a university's staff who might be entitled 'professor'?

These questions can be pursued operationally, so that attention focuses on lines of reporting (such as the relationships between professors and heads of department and faculty deans), on the framing of contracts and on pragmatic adjustment (it just may turn out that particular individuals can lead departments, creatively establish entrepreneurial activities and show a commitment to pushing forward new horizons in teaching professionalism). But the sooner the university brings itself to confront the question, 'what is a professor?', the sooner it will have bearings with which to address its operational problems.

Of course, if the question is pursued seriously, it will expose incommensurable frameworks: amid complexity, supercomplexity emerges. Here, rival definitions of what it is to be a professor arise. Those who see a professor as one who enables us to understand the human condition are not easily going to come to a reconciliation with those who see a professor as an institutional leader who can help the university come to terms with its own situated complexity; and neither will easily form a truce with those who see a professor as one who can operationalize ideas in a changing world. A mass higher education system produces not just rival views but rival factions.

The resolution of such contrasting viewpoints may seem intractable because they often spring from different social positions: not just different institutions but different knowledge fields within the one institution may have contrasting holds on the matter. Yet, unless such 'supercomplex' issues are confronted, even though there is unlikely to be any permanent resolution, any proposed operational responses will just pass each other by. The dilemmas of supercomplexity should command prior attention even though they yield no straightforward resolution. Otherwise, the university will become a site of power plays that are unable to have a purchase on one another other than through the sheer power wielded by the contending factions.

Conclusion: resolving institutional stress

Over the past hundred years and especially over the pa : fifty years, the university has reached out to embrace ever wider definitions of its tasks. It has taken on different stories of itself. In the process, it has not just become embroiled with networks that hook it to the wider world but it has also come to understand itself through competing frameworks of self-understanding. In this situation, the personal and the institutional intersect. Features that present as personal dilemmas or personal stress (such as mid-career 'burn-out') are often reflective of the university taking on these wider conceptions of itself. Individuals become asked not just to do more things but also to do things that have their place in those competing frameworks. Stress in university life is both operational and, although less noticed, *ontological*, a matter of what it is to *be*, to engage and even to live within the academy.[10]

Stress of both forms has a reality to it; it is not imagined. There is overload both operationally and ontologically and the problems that present through both (operational) complexity and (ontological) supercomplexity do not yield to straightforward answers. That is in their nature. They both outstrip the resources for reason, even in the university.

All major institutions in modern society face challenges of both complexity and supercomplexity. We can, therefore, talk of *institutional stress*. The university, however, is in particular difficulty precisely because it sees itself as a site of reason for forming an enlightened understanding of the world. The university has come to stand for a project of reason as such. Now, that project seems to be undermined: complexity and supercomplexity deny that the university can ever get to the bottom of understanding itself. As a result, the university's own institutional stress is deepened.

But just as the university, understood as a site of reason, spawns the anxiety that its *raison d'être* is in trouble, so that *raison d'être* may prove to offer a positive way forward. The university has built into it, and still not vanquished by counter ideologies, a will to reason. This has no distinct form; and nor, under the conditions of our age, replete with its incommensurable frameworks and differential sources of power, can situations ever be a matter of calling forth a particular template for realizing this will to reason. After all, under conditions of supercomplexity, the university's own will to reason is called to account and even within the university itself.[11] But the university's will to reason is a highly flexible organizational disposition, susceptible of taking into account an infinite number of viewpoints and then of producing yet others. It is just possible that the university contains within itself a potential for dealing with the very limits to its reason that its contemporary situation presents.

3

The States of Higher Education

Two theories

There are, as it were, the special theory and the general theory of the state higher education is in. On the one hand, there is the particular issue of the relationships between the state and higher education; on the other hand, there is the issue of the general situation in which higher education finds itself as the twenty-first century gets under way. It is the second to which we must give the greater part of our attention in this chapter.

The challenge before us is none other than trying to chart, in general terms, the character of the overall state higher education is in. Of course, in that task, the issue of the state–higher education relationships cannot be avoided: the general theory must incorporate the special theory. In explicating the state–higher education relationships (in spelling out the special theory), we would have to acknowledge that there are differences country by country even among developed countries. For example, state–higher education relationships in the USA have a different character from those in most other advanced countries. But observations along those lines have to be placed in a wider set of observations about even broader aspects of the structural location of higher education (in developing the general theory).

The term 'structural location' immediately begs the question: does it make sense to conceive of universities as *having* a structural location? As soon as we move from a sense of universities as located within a state-orchestrated patterning of higher education (the special theory) to a broader sense of that location (the general theory), the notion of structure is severely tested. It is tempting to say that the general theory of the state of higher education characteristically shows that higher education is in a state of some complexity. Markets, epistemologies, ideologies, public judgements and institutional relationships: all these elements and others have to be added to the state–higher education relationships and the working out of these relationships is not to be caught by alluding to any simple structure or even structures.

Higher education *is* in a situation of some complexity (as we saw in the last chapter), but complexity does not derive from the absence of structure *per se*. On the contrary, structure – as the complexity theorists remind us – can generate its own complexities. The dynamic inherent in structures can produce an unpredictability, while still retaining a structure. The snowflake has a definite structure, while being of infinite variety. The structures that frame higher education, therefore, do not diminish its complexities but add to them.

We might be tempted to suggest that the general situation of universities is not only one of complexity but that it is *a complexity formed of multiple domains*. For example, the ideologies through which a university moves have features different from its relationships with other institutions within and beyond universities, and these are different in turn from the public judgements that bear upon that same university. At once, therefore, we can differentiate the ideological, structural and evaluative domains and empirical questions would arise as to whether, for instance, these domains are becoming increasingly separate from one another. The difficulty with this tack is that while 'domains' has less definiteness than, say, 'systems', 'structures' and 'networks' in situating universities, all such terms form an unduly limiting vocabulary for the work that they have to do. They *all* contain too much firmness, reliability and assuredness.

Rather than nouns, adjectives suggest themselves: elusive, opaque, transparent, translucent, ephemeral and intersecting. Caught in such multiple elusivities, universities find themselves in a state in which their powers of reason are severely tested, if not exceeded.

Going with the flow

Universities are awash with a particularly intractable set of challenges:

- *Internal/external* – what might be the balance that a university should strike between pursuing its interests as it sees them for itself and framing its activities around the external voices that it hears?
- *Individual/collective* – what might be the balance that a university should strike between permitting staff to pursue their own projects and interests and enjoining them to identify with projects that serve the wider interests of the university?
- *Disciplinarity/interdisciplinarity/practical knowledge* – what are the building blocks of academic life to be in the twenty-first century? Have disciplines had their day as knowledge takes on a more practical orientation?[1]
- *Instrumental/hermeneutical* – to what extent are the projects of the university to be oriented towards material purposes on the one hand and the development of understanding and human development on the other?[2]
- *Managerial/professional* – in what senses can a university as a 'professional' organization be 'managed'?

All these currents run into each other as 'the evaluative state'[3] exerts its multiple and conflicting claims. A university will be judged against its non-completion rates even though most of its students may be mature and increasingly bearing a significant proportion of the costs of their own education: the quality of 'the experience' of those students may have little or no bearing on their decisions to leave before completing their course, as they find themselves on the move geographically or in their careers in even fundamental human terms (they may have undergone a process of personal transformation and come to see their own life projects anew). Equally, the same university may be judged on its employability indices, even though those very students may already have been in employment and may have entered the university in order to leave – if only temporarily – the world of work.

Before long, such 'external' considerations may enter the collective life of that university, impinging on its sense of its own professionalism. The turbulence inside the university is increasingly the result of countercurrents running outside the university but which are now also to be found on the inside. What was exterior and what was interior dissolve into each other.

In this maelstrom, the state constitutes a particular set of currents of uncertain direction and force. Its influences on universities may variously be:

- *direct/indirect*;
- *intended/unintended* (for example, unintended consequences of levying a student fee may be a rise in student non-completion rates or a fall in applications from mature students);
- *corporate* in character/*sectional* in character (a public judgement on the university as such or a public judgement on a department);
- *developmental/judgemental* (for example, encouraging the formation of learning and teaching strategies may offer a positive self-energizing development but yet be subject to external public judgement, which sets in train bureaucratic elements of compulsion and surveillance that undermine the original policy).

The uncertainties of turbulence may cut in opposite ways: endorsement *or* hand-wringing may be the outcome. Universities may rail against the uncertainties caused by a state's research evaluation exercise but, both separately and collectively, they may judge the system in operation to be at least as good as the envisaged alternatives. On the other hand, at the very moment when the state is urging on higher education a wider 'inclusivity', universities that pride themselves on their participation rates among the lower socioeconomic classes may find those achievements marginalized as larger agendas of efficiency and research productivity are superimposed by the state on the policy environment.

The uncertainty befalling a university is that of its currents and its eddies. The university swims in these waters, unsure of the direction or the strength of the currents around it and in it. They threaten destabilization; for the most part, the university avoids submersion, just. Talk of 'mission' in such circumstances becomes cant or a reading of the university's character *post facto*. A mission can barely offer steering capacities: uneven income flows; public judgements at best haphazard and at worst lacking legitimacy; the students now become consumers exerting their preferences and even consumer rights; shifting epistemologies; and insecure alliances springing up – all challenge the idea of strategy and the hope of imparting direction and coherence.[4] Going with the flow seems to be the only option in this environment.

A state of unease

The uncertainties in front of universities are clear enough even if their implications are far from clear. A vocabulary emerges of fragmentation, unpredictability, chaos and even pandemonium.[5] Yet this fragility does not fully capture the state of the university today. For that, we have to go beyond uncertainty to unease.

The university is a moral institution in that the very notion of 'university' stands for a universality of some kind, even if the spelling out of *any* universality is problematic.[6] The concept of 'university' is connected with a penumbra of concepts, such as reason, truth, knowledge, communication, understanding, openness, critique and freedom. Again, each of these concepts is problematic and their problematic character weakens the conceptual force of 'university'. Yet this conceptual hinterland of 'university' endures.

That so-called private or 'corporate universities' or even governments, in setting up new learning or knowledge-producing institutions, choose to use the term 'university' is testimony to the term's continuing value-laden force.[7] In taking the title 'university', those organizations seek to project themselves as associating with the university's long-embedded values. The university is not simply an organization or a corporation, but is also, as MacIntyre (1985) reminds us, a set of practices. As such, universities have their own 'internal goods' requiring certain 'virtues' for realizing those goods.[8] Unease springs up, accordingly, as the university senses that those internal goods are dissipating. That unease, however, has several layers.

The first layer of unease consists precisely of the university finding itself in a set of currents in which it is buffeted. Long-term strategy and planning are made not just difficult but even seemingly out of place: let the university just get through this financial year and preferably without compulsory redundancies seems to be the tacit watchword. This first layer overlies a second layer of unease, namely that some of those currents in which the university finds itself are muddy and impure and even polluted. The ecology of this environment is showing unacceptable levels of contamination. The state is threatening to exceed its otherwise quite legitimate interests in the university; private sector corporations are abusing their interests in controlling the freedom of academics to speak openly; and students wish to define themselves as consumers in calling for 'excellent' curriculum experiences, so much that they neglect their own responsibilities in contributing to the interactive and even astringent pedagogical exchanges characteristic of a university.

But this unease, the unease of the contaminated environment, cannot speak its name. *The university silences itself* in the face of the environmental contamination and on two accounts. Firstly, the university isn't sure, isn't quite certain, that it faces any contamination. Any such judgement, after all, can only spring from a secure value position that constitutes the university itself, but that is no longer available to the university. Secondly, the university has itself begun to swim in those currents; it now contributes its own strength to its movements. Even if it wished to pass judgement on the circumstances in which it finds itself, therefore, the university feels that its voice is suppressed and that that suppression is partly of its own making.

Ethically, too, the university stands unsure of itself. It stood as a key institution in the Enlightenment 'project';[9] now, the very notion that it can stand for any project is called into question, as the university feels itself to be part of an age that is supposedly at the end of ideology. The twin ideas that any institution can take upon itself a project that sets it off from other institutions in a networked age *and* that it can be so sure of its own value base that it can act as a critical set of standards by which the wider world can be called to account – all this now seems preposterous. As a result, so it appears, the university can do no other than to open itself to the claims of its new stakeholders, who extract their demands variously as landlord (the state), as legitimator (the world of work) and as consumer (the students).

The unease that the university feels in being caught up by currents such as these over which it has little if any control reflects its own sense of the emptying out of its identity. The term 'university' is now just that: simply a term, lacking conceptual density, force and direction.

The uncertainty that the Western university faces is real, even though that uncertainty has a variety of manifestations. The university's epistemologies are not merely fuzzy: they multiply and they are without ultimate foundation. Its operational activities and challenges grow, uncontainably, partly because they are prompted by the university's various backers, all with their contrasting agendas (compare the part-time self-paying adult student on a women's studies postgraduate course with the research team engaged on a project for a multinational pharmaceutical company): determining the university's core activities in this milieu is fraught with difficulty. The total environment is too uncertain for the main goals of the university to be identified with any assuredness: the university has a necessarily uncertain mission.

But this uncertainty by no means fills out the spatial and conceptual positioning of the university. For that, as we have seen, we have to draw on the idea of unease, an unease that, too, is legitimate even if it is an unease to which the university has contributed. The fragility of the university's conceptual foundations, the disputability of any ethical stance that the university might adopt (whether in endorsing, or in opposition to, the forces that bear upon it) and its almost necessary activity in going with the flow of the currents that beset it: these are all testimony to the university's part in bringing about its own unease. That the university is implicated in its own unease can only serve to deepen that very unease.

Going to market

Markets are ambiguous in nature. They imply the presence of freely expressed, informed and rational preferences on the part of the consumer *and* of the production and even manipulation of those preferences on the part of the provider. They conjure up notions of consumer power *and* of corporate hegemony. They harbour an ideology of the survival of the fittest, with high levels of product replaceability *and* continuities that sustain brand identities and even brand loyalties. The conjunctions testify to the ambiguities in the markets that universities face.

Higher education systems are, it is often said, becoming quasi-markets in character. The qualifier 'quasi', of course, injects its own ambiguities. We are reminded by it that we are not in the presence of a true market. The caution is normally intended as a reminder of the new state in which higher education finds itself, in which at least one of its backers – the State – is fixing things behind the scenes such that institutions do not start from a level playing field. The rules of the game are designed such that institution X cannot assume that it is equally placed in securing resources for research that match those of institution Y; nor can it set the price of its own knowledge products by itself. It cannot even charge the full overhead recovery cost for much of the research that it undertakes (its key knowledge service actually has to be offered on a deficit-funding basis), and it is also subject to public evaluations by the State that may have little in keeping with the evaluations of its customers, whether past, present or future. In each of these respects, the market is rigged by the State itself.

Both markets and quasi-markets suggest closures, albeit of different kinds. 'Markets' suggest closures brought about by consumers; 'quasi-markets' suggest those brought about by the State. Yet markets also have their own openendedness, that of the unpredictability and even waywardness of consumer preferences. Last year, applicants opted for electronic engineering, whereas this year it is business studies and next year it might even be philosophy. To say that those preferences are the result of fluctuating perceptions of the relative economic value of different subjects in the labour market only throws up further questions as to the source of those perceptions and their substance.

In the internal market of a university's modular degree system, these uncertainties over consumer preferences are compounded as the students decide on their module options, so creating further turbulence within the institution. There may be just enough students to justify offering this module *this* year, after all; on the other hand, that other module, even though it is nested within a well-subscribed course, is failing to attract sufficient students to ensure its viability and it will have to be withdrawn. Such instability cannot be sustained in even the medium term; the market will have to be managed and consumer preferences orchestrated to some degree. Besides, the chemists can hardly allow their 'best' students to abandon the chemistry department for German or archaeology, even if the label of the programme is '*joint* honours'.

Markets and quasi-markets are, therefore, characterized by uncertainties, ambiguities and tensions. The fundamental tension, however, is not a matter of how things work out in practice but is a matter of principle, namely the applicability of the concept of a market in a university.

If a market is a system for allocating scarce goods, usually through a pricing mechanism, a university *qua* organization might legitimately and uncontroversially engage in markets in certain of its activities. A university, for example, may choose to outsource its cleaning or its catering functions to the most attractive bidder. Judgements as to the quality of the services on offer from different companies will need to come into play as well as the price itself, but that is the case with markets typically. Also, issues lurk concerning the general value of outsourcing, for example, as to whether the staff in such bought-in companies will be likely to empathize with that university's mission and its interests in its students. Still, the market as such cannot be said to be anathema to the good conduct of a university *qua* organization. It is in its intrinsic activities where the concept of market presents difficulties to the university.

We can consider the university as a professional setting. At one level, there is no difficulty here: professions have long constituted their own markets, even if they have sought to control those markets. On one definition, professionals are independent, in hock to no-one and, in being independent, they have charged whatever their market will bear. In other words, professionals have signed up to markets. But, still, the professional context is a hybrid for it contains non-market elements. The professional–client relationship has to be in part a non-economic relationship (Downie 1990)[10] in which the professional's judgements are made in the interests of the client. The concept of a market in relation to the university considered as a professional setting is, therefore, problematic: is there still space left for non-market relationships?

The notion of a market also sits ill at ease with higher education as such. At one level, the unease arises in virtue of higher education as a public good. If higher education is a public good, its availability should not be restricted by non-relevant factors (such as the financial resources at the command of a would-be student). Such a consideration has general applicability, for example to one's access to legal or medical services. Markets, however, take on a particular hue in relation to higher education, since universities are social institutions that call for investments of a non-economic kind *from the actors themselves*. It follows that markets not merely limit, on irrelevant grounds, social participation in universities but also skew the character of that participation. Under market conditions, universities are liable to deprive themselves or be deprived of the human *being* that would otherwise add to the well-being of the university itself. Markets, in other words, not merely limit but also diminish universities.

Diminution in this context can take other forms. We have observed that, especially under market conditions, students may come to believe the rhetoric of themselves as consumers and to expect courses of 'excellent quality' to be 'delivered' to them; in the process, they recede from a sense of themselves as contributors to a pedagogical transaction. Here, diminution has two aspects. Firstly, the educational conversation is limited; indeed, it is turned from a conversation to a controlled monologue of provider to recipient. Secondly, the recipient is herself diminished. Learning is reduced to assimilation rather than being a personally authored learning that helps to form the student's identity. A market ethos in higher education is recursive in character: it turns back on the market itself. Students pay an ironic price for casting themselves as consumers.

In higher education, giving the customer what she wants is ultimately a recipe for disaster. We may put the matter in this way: economic epistemologies quickly turn into social epistemologies. The undue shaping of a curriculum by money turns back on the formation of the individual herself; her educational *will* remains unformed. Higher education is thwarted; the university is diminished.

But the world is far from simple. Metaprinciples – of the kind that markets shall not darken the university's portals – simply don't live in this world. Worldwide, higher education is a social institution, the full cost of which the host governments cannot meet. The rise of markets, even if curtailed by states so as to form quasi-markets, is a symptom of this level of cost. There is a logic of sorts, too, to the formation of markets in this sphere, for higher education bestows cultural and economic capital upon its recipients, even if those benefits are seeing their scale diminished in a mass higher education system. It is legitimate that the recipient should in part meet the cost.

It is too easy to focus any angst on the £ sign that appears in the wake of markets. Much more significant are the added strata of complexity that markets also bring in their wake, with their uncertainties, fragilities and conceptual ambiguities. Values, systems, motivations, human development, rights, pedagogic relationships, epistemologies, voice, discursive independence, state–institutional relationships, inter-institutional relationships and academic identities: all are implicated in markets. There can be no complete working out of these interrelationships. Their criss-crossings are too dense, too alive and too recursive in character for them to be unravelled. Complexity here is conceptual, ontological and operational in kind, and gives rise to dilemmas that are not susceptible to dissolution but have to be lived with and lived through.

The state higher education is in[11]

Higher education is *in* the state but not *of* the state, at least not yet. In Althusser's (1971) schema, universities could be seen as an 'ideological state apparatus'.[12] This apparatus acted by fulfilling the state's mission subtly, with those who worked in it 'interpellating' the state's ideologies such that they came to be ideological carriers. This structural perspective was too absolute to be convincing. Was Althusser himself – as a state employee – an ideological carrier? Were his writings representative of a state ideology? And if it was possible for Althusser to extract himself from the state's vice-like grip, how was it not possible for others to do so? If they could do so, how much force did the university-as-ideological-state-apparatus have? Rather little, it seemed.

With, on the one hand, the murmurings of French poststructural and postmodern thought, which has insisted on the particular and the 'genealogical' within the local, *and*, on the other hand, an anthropological turn in higher education studies in which the specific practices that form individuals' academic identities have come to claim attention, the framing of higher education as a state enterprise faces its apparent *dénouement*. The local and the particular may seem to point to a more helpful set of descriptive categories in understanding the contemporary university than the totalizing idea of the 'state apparatus'; this conceptual juxtaposition, however, is misleading.

The point is that we are not in the presence of a zero-sum game. It is possible for the room for manoeuvre of the academic community itself to be increasing *and* for the powers and the influence of the state to be increasing. It may, indeed, be part of the state's agenda to be working in just that way, to free the academic community from any traditional and apparently constraining practices of its own so that, for instance, it can work within freer markets. The state may feel that it has a part to play in, for instance, establishing the conditions under which academics' intellectual products can be 'transferred' to the market for technological and economic gain, even if such technological transfer also means establishing the conditions under which those products can be staked out as 'intellectual property'.

The university comes to move in spaces that it only partly constructs for itself. Those spaces are framed by wider societal – national and global – forces. States play their parts, both directly, in framing the conditions under which universities work, and indirectly, in working with the world of work (especially its high technological segments), *and* in cross-national alliances (for example, over the recognition of academic qualifications). The powers and the influence of the state grow but, to repeat, we are not necessarily seeing a reduction in the scope of university activity. To the contrary, it may be opening out.

The key issue here is whether we can say that we are in the presence of a state agenda such that universities come to construct themselves anew through that agenda. Among the favoured terms of that reading are those of economic growth (Salter and Tapper 1994), performativity (Lyotard 1984), managerialism (Morley 2002), excellence (Readings 1997) and instrumental reason (Blake *et al.* 1998). The underlying angst in these charges as to the character of the state–higher education relationship is evident in a sense of a lack of trust by the state towards universities, especially as it seems in the UK to those viewing the matter from a transatlantic perspective (Trow 1992).[13]

If the state is working its wonders to perform, it does not need to do it overtly; slyness, after all, is often the character of ideological processes. They have all the more power when they are surreptitious, especially when individuals and institutions come to project inwards the state's agendas and so assimilate those agendas that they come to constitute themselves through them. Following Foucault, Jeremy Bentham's spectre of the Panopticon is often wheeled out (metaphorically speaking), but that measure of surveillance is hardly necessary if the inmates are policing themselves.

Against this background, the Jeremiahs talk of the loss of academic freedom. But we should open ourselves to the possibility that academic freedom may be expanding. There may be more space to recruit non-traditional students, to start up businesses, to run up debts in raising capital for new residences, to travel abroad, to engage via the internet with world-wide communities and, generally, to take on multiple agendas and identities. In any discussion of academic freedom, therefore, we need to distinguish kinds of academic freedom. The question at once forms itself: Are universities and their academics, in exploiting these new freedoms (if, indeed, they are present), engaged on their own internal agendas or have they internalized the state's agendas? Are these the freedoms of the lion in the jungle or the lion in the circus?

The question, though, makes an assumption. It assumes that we can distinguish, as it were, between the agendas of the state and those of academe. However, once we allow that the state's agendas may be internalized by universities and academics, then the distinction is in difficulty.

For example, a university may drive forward a project determined to foster students' key skills: curricula, credit arrangements and assessment procedures (complete with profiles) may be developed. It may even do this in the wake of government pronouncements, funded projects and reports, and quality evaluations mounted by government agencies (in the UK, in relation both to taught courses through the Quality Assurance Agency and to research degree students through the Research Councils). How is such a programme on the part of the university to be interpreted? *There is no unambiguous reading available to us.*

Stories of (i) a policy framework increasingly controlled by the state (and of the universities becoming part of the state apparatus), of (ii) higher education coming belatedly to take seriously teaching matters (and for universities, thereby, to exercise their academic autonomy), of (iii) an undue genuflexion in the direction of work (an ideology of vocationalism), and of (iv) academics developing their academic professionalism (a story of academic freedom) may all jostle with each other. Simply to say, too, that they may all have some right on their sides only poses more problems because some of those stories conflict with each other. Yet this is precisely the situation in which universities find themselves, that of multiple and contending legitimate interpretations.

At the very moment that the state appears to be expanding its powers and influence towards universities, so the scope for universities grows. The charge that universities are merely internalizing a state's agendas and have become part of the state ideological apparatus does not bear much weight. It can also be said that universities are freeing themselves from their own self-imposed and even ideological agendas. Their talk of academic freedom, truth, knowledge and academic authority is simply a story to write the world in outworn terms, and many universities and many groups of academics are putting aside those self-representations. Nor is it in the state's interests to circumscribe universities too narrowly. That, in the UK, a state agency (the Quality Assurance Agency for Higher Education) has been doing just that is simply testimony to a lack of both 'joined-up' thinking and policy framing within the state.[14]

Just as with markets, then, the presence of the state introduces layerings of complexities that are conceptual, ontological and operational in character. Multiple readings of the state–higher education relationship are possible, not only from the outside but also from the inside for those in universities. Daily, alternative self-reflexive stories are possible, legitimate and credible, *and* are offered. At one level, this interpretative openness is an empirical matter: it is just rather tricky disentangling all the elements at work. But more fundamentally, this is a matter of the way things inescapably are now. Incommensurable self-readings are signs not so much of confusion, hesitancy or insecurity, but of the multiple and contested readings to which the university's swirling currents inevitably give rise.

Elusive identities

The university, then, moves in spaces that it only partly constructs. Its relationships with its host state are only part of that picture, even if they are taking on a more insistent shape. Its key activities – research, teaching and putting knowledge to use in consultancies, and its being a civic resource – are configured in turn by vigorous currents that swirl around it. These currents include the widening of epistemologies, markets, inter-institutional relationships and state relationships. The intersecting of key activities with these wider currents produces, for each university, an *institutional identity*. It is clear that this identity is not just dynamic but what else it is cannot be captured in any simple way, either by the institution itself (whether in its mission statement or its corporate plan) or by interested observers (such as state agencies). A university turns out to be itself numerous swirls, some flowing into each other and others keeping their distance.

Figure 3.1   Structure of institutional identity

	Epistemologies	Markets	
Research			*Diversity*
Teaching	**Institutional Identity**		*Resources*
Knowledge-in-use			*Participation*
Civic engagement			*Entrepreneurialism*
	Institutional Relationships	The State	

We have, then, something like the configuration in Figure 3.1. The four outer markers – epistemologies, markets, the state and institutional relationships – constitute four domains that significantly structure an institution's identity. But to state the matter in these terms and to attempt to capture such features diagrammatically are to render simple and static what is a complex and dynamic situation. Each of these moments has different strengths and each works both independently of the others and in relationship to them. Expansion in one may not result in the diminution of another. The state may encourage the expansion of markets, institutional relationships and even epistemologies.

On the left-hand side are the university's key activities, the character of which reflects the university's identity but the working through of which also helps to constitute that identity. On the right-hand side appear just a few of the many pressing 'issues' that concern the sector as a whole and to which each university will find its own response. Within a multifaculty university, there may be several responses to any one issue. The single university turns out to contain a multitude of identities. Gilbert Ryle posed a nice philosophical question: Where is the University of Oxford? His point was that we can make intelligible utterances about an entity such as the University of Oxford even though it cannot be identified in any straightforward way. It is not to be identified by walking around Oxford with a map of the University's colleges in one's hand. What is clear, however, is that when we talk of the University of Oxford, we are not talking of the University of Cambridge (or any other particular university). 'University identity' may be elusive, but it is not, thereby, an idea that we should discard.

Conclusion: the limits of 'Foresight'

In the UK, the government has set in hand, in several of its departments, a Foresight initiative.[15] Foresight initiatives are intended to identify developments in the wider society or even globally that affect the enterprise in question (transport, health, defence) and, on that basis, to work out potential scenarios for the future on which sound planning can take place. Some universities are engaging in Foresight-like initiatives, attempting to chart the state of the world that bears on them. Such exercises are not misguided but their name is misleading. Foresight is not available, if it is taken to mean a capacity for seeing in advance what is likely to transpire. In the networked world in which the university is placed, the variables are too many, and their interrelationships too dense, for such prior knowledge to be possible.

A response will be that, on the basis of the available intelligence, a number of plausible scenarios could be developed. The difficulty here concerns the status of such scenarios. The university is beset with the limits of reason: amid uncertain ontologies, epistemologies, expectations and responsibilities, any so-called scenario has to be a work of fiction or of hope. It is an imaginative reconstruction, and simplified at that, of a possible situation in which the university might find itself. To invoke the idea of 'the future' conveys an unwarranted substance to any scenario. Reason runs up against its limits not so much through the difficulty of seeing into the future but more in attempting to describe the world in which the university finds itself. The problem lies not in trying to dress up a future scenario as a 'projection' of the future but in the tacit implication that it is even possible fully to describe the world in which the university struggles to survive.

The vortices that propel a university this way and that do not stop it trying to catch its breath to give itself some direction, but they rob a university of even the fiction of maintaining any particular direction. They also rob a university even of describing itself, its character and its conditions. An infinity of descriptions and interpretations is in front of every university. The state itself shapes the range of plausible descriptions, attempts to arbitrate among possible descriptions and even tries to impose its own descriptions (not least in its public judgements of universities). But it is only one actor and it frequently utters messages with different voices even of the same institution. The state that higher education is in is elusive; more accurately, the states higher education is in are sets of elusivities. Their description exceeds the university's reason.

Among the currents with which the university contends, some run more swiftly than others. These are ideologies and it is to them that we should now turn.

4

The End of Ideology?

The end of the idea of ideology

Many have been telling us that ideology is at end. We live, we are told, in a post-ideological age; in an age without ideology. Different stories are adduced to lead to this proposition.

For some of a postmodern persuasion,[1] a line of thought can be observed as having something like the following four steps:

1. An ideology harbours a large claim or claims about the world – 'a grand narrative'.
2. Large stories claim some kind of universality, some attempt to construe and even reconstruct the world in a particular image.
3. In a world without foundations (a fundamental postmodern belief), we are left with only local or particular stories ('paralogies' as Lyotard called them).
4. Ideologies, therefore, have no location from which to gain a purchase: they are like dinosaurs whose environment has overtaken them and that are bound to die.

Such a line of reasoning contains four questionable assumptions. Firstly, it assumes that ideologies are grand affairs; secondly, it assumes that ideologies cannot exist in a post-foundational world; thirdly, it assumes that the stories in the world are of equal weight and that none is seeking to extinguish any of the others; and, fourthly, it assumes that each local discourse is discrete unto itself. Each of these four assumptions is suspect. Even in a post-foundational world, there is room, lots of room, for ideology.

A second critique calls into question the concept of ideology itself, at least as it has been depicted in its classic formulations. A key concept in the story of ideology is that of false consciousness, the idea that a community or a group could fall into a deluded state about itself. The working class could come to believe that the social order was preordained: 'the rich man in his castle, the poor man at his gate'. Many counter-claims have been made to the effect that the whole idea of false consciousness is misguided or muddled.

If a community could be suspected of falling into the mass deception implied by the idea of false consciousness, questions would arise as to whether that deception was voluntary or involuntary. If the former, we would be in the presence of a cult, not a community *willing* to undergo self-transformation; if the latter, we would be in the presence of a mass hypnosis, not a community *capable* of undergoing self-transformation. In either case, there would be no possibility of obtaining release from the deluded state in question. Furthermore, the prefix 'false' implies the availability of some independent point, from which a 'true' consciousness could be identified and which could serve as the consciousness towards which this benighted community should be heading; but how, amid 'false consciousness', would such a non-ideological position be possible?

The notion of false consciousness will not bear much weight, therefore. But a repudiation of the notion of false consciousness need not lead to the end of the idea of ideology. The idea of false consciousness is not a necessary component of ideology. While an ideology makes truth claims, it does not necessarily entail a total *Zeitgeist* of the kind implied by 'false consciousness'. Ideology can be a much more local affair. It can have a specific *locale*; for example, universities may turn out to be just such a site of ideology.

Yet other efforts to put paid to the notion of ideology have been variously sociological (Bell 2000) and historical (Fukuyama 1992). On the one hand, it is suggested that, with the collapse of Marxist-inspired politics and societal arrangements, large political ideas are 'exhausted' and 'have lost their . . . power to persuade' (Bell 2000: 402).[2] We are, therefore, at the end of ideology. On the other hand, it is suggested that we have reached a state of political maturity that has taken global politics beyond nationalism (the last vestiges of which on a grand scale was the Cold War). There is now 'a . . . consensus concerning the legitimacy of liberal democracy . . . as it conquered rival ideologies like hereditary monarchy, fascism, and most recently communism' (Fukuyama 1992: xi). Here, history is at an end in the sense that society, through liberal democracy, has achieved its apogee: there is nowhere further and certainly nowhere higher for society to go.

On either account, ideology is passé, a stage of social evolution beyond which we have thankfully progressed. We have emerged into the sunny uplands,[3] free of dogma, non-rationalism and downright dangerous societal beliefs. Now we live in a non-ideological age, characterized by reason, pragmatism and even progress. That, at any rate, is one set of views on the matter, a set of views, indeed, that we might be tempted to adopt in relation to higher education.[4]

Ideology on campus: an end without a beginning?

It is apparent that the theory of ideology is a large and complex set of understandings. It constitutes a literature that has grown steadily over 200 years. Its origins, by all accounts, seem fairly well established: in 1797, in the wake of the French Revolution, de Tracy coined the term 'ideology' to refer to a new science of thought that he sought to establish. The Institut de France that de Tracy founded quickly came to be the home of a group of 'ideologues', as they became known. In turn, Napoleon turned the latter word into a term of abuse in pouring scorn on the group: for him, they were wasting their and everyone else's time, spending effort on intellectual labours that could have no practical value (except, perhaps, to offer the seeds of a critique of his grand projects).[5] The earliest and perhaps most famous classic statement on the term was that of Marx and Engels, whose extended essay on *The German Ideology* began a literature that was to run until the present time. *The German Ideology*, in fact, owed at least as much to Napoleon's position as to that of de Tracy, for Marx and Engels argued that in an ideology the world was turned upside down. Those who fell under the sway of an ideology were not living in the real world: it was in the interests of the ruling class that the world be misrepresented.[6]

So began a literature that was to last 200 years. The question is: Is that literature at an end? As we have seen, many are trying to put it in its coffin. Both philosophically and more empirically, we are repeatedly told that the idea of ideology can do no useful work for us. If we have reached the end of ideology, we have also reached the end of the idea of ideology.

The end of ideology thesis is entirely explicable; it serves many interests, inside and outwith the universities. It forecloses on some rather difficult and even embarrassing issues. It pretends that universities are guided only by the force of the better argument; it implies that universities are as they portray themselves. It is a WYSIWYG philosophy: what you see is what you get. As such, the end of ideology thesis discourages any consideration that the university may be offering somewhat other than what you see.

For those who are trying to comprehend the university, this view that we have reached the end of ideology is a nice let off. Much as it has developed over the past twenty years, the literature that seeks to understand the university has – with just one or two exceptions – fought shy of tackling the concept of ideology.[7] It has not felt it worth embracing the possibility that the concept of ideology has anything much to offer in helping us to understand the university. Now, it seems, the effort does not even have to be made, for the story comes from many directions that the idea of ideology has had its day. Any attempt to understand the university can do so without even a passing nod in the direction of 'ideology'.

All this is extraordinary and regrettable. It is extraordinary because the concept of ideology invokes a cluster of terms such as 'knowledge', 'reason', 'truth' and 'communication' – and so does the concept of university. Certainly, that cluster of terms works diagonally across the two concepts: 'university' plays up that cluster of terms, essentially those of the enlightenment, and 'ideology' calls up presences that fall short of such rhetoric. But, in that case, there is all the more reason for an understanding of the university to confront the idea of ideology because the concept of ideology offers a searching critique of the university. Essentially, to place 'ideology' in the company of 'university' is to cast doubt on the university's claims about itself. It is to suggest that the university is not all that it may seem or may present itself as being. It is to hint that the university may be an emperor without clothes.

This absence, this disinclination, may be understandable – scholars of ideology usually have their livings in the university and are not going to rush, we may venture, to cut the branches on which they sit – but it is also regrettable and for two reasons. Firstly, not just the scholars but, more importantly, the university as well is let off the hook. It is saved from being exposed to a potential critique and can more easily continue to represent itself as a haven of pure, objective reason. Secondly, our understanding of the university is diminished. A literature that could have enlarged our understanding of a key social institution is put in a box, the lid locked and the key thrown away. Of course, the irony is that this very blankness could itself be indicative of an ideological presence on campus.

Full of interest?

The story of ideology is a story of reason and non-reason both at once. Strange as it may seem, ideology and reason go together. An ideology gains its spurs through its being a plausible claim about the world. It is a truth claim or, more probably, a set of truth claims; it is a reading of the world.[8] The view that immigrants or members of a certain group are gaining jobs and are, in the process, displacing others who believe that they have a right to those positions is a set of beliefs with a truth content. However, it can be termed an ideology on three counts: firstly, it springs from a collective interest on the part of its subscribers; secondly, it is – at best – a partial reading; and, thirdly, it harbours a social project, namely to lessen or even remove altogether the presence of the group against whom the claims are being made. Reason is present, but it is contaminated by the interests of those who espouse it.[9]

Reason can never be free of interest, so the presence of interest is not in itself an indication of the presence of ideology. Habermas, after all, in one of his early major works (Habermas 1978), distinguished different 'knowledge-constitutive interests'; in other words, interests are necessarily present in driving the quest for knowledge and cannot, therefore, be indicative of ideology in themselves. Ideology emerges when interest seeps into the offering of accounts of the world *unduly*.

What counts as 'undue interest'? One move that recent philosophy and social theory may prompt is to say that it shows itself in a partiality that is the result of a particular perspective. But the perspectival theory cannot work *by itself*. A perspective is just that: a view of the world, or a slice of it, from a particular vantage point. A perspective may yield worthwhile insights and is not to be repudiated as such.

For Habermas, ideology is an indication of a distorted communication process.[10] Such a view from Habermas is hardly surprising, given his concern to play up the communication process in understanding human rationality. *This* theory of ideology implies that undue interest is present when reasoning processes are of a certain kind, namely those that thwart open communication. Ideology is inherent less in particular beliefs and more in the processes of communication out of which they emerge. In our present context, of understanding universities, this is a helpful idea. It suggests that ideology is likely to be present on campus if and when there are communicative processes present that hinder open communication. It suggests, too, that neither an interest nor a perspective is in itself a harbinger of ideology; for that, the processes of communication by which knowledge is generated have also to come into the reckoning.

This Habermassian view of ideology – as a matter of distorted communication – has its virtues. It indicates that the presence of ideology cannot be read off any particular knowledge claim and it turns us to enquire into the aspects of the social processes that gave rise to any such claim. It implies that we should be cautious in forming the view that an ideology is before us. But its strengths also hint at ways in which it needs to be buttressed. A distorted communication process may or may not produce an ideology; it may, after all, simply produce a deformed theory or a partial set of knowledge claims. A distorted communication process cannot be a sufficient condition of ideology being present; at most, it is a necessary condition.

Undue commitment

Assume a university that has come to be awarded high marks for its research profile (and may even have come to do well in national research rankings). Assume, too, that in that university the professors have been provided with conditions of work that allow them to focus their intellectual efforts on research; they have also come to believe that their time is better spent on research than on teaching. In explaining their collective position, our professors may say that it is in the university's interests that they concentrate their intellectual energies on research. Pressed to justify this position still further, they may say that their position as 'professors' is in itself testimony to the university having already declared itself on the matter *in their favour*: their titles (of 'professor') having been conferred indicates their worth to the university and even to the wider society and so they should focus their energies on research. It may even be said, by the professors themselves, that their time is best spent on the activity that is likely to generate the greatest economic return to the university, namely research. On this exposition, our professors' interest in research is a matter not of personal interest but of the university's interests.

All of the reasons adduced are debatable. Firstly, professors presumably profess and where better to do so than *qua* teacher and immediately put their intellectual and personal wherewithal towards nourishing the development of students. Secondly, teaching that captures the full spirit of university life is *necessarily* more demanding than research since it calls for a research capability but much more besides: professors as teachers have to open their being to the beings of the students. Pedagogical transactions that are genuinely characteristic of higher education are ontologically open-ended and risk laden. Thirdly, far from research being economically profitable, it appears that – in the UK at least – research has become a kind of loss leader: the volume of research in universities is possible only through its being partly subsidized by teaching.

But our professors are not to be deflected by any such arguments. Such arguments are likely to prompt yet further retorts in efforts, *post hoc*, to justify a position that is already entrenched. The military metaphor is apt here: the professors may feel beleaguered, under siege and as if they are simply being directly attacked. The questions are perceived as if from a hostile force. In turn, such questions are met with resistance from our professors. This is an ideology in full flow. A battery of reasons may be advanced to justify their position but, ultimately, we are not in the presence of a position that is grounded in reason. Our reasonable professors are hardly reasonable, so confronting their position with reason cuts no ice. The position is one to which the professoriate is committed. There is at work an *ontological commitment*. This commitment will not give ground to reason; at least, not immediately. How can it? This commitment has a collective predisposition written into it: it is an orientation that springs out of a collective emotion.[11]

This ideology is neither just a Nietzschean will to power nor a 'fantasy' as Zizek (1999) has recently urged. Certainly, both ideas have their traces here. There is a will to power *and* this ideology is an expression of a collective fantasy, a desire of the professors to see themselves and to project themselves to themselves as well as to others as enjoying a certain kind of collective position and status. Ideology is the structuring of a collective identity in which individuals come to share.[12] Those individuals – here, our professors – both give to and take from this collective identity individually. It is a fantasy because these professors would project onto the world their own image of a world as they desire it.[13] Yet, beyond these ideas of commitment, will, power, fantasy and identity lies a yet further element.

In an ideology, its holders place themselves in the centre of the world, *their* world. Their world is configured through the ideology. An ideology is, therefore, even more an ontological matter than it is epistemological. Ultimately, the resistance in which ideology reveals itself is ontological in nature; it is a sign of a commitment-in-being in which there is an undue investment. The ensuing identity is *ontologically overloaded*. Here, ontology trumps epistemology. Our professors come to construct the university by placing themselves at its centre, acting out their fantasy, which they attempt to project onto all around them. The university would be much better off if only the world could be experienced through their fantasy.

The irony of this analysis of ideology will be clear; indeed, the double irony. In ideology, ontology is over-freighted; epistemology is side-tracked. Our professors advance their ideology not through rational argument but through a commitment-in-being – *their* collective being. The university that constructs its self-image as a reasonable institution *par example* turns out to house strains of non-reason. More than that, in this example, our professors who owe their institutional image to their disinterestedness as scholars have to be understood as being *unduly* committed in such a way that it is difficult, if not impossible, for reason to have a hearing.

Ideology, it turns out, has three moments: the epistemological, the communicative and the ontological. Of these, the ontological is the most significant. In ideology, truth claims are made; an attempt is made to offer us a view of the world. Ideology is epistemological but that cannot be the full story.[14] Habermas was right to point us to communication processes: an ideology does not announce its presence in the character of knowledge claims in themselves; but neither does it do so purely through communicative processes. For that, we have to find ourselves in the presence of a collective view of the world to which there is an undue commitment, a commitment held collectively and so strongly that it becomes the identity of those espousing the ideology.

Ideology, then, betokens the presence of a collective commitment-in-being. Our professors come to know themselves and to constitute themselves through the stories they tell of themselves. Our disinterested professors turn out to be not only overly interested but also overly interested in themselves. No *hubris*: no ideology.

Voluntary servitude

A key question in the early part of the unfolding of the story of ideology was the following: Why is it that certain groups (for instance, the working class) appear to believe fables about themselves that have the effect of rendering legitimate the conditions of enthraldom under which they labour? That which is contingent is seen as inevitable. That which is iniquitous is seen as just. That which is imposed is seen as natural. Within the theory, the response to the question, as noted, is that the world is represented as that which it is not; this consciousness is literally false. Since alternative perceptions are not taken on board, and since it seems as if all that is necessary is a collective opening-of-the-eyes, this 'false consciousness' has in part to be self-imposed. Ideology is a form of 'voluntary servitude'.

Later theorists came to modify this Marxian heritage. For Althusser, the servitude was, rather, involuntary, the result of an enveloping structure of cognitions, patterns of action and symbols, such that individuals were 'interpellated' by the ideology.[15] Ideology came to structure individuals as such. Institutions such as universities were part of an 'ideological state apparatus' that acted to sustain this all-pervasive structure.[16] Ideology not just wrapped itself around individuals but also insidiously inserted itself in and through individuals. While such institutions worked 'effectively', a general docility could be assured.

More recent theorists have tried to boot all this into touch. Led by Foucault, the self-declared 'anti-structuralist', the view developed that ideology smacked too much of both truth and untruth (who would draw the line and where would it be drawn?). Instead, we should speak rather of 'discursive regimes' that would brook no distinction on grounds of 'truth'; 'power', on the other hand, was to be an approved means of distinguishing positions amid such regimes.[17]

Foucault protested too much. His discursive regimes *were* structures, even if layered in all their genealogical complexity; his allying of truth with ideology was unduly tight since, as we have seen, the truth content of ideologies is only one of its several properties; and ideology and power go rather nicely together. So Foucault's attempt to bracket off ideology as an unhelpful concept should not be treated reverentially.[18]

How does this excursion into the theory of ideology help us here? Ideology *is* a structure – a structure of collective belief.[19] Structures can capture, can impose themselves; but they can usually be entered willingly, they can be abandoned and they can even be demolished and new ones created in their place. Structures are not immutable. University ideologies can be changed.

We may distinguish two kinds of ideology: that which is generated by an immediate community and that which is generated by others. The professors' ideology that we have just looked at is an ideology of the first kind; the idea that universities might become part of an 'ideological state apparatus' (by, for instance, swallowing hook, line and sinker the agenda of a national evaluation agency) is of the second kind. The university has more freedom to change the first kind of ideology, a *self-imposed* ideology. However, the university is not bereft of room for manoeuvre even in relation to the second kind of ideology, an *imposed* ideology. In democratic societies, universities have considerable degrees of freedom. (As we noted in the last chapter, those freedoms may be shrinking but others may be opening and it is in the state's interests to permit its universities to have freedoms, even if some universities are more free than others.) Even in relation to external ideologies coming their way, universities have space to determine their stance.

Ideologies on campus, therefore, are forms of voluntary servitude.[20] Their presence on campus – whether internally or externally generated – is an indication of a degree of wittingness: the university may protest loudly that it had no choice in the matter (in becoming an 'entrepreneurial university', for instance) or that 'money talks' (in its deciding to place research well above teaching in its priorities). It may even believe its own rhetoric on these matters. Even so, we remain in the presence of *voluntary* servitude. *All* ideologies on campus are self-imposed; the only difference between them is the degree to which they are self-imposed.

The term 'voluntary servitude' suggests rather too much. The 'voluntary' is fine; it's the 'servitude' that is problematic. The term suggests total capture and a master–slave relationship. But sometimes, the slaves can escape their bonds and they can come to see themselves differently.

'Servitude' places the responsibility for the relationship on an 'other'; the subject becomes an object. In an ideology, there is a characteristic displacement at work, with responsibility being turned away from the self, if only in saying to oneself, to one's collectivity and to others that 'this is how things are; there is no alternative'.[21] Our earlier professors will be clear in their collective minds that their perceptions are describing the world as it is; correspondingly, the managers of the university in driving through the agenda of the national Quality Assurance Agency may content themselves that that, too, is how the world is. A view of the world is internalized *and* the responsibility for driving that view forward is projected onto others.

In so far, then, as there is servitude, it is voluntary; but in so far as it is voluntary, the servitude is barely servitude. It is more a case of voluntary bad faith.[22]

The forces of reason

The university prides itself on its reasonableness. This, too, is an ideology. There is, here, a collective structure of beliefs that promotes the interests of those who work in 'universities'. That a range of organizations, especially those in the corporate world, want to claim the title of 'university' is testimony to the widespread subscription to the ideology; or, at least, to the wish to be seen to have embraced the ideology.

Reason harbours a force in itself: the institutionalization of reason, by definition, is a force for the development of the rational society. For Habermas, the first utterance contained its own inbuilt will to reason: reason is embedded in language as such. There is no ideology here. But reason can become an ideology by being erected as a project under which collectivities shelter. A university, as a community, is just such a collectivity. Universities put up the project of reason in neon lights: they celebrate it; they promote it; and they claim to be society's favoured institution for protecting and furthering the project. Or they *did*.

On campus, other ideologies now usurp the ideology of reason: research, entrepreneurialism, excellence and participation. They provide motivating banners, emblems of attachment and new forms of academic identity. Reason is displaced from the centre of the ontological space of the university. Perhaps, then, not centre stage, but it is still *there*. Universities cannot bring themselves to abandon the flag of reason. Its ubiquity (institutions of diverse kinds subscribe to it) and its embeddedness as a common sentiment claim a continuing ontological space for it.

But to point to its ubiquity and embeddedness describes only certain of its features. That it endures across centuries, across countries and across institutions is testimony to reason having some *force*. Still, the force of reason on campus calls for yet a further account.

Universities are institutions that have come to nurture communication systems that are characteristic of reason; reason is none other than particular kinds of human interaction involving the mutual giving of accounts. In structures of reason, the 'I' gives way not to the 'other' but to interesting stories. Stories gain their interest from their suppleness, their inventiveness, their boldness and their security. It is not that the reasons are separate from the stories; rather, the interest in the stories derives from the qualities of the stories (which have reasons within them).[23]

Yet, even this does not capture the full force of reason for, so far, this account is purely an epistemological account, albeit a generous epistemology allowing for stories to carry with them their own reasonableness; it is an epistemology without the hosanna of 'truth', except for a sense of truth as interest, as inventiveness, as backing and as complexity. To this generous account of epistemology, reason calls in aid ontology. Through storytelling of this kind, individuals on campus construct themselves as being party to one set of stories and as against others.

'Academic identity' has become a recent matter of interest in its own right.[24] For the most part, however, that literature has overlooked the binding force of reason as an ontological force. The assertion that 'I am a chemist' or even 'an organic chemist' or even 'a chemist who is interested in certain kinds of compound investigated through certain kinds of technique' is testimony to a wittingness to subscribe to a life form with its own kinds of storytelling and its own kinds of collective exchange. The force of reason is thus a product of ontological investment in reason; as a result, reason captures subjectivities but subjectivities also capture reason. Epistemological changes trail in the wake of dispositions to retain one's hold on the world. To the extent that academics work largely in taken-for-granted frames, to that extent is revealed their disinclination to change themselves. Ontology, to repeat, trumps epistemology.

Reason, we see here, is both institution and ideology. It is an institutionalized set of symbols, claims, forms of interaction, activities and account giving. It generates its own syntax, discourse and genres; and these are dynamic, never still. But it is also an ideology. Communities are formed, subscribing to this life form of grounded storytelling. Communities come to form themselves certainly by their institutionalized practices, their journals, their networks and their conferences. But they come principally to form themselves by their mutually sustained self-understandings to which they wittingly subscribe. They assent to the life of reason, albeit reason filled out and interpreted in their own image. These communities endorse the life of reason and are taken over by it to some extent. It is an ideology, but one that is justified through the idea of the university itself. Reason, therefore, can offer the makings of a virtuous ideology on campus.

Two objections form. It will be said that this view of the force of reason on campus is past its time. It looks back to a golden age that is no more. As stated, other ideologies have supplanted reason. It will also be said, even more tellingly, that this idea of the force of reason on campus is just an ideal; it never did exist as such. Academics may have liked to have projected the academic life as one of reason but, in reality, the academic life has *always* been characterized by unreason, by inequalities of power and by micro-politics: back-stabbing, the undue presence of gender, manipulation and authoritarianism have been the order of the day, *tout court*.[25] Modern managerialism is only a past machiavellianism on campus, now become explicitly on show.

The campus has seldom, if ever, been free of distorted reason. The university's own ideology has never been fully institutionalized; and now, under the force of societal and global forces of audit, income generation and entrepreneurialism, reason is placed even in further jeopardy. But this set of rejoinders carries its own limitations. As an empirical story, it serves to test the ideology, true enough. But, still, the ideology itself serves as a critical standard by which to assess the unfolding of an age. By matching the university's practices against its ideology, we can see whether the university lives up to its own ideology of itself as a site of critical reason.

Reason as ideology, therefore, carries two kinds of force. Firstly, it produces an ontological force, not exactly binding or compelling but persuasive and influential. Through the ideology of reason, interpreted in all its manifold forms across campus, individuals and the community *qua* academic are formed simultaneously. Individuals are able to see themselves as, and *become*, academics in so far as they subscribe to the rules of reason of their immediate community ('rules', as we have seen, being understood generously). The community gains its strength through the strength of the networks that develop among the individuals so constituted. Such networking can be encouraged by suitably active institutional leadership. This can be a community-in-the-making.

Secondly, reason as ideology forms a critical standard by which practices can be examined. The ideology might be imaginary; it might look to a community that does not completely exist; and the rules of reason might be bent or even broken. But the ideal in the ideology can still serve as a critical standard for scrutinizing and even for reorienting so-called academic practices, where they fall short of the standard.[26] By recalling its own ideals, the university can become other than it is and other than it is shaping to be.

Two forms of ideology

Let us put it plainly. Ideology is alive and well on campus. However, ideology on campus comes in two forms: pernicious and virtuous. Pernicious ideologies are those that undermine the realization of the historic idea of the university as a rational institution, as an institution that is playing its part in the continuing formation of the rational society. In contrast, virtuous ideologies on campus are building ideologies ('building' here being an adjective): they take the project of the university forward. Even amid the challenges of the contemporary world, they attempt to retain a university project as such. There are a number of qualifications to make to this statement.

Firstly, we have seen that ideology has three elements: communicative, epistemological and ontological (and, of these, it is the ontological that is the most significant). *Secondly*, ideologies are projectional: they embody a social project that they carry into the world. Such projects may be conservative or transformative: they may be projects that further existing ideas of the university or they may be projects that seek to usher in new kinds of university. This is a different axis from our pernicious–virtuous distinction: it is by no means the case that conservative ideologies are all virtuous (witness our earlier group of professors) or that transformative ideologies are all pernicious. Accordingly, we can superimpose these two dimensions on each other and we can attempt to locate contemporary ideologies of academe in the grid space: refer to Figure 4.1.

Thirdly, I have argued that ideologies serve as critical standards by which contemporary practices and their associated ideas – or historical ones, for that matter – can be scrutinized and perhaps found wanting (whether against pernicious or virtuous ideologies). Picking up on our last point, it may turn out that the Western university has never been fully realized when assessed

Figure 4.1 Two axes of ideology

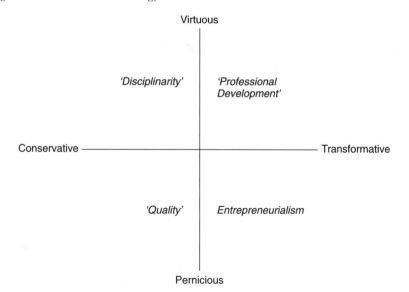

against its own (virtuous) ideologies. Accordingly, transformatory ideologies are going to be needed if the university is to become what it claims it is and has been.

Lastly, our tying of campus ideologies to the idea of the university as a vehicle of rationality is a shorthand. Ideology is, as we saw, a collective construction that requires imagination, fantasy and creativity. Reason on campus has to look to the telling of new stories, stories that capture the imagination and that win hearts and minds: only then can a collective construction and reconstruction take place. In giving a key place, therefore, to the concept of rationality in the spelling out of ideology on campus, the idea of rationality will itself have to be generously interpreted. On campus, reason can even be accompanied, and quite legitimately, by passion. Ultimately, ideology is beyond all reason. Ideology has its rational elements but it also has its non-rational elements; and the latter are both in being and in ideology's imaginary qualities.

Summary

Ideology is alive and well on campus but its presence is neglected, partly because it has done its work *as* ideology: the projects that are sweeping across universities world-wide have come to be seen as natural, as the way things have to be. Partly, too, ideology on campus is neglected as ideology because ideology itself is misunderstood. For too long, ideology has been felt to signify a shortcoming of some kind. Its 'truths' were only partial and put in the service of questionable ends. The result of this double neglect is a largely unquestioned stridency and babel of interests driven by the dominant forces.

But why let the devil have all the best, or at least the loudest, tunes? If ideology can be a force for dubious ends, so it can be a force for positive ends. If communities can come to understand themselves and motivate themselves through ideologies that have limited or even deleterious effects, they can also come to understand and motivate themselves through ideologies that have positive effects. And so it is on campus. If ideology cannot be extinguished on campus, let its expression include virtuous ideologies that are likely to further the project of the university.

If it is honest with itself, the university knows that it cannot expunge ideology from itself; the university, accordingly, is itself beyond all reason. Reason itself can become an ideology on campus: it can help to frame the organizational culture of a university in which not just the academics but also the managers call themselves to account. As an ideology, reason has to be taken on trust to some extent, but this trust can be seen to work. The generosity embedded in reasonableness can be seen to pay off. The university of reason can enable the university to live prosperously with ideology, for the university of reason can itself become an ideology; indeed, a virtuous ideology.

Part 2
Pernicious Ideologies

5

'The Entrepreneurial University'

The go-between

The *entre*preneur is a go-between. The entrepreneur not just undertakes a venture but is intent on taking himself and often others from the present state to a new one. The undertaking involves personal and organizational change, but it also involves an investment and, thereby, personal or organizational *risk.*[1] That the idea of the entrepreneur has come to be applied separately to the worlds of commerce and entertainment is not without point, too, in the idea of entrepreneurialism now coming to have application in relation to universities as well.

To say of a university that it is entrepreneurial is, therefore, to invoke sentiments of undertaking, venture and risk. Such a university is prepared to become other than it is, and in two senses. At a surface level, its new ventures may take it into uncharted paths. It may try electronically based programmes of study, incurring high up-front costs. The venture, undertaken systematically, has profound changes for the university: its pedagogies change, its educational relationships with its students change, the relationships that students have with each other may change (the students may become *more* interactive among themselves) and the identity of the tutors changes (less a visible authority, aided by an immediate physical presence, and more an enabler of learning tasks and opportunities).

Entrepreneurialism also extracts, therefore, change at a deep level. In our present example, the university changes as such. There is not simply an absence of students bodily on campus, for this university is marked by new kinds of identity (of both tutors and students), relationships and communicative structures.

Entrepreneurialism invites, therefore, both surface and deep levels of change. Universities add to their repertoire of undertakings and undergo fairly visible *performative* change but, in the process, they may also undergo *constitutive* change and, in the process, offer new forms of belonging.[2] Such constitutive change is not captured by talk of mission change or even mission 'creep'. On the cards here are changes that bring forth a new entity, even while it might continue to take the name 'university'. After all, it is not obvious that the entrepreneur has any limits to his undertakings other than his willingness to accept the risk involved.

Risk, accordingly, for the entrepreneurial university is ambiguous. At the surface or performative level, a venture may simply not come off. The students for a new electronically based programme may not materialize. The human and physical resources expended are at risk, but there are opportunity costs too. The total capital at stake – intellectual and financial – may be surrendered. But there is risk embedded at deeper levels of this 'university'. At risk is a change in the university as such. *Firstly*, in the changing of its pedagogies, its academic and student identities, and its educational relationships, unpredictable changes are let loose. The outturn of those changes cannot be comprehended in advance. The changes are literally complex in nature, the intersecting elements are so numerous, and the webs of identities and relationships so intermeshed, that the outcome of their transformation cannot be computed. *Secondly*, having been let loose, such changes may be irreversible in any straightforward way. Yes, the university may decide to return to conventional curricula but identities and their associated perceptions, values and orientations, once dislodged, will not easily be morphed back to earlier patterns.[3]

The entrepreneurial university is engaged, therefore, on an especially risky course. It may be risking more than it understands for it may be risking *itself*. In coming to be a different kind of institution, it risks coming also to live by new sets of values. The risk may still be felt to be worthwhile, however; although that consideration implies that the risk to the university's value structure has been actually identified and weighed.

The entrepreneurial university is one that is being placed between states of being but no new stable state of being is available. A particular form of performative change may be identifiable as a goal and it may be reached self-evidently (the new centre is opened, perhaps even in another country) but the entrepreneurial university is never at rest. Institutional energy is galvanized at a deep level: the entrepreneurial university is a restless university. At a deep level, there is no going-between: the entrepreneurial university has left point A but there is no arrival at any point B. The entrepreneurial university is always on the move, transforming itself as a university.[4]

Making it in the world

Can an entrepreneurial university be a university? If the entrepreneurial university is not so much moving from one state of being to another but is always characterized by change-in-its-being, is there any residue to which can attach the name of 'university' (whatever that term might mean)? Entrepreneurialism brooks no limits on the ventures that might be undertaken. The only limit is that of the risks that might be tolerated. Does the entrepreneurial university have any 'core business' that attaches to the university as such? Are there *any* principles that might claim its allegiance?

Risks come in many shapes and sizes. The financial risk probably attracts the most attention but others are equally significant (even if they come less into the reckoning within the Vice-Chancellor's senior management team). In mission risk, the university lays on the line its image, reputation and positioning – all of which may be global. In intellectual risk, the university opens the way to losing its key resource, its intellectual capital. (If its professoriate is uneasy with certain aspects of the new entrepreneurialism, the global academic labour market lies waiting to capture the university's dissidents.)

The motto of the entrepreneurial university is 'seize the main chance': it takes whatever opportunities come its way. Yet it does more than this: it creates its chances. The entrepreneurial university is imaginative: it not just brings the future into the present but also creates the future. The entrepreneurial university is in a perpetual state of transition between the now and here and some imaginary potentiality. Its imaginary qualities enable it to be ahead of the game; at least, that is what its managers would have us believe. The entrepreneurial university creates the future by living in the future. It cannot afford, from its point of view, to live for the moment. It always has its eyes on the next, the new and the imaginary. The managers who are really prized are those that can apparently do this living in the future and bring it in amid uncertainty, resistance and conflicting viewpoints: these are the *leaders*. If management is the art of the possible, leadership is the art of the impossible.

Stasis is anathema to the entrepreneurial university. The idea that a university is a set of continuing conversations[5] is marginalized in this university. Ever onward, ever forward, ever reaching out – for new markets, new forms of collaboration, new pedagogies, new client groups and new front-line activities. The changes may be made palatable through being adopted under existing headings; consultancy, for example, is embraced by being labelled, at best, as an extension of research. At worst, consultancy remains visible but is legitimated by means of an indistinct boundary between it and research: it is quasi-research.[6]

The university is 800 years old: its survival is testimony to its adaptability. Now, the watchwords are those of innovation, flexibility, adaptation and change. This is a discourse not without irony, with its suggestion that, despite its capacities for adaptation, one of the longest-lasting institutions has been insufficiently adaptable. The implication is that survival now requires, as a matter of explicit faith, a willingness to embrace fast-moving adaptation. Turbulence and riskiness have to be in the shop window.

As we saw, the implications of many new ventures are beyond calculation. They are systemic in character but they are also conceptual: How much change can be tolerated conceptually (not just psychologically or in the management of its systems)? If the university decides that it is too expensive to have a teaching mission and that its intellectual capital is better spent on research and consultancy, would we still be in the presence of a university? Can the entrepreneurial university really do what it will? Are there no boundaries? Does it have no responsibilities, other than to its financial stakeholders? In making it in the world, can it do as it pleases?[7]

Ventures involve risk where uncertainty attaches to them.[8] The entrepreneur is prepared to take the risk; the entrepreneurial university is prepared to chance its arm by going where other universities have not yet gone. The entrepreneurial university is, by implication, one that wills itself to become different from other universities. If it was simply following other ventures that had already been tried by other universities, the risk would barely be a risk. The ventures would be rather tame affairs.

The entrepreneurial university, accordingly, wills itself to become a new kind of university.[9] It does so by making it in the wider world. It places itself in the wider world and seeks to hear the voices of that wider world – for certain kinds of training, for particular kinds of knowledge transfer and for special kinds of consultancy. But market testing is fraught with difficulty: until the new forms of collaboration, the new reaching out to the community or the new programmes of networked learning have been tried, their success cannot be certain.[10] The risk cannot be computed in advance; the risk in resources can be calculated – though even there, there are difficulties[11] – but the likelihood of success remains uncertain.

This uncertainty arises out of the university placing itself more fully in the world. The entrepreneurial university endorses the idea of the networked society, for it seeks to extend its networks in society and even across the globe. The entrepreneurial university reaches out, and even beyond the academic world as conventionally understood, to foster new audiences, new publics and new clients. The entrepreneurial university surrenders to the claims and requirements of that world. The webs of its networks with the wider world grow ever thicker: its dedicated mailing lists grow daily, as new corporations, professional bodies and community groups are added. Its potential clients are virtually limitless: almost anyone and any group might have a use for its knowledge services. The entrepreneurial university thus displaces itself into the world.[12]

The market is the test

The test of the validity of the ventures that the entrepreneurial university undertakes is that which the market will bear. Can the venture elicit an income stream sufficient not only to cover the immediate costs but also to make a contribution to the university's overheads? That is the test.

The entrepreneurial university, therefore, yields itself to the *exchange value* that its resources can command. Its intellectual capital might command a *use value* in the wider community but one that does not provide a full return on the resources expended in the process; but, then, this value is marginalized in this university. 'Reach out to the community' has to have a price tag for the entrepreneurial university. It may offer much use value to the community but, unless it can generate income, the value will be discounted: an exchange there has to be, with an income stream into the university to justify the resources expended. The academics of the entrepreneurial university could provide all kinds of knowledge services to the community – in legal services, business services, creative activities and services to museums and galleries: an infinite array of clients could utilize the knowledge capacities of the university. Unless that *use value* generates an *exchange value*, however, it is as if it has little or no value.

That the entrepreneurial university's knowledge activities have to have exchange value has multiple consequences. *Firstly*, the clients of the entrepreneurial university have to be able to afford its services: the entrepreneurial university is not inclined to put its capabilities at the services of just any client. A local community group might wish to take advantage, one evening, of the university's heated but underused rooms, but it will have to be able to afford the going rate. *Secondly*, that the university's knowledge services have to acquire a particular kind of recursive capacity – in generating an economic exchange with the recipient – imparts its own influence on the knowledge itself. Knowledge, as Lyotard (1984) put it, acquires here a 'performative' character. No longer is knowledge its own end;[13] it has to have a pay-off. In turn, what counts as knowledge is itself affected. Truth criteria and the validity of concepts take on a pragmatic tinge. *Thirdly*, inquiry and the formation of knowledge are oriented towards client satisfaction. Critique is necessarily downplayed in this market.

In the entrepreneurial university, in its market setting, the Finance Officer performs a key function, but a function relatively new to universities. It is not that of balancing the income against the expenditure *per se*, but of providing the 'business plan'; or, rather, lots of business plans. For every new venture, there has to be a business plan. The advent of the computer is more than a marginal help. By means of a spreadsheet, varying values for different elements can be inserted and the consequent potential outturns can be computed instantaneously and compared. Varying assumptions can be made about market behaviour, such as the possible flow of students for a 'full-cost' course and the fees that they might be prepared to bear. In the past, the Finance Officer lived largely *in* the past, looking back at last year's performance; in the future, the Finance Officer will live *in* the future. It is a fictive future or set of futures, however.[14] By means of the Finance Officer's ability in juggling the spreadsheet, the risks of possible future ventures can at least be minimized.

The entrepreneurial university, therefore, does not just live amid markets; it creates markets for itself.[15] It ventures forth, seeing where opportunities might be worked on and developed. The entrepreneurial university realizes that it has considerable capacity locked up in the minds of its academics. The knowledge society, by definition, is one that values and creates knowledge. Certainly, the knowledge society, again by definition, is one in which knowledge is produced *generally*; knowledge production is no longer confined to formal institutions (Gibbons *et al.* 1994). But the university still has much to offer; it remains, even amid myriad knowledge producers, a major knowledge producer (and even if the clients are looking for knowledge services that the university seems unable or unwilling to provide).

Yet, many in the wider society have old-fashioned images of the university. They assume that universities are institutions characterized by research and teaching, and particular kinds of research and teaching at that. They do not realize that universities have gone into the marketplace, advancing their causes wherever they can find a return on their investment. Universities, therefore, have appointed 'marketing officers'. Their purpose is less to market particular 'product lines' that the university has to offer than to advance the cause of the university as such. It is to project the university – and its capacities to provide knowledge services – into those parts that it has not reached.

It is no coincidence, therefore, that the country in which universities have most markedly assumed a market orientation – the USA – is one in which the term 'advancement' has emerged as a symbol of educational effectiveness. Clearly, in a market setting, the successful university is going to be one that is able to *advance* its causes, perhaps in the most unlikely of places. Amid markets, the entrepreneurial university becomes adept at projecting itself. Image, badging, branding and positioning: this is the new vocabulary of this form of university life. What counts is the perceptions of others. Amid markets, the entrepreneurial university has to care what others think of it. Our logo is recognized, therefore we exist.

The entrepreneurial university lives outside itself but not just through its communicative webs and activities in the wider world. It lives outside itself in its being constructed by others. Out of its direct experience, the university knew about 'constructivism' before the term was coined by its own academics.[16] The function of the marketing officer is to assist that image construction. The marketing officer's account may be that she is simply 'mediating' the real character of the university to its client groups. But, if it is to be 'effective', the mediation cannot be one way; the outer has to be turned inwards, such that the university comes to understand itself and construct itself in the images of its client groups.

The market, then, is not benign, is not merely there outwith the university. The market comes into the university. It is not just a test of the validity of the university's activities; it comes to construct those activities and, ultimately, will come to construct academic identities. Those who live by the market will see the world through the market. They will live outwith the university. Their identities are, to some extent, displaced *into* the wider world. Ultimately, then, the entrepreneurial university will dissolve into the wider world, with its activities, identities and values indistinguishable from the wider world. How could it be otherwise?

Entrepreneurialism as ideology

Recall some of the distinctions that we observed in our last chapter. Ideology has, it was urged, three moments: communicative, epistemological and ontological (and, of these, the ontological has the upper hand: ideology is ultimately a matter of a kind of *being*). On top of this analysis, three distinctions were drawn:

- ideologies that are derived largely from outside *or* from within the university;
- ideologies that are conservative *or* transforming in character;
- ideologies that are pernicious *or* virtuous.

How does our analysis of entrepreneurialism map on this analytic framework?

On our three distinctions, entrepreneurialism is, firstly, an ideology that comes from outwith the university, but it is one that is being increasingly accepted and endorsed by the university, at least in its managerial domains. What began as an external ideology is being internalized: an ideology *for* the university is becoming an ideology *of* the university. Secondly, entrepreneurialism is transforming in character. Through being entrepreneurial, the university is becoming something other than it has been. In living others' agendas – as the entrepreneur must do – the university is surrendering its integrity. Literally so: the entrepreneurial university is becoming a university without integrity as its inner callings are emptied out to be replaced by the callings of others. Thirdly, entrepreneurialism has its virtues – which we shall come to – but, in its present incarnation, it is largely pernicious.

What of the three moments of ideology? How might the communicative, epistemological and ontological moments of entrepreneurialism be understood? It is in the spelling out of these moments that the pernicious nature of entrepreneurialism on campus reveals itself.

Entrepreneurialism wears much of its communicative character on its sleeve. Entrepreneurialism depends on communication; it lives through its communicative achievements. But the communication that is characteristic of entrepreneurialism is limited: it is non-dialogical. To pick up a Habermassian distinction, entrepreneurialism bequeaths a form of communication oriented not towards achieving mutual understanding but towards success. It is true, as remarked, that the entrepreneurial university, if it is serious about its 'marketing', will listen to the voices of its customers, but the purpose of that set of exchanges is not to promote understanding as such. The purpose of the entrepreneurial 'communication' is that of bringing off the venture that the university has underwritten.

The counter to this position is that it goes too far. With the support of a private donor, a university may seek to set up a research institute intended to produce marketable products. It will engage in negotiations with its potential donor and those negotiations are surely reaching for an understanding. Yes, but the understanding in question is precisely one of understanding the likelihood of success rather than arriving at an open-ended mutual understanding. The negotiation is focused outwards, to the outcome of the venture. This is not a dialogical conversation as such in which any kind of respectful utterance may find a place, but is an exchange that is validated by external criteria – of income growth, of the markets that may open and even of projecting the university's image.

The validity conditions of this conversation have nothing to do with truth, understanding and the mutual development of the parties and everything to do with success, achievement and market viability.[17] This bending of the communicative structure of academic life is not peripheral but, as we have just seen, affects the standards of its judgements and the composition of its cognitions. Ultimately, this has to be an unacknowledged consequence of so-called Mode 2 knowledge finding its way into academic life.[18] Disciplines come to live in that wider world and their concepts have an exchange value in that world, embodying hopes of markets yet to materialize. In certain subjects, employers come on campus not just to describe the world of work but also to show students, within their programmes of study, that there is no boundary between their discipline – chemistry, electronic engineering, computing – and the wider world of entrepreneurship. Some universities establish courses in entrepreneurship itself: it takes on a knowledge form.[19] The marketization of higher education has epistemological power: its knowledges take a market turn.

Entrepreneurialism distorts both the communicative character of universities and their epistemologies and it does so by altering the validity conditions of their conversations.[20] A university may be approached by an organization to run a specially designed course, intended to develop its employees' capacities. That the capacities in question might be associated with particular practical ends is not at issue. What is at issue is the potential for the market components of the venture to furnish the conditions whereby the curriculum is reduced to the production of an 'entrepreneurial self' (Giroux 2001a: 3) in which critical thought is silenced. In such a fusion of the corporate and academic worlds, therefore, there arises a risk that 'the corporate model . . . [could undermine] forms of theorizing, pedagogy, and meaning that define higher education as a public rather than as a private good' (Giroux 2001b: 36).[21]

The market becomes the driver but in more than one sense. There is a speeding up of academic life; what used to be the normal rhythms of academic life, allowing due consideration to matters that came before it, are now dissolved. But the market creeps surreptitiously into the collective subconscious. The managerial ontology becomes that of the market: the managers not just think but construct themselves through market considerations. There is talk of 'winners', of 'opportunities', of 'enterprise' and of 'income streams'. At the senior levels and in certain offices, at least, the market comes to configure identities. But the market finds its way into identities right across the campus. Academic departments, at times of reducing unit costs and devolved budgets, look for opportunities to increase their income. At the same time, increasing proportions of staff are employed on short-term and self-funding contracts: these staff have to live in the market or fall by the wayside. So the market comes to have an ontological existence on campus: the market is *ontologically diffused* across the university.

Entrepreneurialism is an ideology that can, if unchecked, corrupt the key dimensions of academic life and nullify the universality of the university. That is the point about the pernicious character of entrepreneurialism; not that entrepreneurialism is problematic in itself, but that its adoption as a self-assured mission would have the dual effect of rendering the university as something other than it is and, in the process, causing it to become indistinguishable from the wider world. The discursive space that the university has enjoyed would close. As a result, the intellectual autonomy that the university has had over 800 years would diminish. In turn, the capacity of the university to hold up its own discourses to society and to go on subjecting them to critical scrutiny would shrink. Under conditions of marketization, the university could lose its potential as a vehicle for collective social learning, assisting public debate from a disinterested viewpoint. The university as a means of societal *Bildung* would be at risk.

Entrepreneurialism, therefore, has the makings of becoming a full-blown ideology on campus. It exhibits the three moments of ideology, being found in the communication process of the university, its epistemologies and the identities of its members. Through entrepreneurialism, individuals come to live a hybrid existence, partly in the academic world and partly in a wider world of entrepreneurial*ism*. Not surprisingly, the willingness to say of oneself 'I am an academic' dwindles. The category of 'academic' speaks of closed boundaries and of a form of life sure of its own standards and practices.[22] The market breathes new and different life forms into the university. The identity marked out by the term 'academic' is neither sought after nor much available, but what then are the identities made possible on campus in the twenty-first century? The entrepreneurial university is ontologically challenging.

Let us summarize how entrepreneurialism fares against our three distinctions (recalled at the start of this section). Firstly, the ideology of entrepreneurialism has come into the university from *outside* but, in many quarters at least, it has been assimilated and often – but by no means universally – with ease. Secondly, it is *a transforming* ideology, spilling out into all of the university's activities (even if not yet into all of its sites, as some disciplines put up their resistance). Thirdly, it is a *pernicious* ideology in that it distorts the conversations of the university. The discursive space that the university provided and through which it could offer its own take on the world, its critical judgements on the discourses of the world, is now shrunk and, in some disciplines, largely dissolved.[23] Through the ideology of entrepreneurialism, the university's particular place as a critical forum is being undermined.

The virtues of entrepreneurialism

Entrepreneurialism challenges the university: it challenges its epistemologies, its communicative processes and the identities that have emerged within its spaces over the last several hundred years. All of these, as they have come to be associated with the academic life, are now called in question and sometimes explicitly so. Governments and institutional managers urge the callings of the marketplace. Inevitably, these urgings generate some resistance even if, as we have noted, the response is assuredly mixed. Many, especially those in the humanities and the social sciences, sense in the market a betrayal of all that is good in the academic ark.

The distrust of 'the entrepreneurial university' has right on its side but it can be, and often is, overplayed. The resistance that such a mission attracts is not mere show: the sentiments of betrayal and of undermining are real enough. But these sentiments can themselves be expressive of an ideology, namely an academic ideology. For 800 years and especially over the past 100 years, the academics have been accountable largely to themselves. Now, the market carries new demands, of the bottom line, of consumers and of knowledge-that-works-in-the-world. The academics are asked to see themselves as expensive resources and to recoup not just their salaries but also the 'overhead' costs of keeping the university as an organization afloat. The feelings of resentment, accordingly, are likely to reflect several responses. There just may be some considered responses, sensitive to the distorting character of markets on academic life. Mixed up with those responses, however, are likely to be others springing from an admixture of resentment at being constructed as an economic subject and at being called upon to listen to voices other than those in the academic community.

Through such sentiments, the academic community reveals its inwardness, its closure and its assuredness of its own character and values. Particularly poignant is the appearance of the sub-communities in the humanities and the social sciences when, displaying their academic credentials, they spawn texts that implicitly draw attention to the problematic character of academic life itself.[24] The difficulties of providing *foundations* for any description of the world, the *contamination* of any description of the world through tradition and partial interest and the writing of one's stories through *local acts* may be the plots of the postmodernists, the poststructuralists and the pragmatists respectively,[25] but these sensitivities somehow rule entrepreneurialism entirely out of court. With entrepreneurialism, it appears that our self-critical academics are able surprisingly often to come to definite and large judgements. Entrepreneurialism, it seems, can be judged and presumably in a non-contaminated way. And, lo and behold, the judgements just happen to permit our critical academics to continue to practise their form of life unimpeded by any challenges that the market may bring.

The virtues of entrepreneurialism are precisely that it calls in question academic inwardness and assuredness *and* does so by obliging the academic world to engage with the wider world.[26] Entrepreneurialism requires academics to communicate with the wider world and, for that, the academics have to speak to new publics in ways that those publics can understand. This, perhaps, is the real message of the academics' resistance to entrepreneurialism: that it calls upon academics – who pride themselves on their communication skills – to find ways of communicating to multiple audiences. Of course, in that process, the boundaries of academic life are made fluid; identities are made virtual, living in the space and time of serendipitous markets; and the rules of the discourse have to be negotiated *in situ*, as an exchange with a client develops.[27] This marketized world extracts a psychic toll on academics: their identities and the rules of their discourses are having to be made and re-made.

It is hardly surprising if the academics exhibit resistance: to welcome entrepreneurialism invites into academic life the dissolution of its boundaries, discursive uncertainty and communicative ambiguity. This is a NIMBY response, a 'not-in-my-back-yard' stance. Entrepreneurialism may be acceptable for the university up the road (if at all) but certainly not for my university.

Conclusion

'The entrepreneurial university' is an ideological project. Even if it does not carry all before it, it carries much before it. It contains momentum, built up as a direct and an indirect outcome of public policy. That policy context is itself a hybrid, looking to universities both to supplement their income from non-state sources *and* to provide knowledge services that are actually desired by the market. Many academics, especially those in the biosciences and the geological, the chemical and the computer sciences, have responded to those promptings with alacrity: it is not unusual for academics in these disciplines and others to have set up or collaborated in the setting up of private companies such that their earnings exceed those of the vice-chancellor. It would be understandable, though oversimple, to see the resistance being shown by their colleagues in the humanities and the social sciences as sour grapes.[28] Market opportunities, to convert one's knowledge into knowledge capital, *are* more readily available in the sciences and the technologies, but entrepreneurialism does raise matters that concern the nature of universities.

Entrepreneurialism is a full-blown ideology that works in all the main media of the university: its epistemologies (in the structures and truth criteria of its knowledges), its communicative processes (as the criterion of success tends to supplant understanding) and its ontologies (as identities are formed around the realization of market opportunities). Since the marketization of universities is still a relatively recent phenomenon – the USA notwithstanding – universities that are intent on maximizing their knowledge capital need to undergo major internal readjustment and reorganization.[29] After all, the markets that can exploit the university's knowledge capital are not 'mature': they have to be fostered and even created

Table 5.1   The ideological structure of entrepreneurialism

	Epistemology	Communicative processes (CPs)	Ontology
Transforming/ conserving	Success supplants consensual truth	Distorts CPs in transforming them	Market identities emerge but are skewed vertically and horizontally
External/ internal	External (see below)	CPs focus more on external outcomes than internal processes	Largely external in origin but internalized within the university
Pernicious/ virtuous	Truth as such sabotaged as it becomes subject to the test of the market	Surrenders discursive space to the wider world but requires academe to communicate beyond academe	Challenges taken-for-granted values but pernicious in imposing instrumental values

anew. The entrepreneurial university is one that is prepared to remake itself, to become a different kind of institution.

The ideological structure of entrepreneurialism takes the summary form shown in Table 5.1. Entrepreneurialism has its virtuous qualities but it is largely pernicious. It cannot be silenced; this genie will not go back into the bottle. Sheer resistance is itself neither a legitimate response nor a politically adept response. Resistance lacks legitimacy by refusing to countenance that entrepreneurialism may have some virtues of its own (both discursive and economic) and it lacks political *nous* by allowing academic life to be portrayed by others as not living in the real world. Sheer resistance betrays its own ideological character: it is a stance that seeks to refute another ideology but is oblivious to its being an ideology – an *academic* ideology – in its own right.

Entrepreneurialism is an ideology that calls for responses that are appropriate to the supercomplex nature of contemporary life. A supercomplex university would ride with entrepreneurialism, extracting from it its virtues while confining its tendencies to displace itself across the campus. If managers have a responsibility to inject a market responsiveness, they also have a responsibility to sustain discursive spaces relatively free of such considerations.[30] Of course, in being an ideology, entrepreneurialism has found effective ways of legitimating itself. It will dress up its openness, its own responsiveness (discounting that money talks) and its energy-generating qualities. Those claims can be seen off but the deeper claims of entrepreneurialism remain.

Entrepreneurialism provides academic life with epistemological, communicative and ontological challenge. The challenge is that of placing boundaries around it, discursively and organizationally. It is that of living prosperously with it, of keeping it on tap and of not allowing it to get on top.

6

Anything You Can Do

The Pontius Pilate syndrome

Universities have always competed with each other. Now, however, they are encouraged to do so. In this, the state is the most influential encourager, as its monitoring exercises address increasingly wider aspects of universities' functioning. In the UK, not only are a university's key activities – teaching and research – placed under the microscope but its workings as an organization also come in for close scrutiny. If it moves, and even if it doesn't, audit it: that seems to be the dogma. The proportion of income raised with non-state agencies, the proportion of student entrants from homes with particular postcodes, and the proportion of staff on fixed-term contracts: these are just indicative of the dozens of performance indicators by which universities are judged. Inevitably, in this audit milieu, the performance of universities becomes both a public and a comparative matter: universities are placed against each other in the volumes of statistics. In turn, it is hardly surprising if universities come not just to improve their performance but to do so with their eye over their shoulder. Not just improvement but comparative improvement: this is the tacit injunction of this world of public scrutiny. *Competition* is an understandable response to the situation in which universities have been placed.

The state will seek to evade its responsibility in the matter; the public league tables that appear in the mass media are not its tables, after all. This is the Pontius Pilate syndrome. The state washes its hands of a situation in which it is culpable. The whole point of its various evaluation exercises is to bring the universities into the public light, to render them 'accountable' and to demonstrate that they are giving 'value-for-money'. The state's tears are false: the competitive climate among universities owes much to its policies and it knows that to be the case.

The state, however, is not the only player in all this. Certainly, the interest of the wider public in higher education is heightened by having sight of league tables, in which universities are pitched against each other. The mighty might not have fallen yet, but they may do so in the next issue of the tables. But critical in this climate of competition are the universities themselves. Some know that they are going to come out well in, and perhaps even top, the league tables. Others can hope, at least, to find themselves well up certain other league tables. Even if it is not yet a case of 'all must have prizes' (Phillips 1996), the modes of judgement in a mass higher education system are such that each institution can reasonably expect to see itself performing comparatively well under *some* aspect or other. The competitive urge may be encouraged by the state and fanned by the wider public and its various 'stakeholders', but the universities connive in the process: they bewitch themselves in favour of public competition. A university may declare that it doesn't believe in league tables and then a league table appears in which the university finds itself in number one spot: its views on league tables are likely to be softened at this point. The Pontius Pilate syndrome, accordingly, is also to be found in the academic community itself.

The logic of competition

Hospitals may compete to process patients through their wards, to treat quickly patients in accident and emergency units and to ensure that patients are seen promptly by consultants following a referral by a local doctor. In doing so, they compare themselves with other hospitals and their relative performance is assessed by others too. In public services funded from the public purse, in an age replete with evaluation instruments and computerized data, public audit and public outcomes are surely here to stay. Notice the link and the way that it works: the *public* audit leads to competition. To say that this is an unintended consequence is to be too generous. The audit process is intended to bring institutions to the point of placing their performance in the context of the performances of other institutions.

Competition is an inevitable outcome of public audit. The *practical logic* – as it might be termed – is not hard to fathom.[1] Public audit is, in itself, a comparative process: institutions are evaluated against some benchmark or standard.[2] That benchmark or standard may be the performance of other institutions or may be some independent benchmark or standard: in *both* cases, institutions are being compared one with another (the one directly, the other indirectly). The public disclosure of the 'findings' only heightens a sensitivity to the performance of one's peers which such evaluation is bound to engender. The competitive drive is endemic in the very processes of comparative audit.

Higher education has *not* been picked out for special treatment in this development (although there might be felt to be something curious in supposedly autonomous institutions, each with its own 'mission', being subject to comparative evaluations). The development is, as stated, now part of the structuring of public services as such. The price of public financial support is public audit and part of its cost is heightened competition.

The empirical question arises: To what extent does any particular form of competition come to structure, if only in part, a university's key activities? If it does so structure its key activities – teaching or research – the further, more evaluative, question arises: Does it matter? Ever since research came to be institutionalized in the nineteenth century, scientists have come to compete with each other and even internationally.[3] Such competition could break out into priority disputes; and so, today, many journals flag the date of receipt of paper manuscripts to head off such contestations. The more positive consideration is that such competition propels science forward; it injects intellectual energy. The world of knowledge is better off for competition among researchers.

In a competitive milieu, are we perhaps in a win–win situation? The public service achieves its ends – more patients are treated, more papers are produced – *and* these outcomes are visible for all to see. Before we run up the flag for competition, let us rehearse the conditions under which this competition is being orchestrated.

Firstly, this competition is *explicitly* public; that is, the outcomes of this competitive process are publicly evaluated, being released into the public domain. Secondly, these public audits are mostly conducted by the state *or* major agencies that are underwritten by the state (such as professional bodies that often have royal or state charters, or accrediting agencies that are sanctioned by the state). Thirdly, the criteria around which this competition is framed are not fully under the control of the academic community. The criteria may speak, indeed will speak, to features of academic life but only to some features. Fourthly, the criteria that set the competition in motion characteristically yield numerical evaluations against which the performance of universities can be plotted easily. The histograms can be produced.

Lastly, competition among universities is typically orchestrated by the state. For the state (especially in the UK, but in many other countries as well), competition promotes efficiency, consumer-responsiveness and a reduction in the powers enjoyed by the academic class. This competition breaks open the inwardness of the academic community and its associated self-assuredness. It requires the academic community to put its norms, standards and outputs to the test. This competition pits university against university and, in so doing, renders their comparative success transparent.

Ever since their mediaeval foundation, universities have competed against each other, but that competition was founded on the inner values of the academic community itself. Now, this state-orchestrated competition is founded on externally driven values of efficiency, consumer-responsiveness and accountability. These values are not, in themselves, problematic. Their problematicity arises when they are put into the context of the value structure embedded in the idea of university. On this reckoning, the extramural values now associated with competition can easily come to acquire a character disproportionate to their likely benefits.

The idea of university points to institutionalized processes of communication governed essentially by the force of the better argument and for human development. Competition – *this* competition – cuts across such hopes. Its three sources – considerations of efficiency, consumer-responsiveness and accountability – are key in that, through them, the contours of reason and of human development are configured, at least in part, by *those* considerations; that is, considerations other than reason and human development. Students come to be 'processed' quickly so as to improve a university's comparative position in regard to its progression and non-completion rates, but this may sit uneasily with the students' educational experience. Research comes to be governed by a determination to use resources sparingly, but this may just prejudice the integrity of the methodology.

It will be rejoined, perhaps, that the hypothesized situations are a poor representation of the way that things are. Only at the margins might the integrity of the university's key activities be affected: the university retains much of its educational space, enough at least to ensure that those activities are still structured largely under academic (truth) and educational (developmental) purposes. That may be so, but then the issue becomes an empirical matter. The rejoinder concedes the *a priori* contention that these developments are themselves problematic so far as the embedded aspirations of the university are concerned. Considerations of consumer-responsiveness, efficiency and accountability have the *potential* to run against considerations of truth and human development: that is all that needs to be said.[4] The issue is one of principle and not of how matters might play themselves out in particular situations. In a mass higher education system, there will be bound to be differences in practice. That the point can be made *a priori* as indicating sources of possible tension is sufficient for our purposes here.

The further rejoinder may come that the argument has set up a straw man. At most, all that has been achieved so far is the lodging of a few cautions in the direction of what may be some of the ideological baggage accompanying competition in higher education. Indeed, as we observed, competition may well bring benefits, fuelling an urge to inquire into an institution's educational efforts and to demonstrate to the wider world that they are sound and even 'excellent' in character. Competition, it may be urged, has not as such been ruled out. Its ideological structuring may have been dented a little but that is all; the worth of competition as yet appears to be relatively intact.

The idea of competition

Suppose we were to say that a competition is characterized by a process in which two or more parties contend against each other in relation to some standard or element of their constitution. The definition presupposes a number of conditions, for example that the parties have the element in question in common: an institution of higher education that lacks a research capability can hardly compete in relation to that domain. A further presupposition of our definition is that the parties are so placed that there can be a genuine competition. In our example, if two institutions possess something of a research capacity in, say, astronomy, but one institution not only has its own radio telescope but also enjoys access to key telescopes at sites around the world whereas the other just has limited access to a local telescope, we would have to say, at best, that the competition is not real; we might even wish to say that the competition was unfair.

The judgement that we are in the presence of competition requires judgements that are beyond a formal conceptual analysis. Those judgements are made daily; language is caught up in discursive plays between different groups. In a mass higher education system, with differential financial and symbolic resources, one group's 'competition' is another group's 'unequal playing field'. A term such as 'competition' is pulled this way and that depending on its user; its application reflects, here, the political economy of higher education.

There is a double irony at work here. There is competition over 'competition': different groups compete to advance their own interpretations and applications of the term 'competition'. Behind any particular Competition (with a capital 'C', as it were) in higher education (say, over research) lies a discursive competition, and that discursive competition is linked, in turn, to strategic forms of competition over financial and symbolic resources. Behind any particular competition stand other waves of competition.

The work of the conceptual analyst is not redundant, however. The idea of competition calls for conceptual analysis precisely *because* such work is cut adrift from empirical conditions. Conceptual analysis gains its value through its separation from empirical affairs. It does so by offering critical standards through which applications of the term can be judged.

Suppose, to take a further example of conceptual exegesis, it was suggested that a condition of a competition is that the parties involved must each feel in some way committed. We could not say we were in the presence of a competition if a party had no interest in the matter. League tables might even be produced showing institutions' comparative performance in different kinds of competition, but if the institutions in question are indifferent to the performance indicators in question – say, proportion of mature students or non-completion rates – the competition could be said to be a phantom competition.

An implication of the three conditions of competition so far adduced – as to commitment, capability and the constitution of the parties – is that situations of 'competition' are often so portrayed *spuriously*. What is claimed to be a situation of competing institutions turns out to be a situation in which institutions are *said* to be competing one with another but in which the institutions are not *in fact* competing with each other. A purpose of the league tables, it might be judged, is precisely to promote competition, *especially* where none exists. 'Competition' is perhaps evident more in the breach than in its fulfilment.

Yet, where our three conditions – the three Cs of commitment, capability and constitution – are actually present, we can reasonably conclude that we are in the presence of a genuine competition. If two or more institutions share elements in common, enjoy comparable resources and are intent on measuring their performance against each other, then we would have to judge that these institutions were competing with each other. Such a situation obviously obtains. There may be only one institution against which an institution would pitch itself in this way (there may only be one other 'like' university with a mediaeval foundation) or there may be several comparable institutions, but all to be found in other countries.

Beyond these conceptual points, how are we to make sense of competition in higher education? Let us say, crudely, that there are certain activities that are characteristic of universities, namely engaging in critical inquiries intended to (i) advance our public understanding of particular matters (research), (ii) foster particular human qualities at an advanced level (teaching) and, more recently, (iii) put intellectual capital at the disposal of clients in solving particular problems (consultancy and technological transfer). Competition finds its way into each of these three activities. Within research, not only may research teams compete for contracts or for funds but they may also compete during the research process itself, even while retaining close contact with each other; and the competition may take place globally. Within teaching, not only may universities compete for incoming students but they may also compete for advantage in quality evaluations. Within consultancy and technological transfer, universities may compete for the most prestigious clients and for economic returns.

These forms of competition may be felt to be benign and even positively beneficial. Students gain a higher quality of education, funders procure their research at minimum cost and knowledge capital has its due impact on the world. In the process, so the ideology declares, the academic activities are enhanced in quality *and* efficiency and there emerges a proper affinity between university and client. The university finds its true clients *and* client satisfaction is enhanced; and – *sotte voce* – universities even secure access to new 'funding streams'.

Within this ideology are empirical assumptions as to the efficiency of markets (that potential clients are so positioned as to make informed judgements), the calculability of the costs and the quality of the services on offer, as well as the economic relationships between academic activities and the position of the client. Put all those aside. Here, our focus is on the appropriateness of competition as a matter of principle.

The otherness of competition

The idea of competition strikes at the integrity of academic activities for, in a competition, attention is focused on *an-*other. The rejoinder will come that the presence of an-other is characteristic of academic activities in any event. A teaching act demands the presence (however virtual) of both teacher and taught; a research or scholarly act requires the presence of a research community. Academic activities can never be private acts.[5] To point to the student as autodidact and the lone scholar in the garret or even in the library mistakes individual bodily presences for the acts of communication with others that 'student' and 'scholar' require. The terms point not to persons but to roles that, in turn, invoke networks of relationships. 'Others' are necessary components of academic life; it can be no criticism of competition, therefore, so the argument may run, that it calls up yet other 'others' into the academic life.

The argument is spurious, however. Students and the academic community constitute *necessary others* of academic acts. In contrast, the *others* summoned forth by competition are *non-necessary others* of academic acts. There are two kinds of non-necessary others. Firstly, and more obviously, there are those universities that can be said to be party to the competition. (As we observed, certain conditions have to be fulfilled before universities can be said to be engaged in competition: they have to be witting participants, willing to recognize that they are engaged in a competition, and have to have the resources to do so.) Secondly, there are the parties that keep the competition going. Typically, the state is a significant player, but several other parties can come into the reckoning, including alumni, parents and employers.

Non-necessary others to academic acts are liable to distort academic acts. As players that participate in, or who help to fuel, a competition, they are liable to inject expectations that disfigure the integrity of academic acts. An academic act is one propelled by a desire to develop understanding, either the collective understanding of a community (as in research) or the individual understanding of a student.

The issue arises, therefore, as to the nature of the considerations that the competition may generate. Little can be said *a priori*. It would be tempting to argue that competitive considerations that emerge either from the academic community or from students – that is, from necessary others – would be less injurious to academic acts than those that emerge from the expectations of non-necessary others, such as the state, employers or collaborators in technological ventures. No such assumption should be entertained.

Even necessary others – that is, the academic community and students – can contribute to forms of competition that corrupt the nature of academic acts. Academics can announce their 'success' in a research endeavour, perhaps to the world's press, only to realize that the announcement has been with undue haste in a bid to beat a rival team. Students, wanting their degrees, can tacitly connive in a university's determination to maintain its comparative completion rates, even at the price of the standards required to gain those degrees slipping downwards. Competition is, therefore, increasingly fuelled by the immediate parties to academic acts. But notice that beneath both examples lies the influence of non-necessary others (the academic marketplace and the state, respectively). In other words, we cannot easily separate the *others* that are party to competition.

In an age in which higher education and society are intermingled, no demarcation is available that separates the benign otherness of competition from more insidious otherness. The internal/external distinction dissolves as the boundaries separating higher education from the wider society dissolve. In the process, forms of competition run into each other: insiders and outsiders collude – with greater or lesser degrees of wittingness – in stoking up competition, both within and across institutions and both within and across disciplines.

What can be said more definitely is that competition has recently been transformed from being a peripheral element in the practices of higher education to being an ideology that enters into the character of the central practices of academic life. In the process, individuals come to understand their practices in just that way: academics will be heard comparing the performances with which they identify – of their department, their course, their subject and their institution – with those of others.

In the process, too, the idea of competition itself changes from 'game' to 'enterprise'.[6] Analogous to the Olympic Games, competition had an amateur status in higher education; now it is professionalized. Whereas academics could compete against each other in the shadows of their activities, now competition has come at least partly to frame those activities and, in turn, it has come partly to frame the identities of the players themselves. Whereas relationships were ones of community, of joint recognition of mutual purpose, now competition surges to infect the relationships themselves. Academic life becomes 'othered' in a pernicious way.

This is an ideology in its fullest sense, embracing purpose, identity, communication and forms of evaluation. As ideology, competition threatens to corrupt the integrity of academic acts. Academic acts are no longer to be characterized as a matter of promoting understanding – whether of a community (research) or of individuals (teaching) – but are broken open to allow in extraneous considerations that constitute forms of competition. In turn, those acts of understanding are now invaded as considerations enter, with an eye to the impact on a standing in the competition. In asking the academic world to take on this ideology of the wider society, the very characteristics of the academic world that are valued by that wider society are put at risk.

Anything you can do . . . ?

This competition sponsors institutional takeovers. It promotes an interest in size as such. It is assumed that greater size is accompanied by greater efficiency and greater impact of product. In many league tables, the smaller specialist institutions are siphoned off into league tables of their own, which are placed after those of the larger multifaculty universities. The tacit messages are clear enough: greater size is of value in itself; specialist missions are marginal to the main enterprise, the performance of such institutions being difficult if not impossible to assess by the standards against which multifaculty institutions are judged. The accompanying policy drive is inevitable: let the larger institutions sweep up the smaller ones. Big is not particularly beautiful but it is more efficient, easier to assess and, therefore, less problematic.

In the private sector, competition is characterized by a Darwinian struggle: the weak simply go out of business. *This* competition is more subtle. The prospect of going out of business is not seriously on the cards, even though it may hover in the background. Indeed, few universities have gone out of business in Western higher education. In this competition, it is assumed that the making public of an institution's comparative performance will both increase directly public understanding of the sector and of individual institutions in it *and* serve indirectly to encourage institutions to improve their performance on the identified performance indicators. This is a quasi-competition in that the rules of the game (the performance indicators) and its processes (the forms of the evaluation) are shaped by a third party (the state). Even as it voices the virtues of the market, the state may not allow institutions to charge a 'market' fee for their courses owing to the inequalities of access that might result.

This state-managed competition has a tendency to become more and more complex. Not only may the performance indicators lengthen but so, too, may the procedures by which this competition is framed become ever more intricate: the 'benchmarks' may grow, the 'key skills' may lengthen and their status become more ambiguous, and so on and so forth. This is a controlled complexity within which the competition is urged forward but it is, nonetheless, potentially infinite in scope at the same time.

Anything you can do, I can do better. This may seem to be the prompting at work but it is not quite that. It is more a tacit message of 'No matter how good you are, I am good, too, at *some* thing'. This competition is intended to sponsor diversity across the sector. Certainly, there are doubts as to the development of diversity; indeed, for some commentators the reverse is the case, this competition sponsoring sameness.[7] Nevertheless, this competition and its associated evaluation mechanisms are bound to yield spaces in which institutions can claim their own excellence. That, after all, is implicit in part of the logic at work, that of 'fitness for purpose': in this competition, institutions compete both against other institutions and, crucially, against themselves. Each institution is to be assessed against its own purposes, its own priorities and its own goals. That is – or, at least in the UK, was – the rhetoric.

Mixed messages

It may be said that the discussion so far has been ambiguous. This is explicable. The ideology of competition in higher education contains mixed messages: closure and infinity; excellence and evaporation of standards;

diversity and commonality; and competition driven by the state and competition driven by universities themselves. In *this* competition, institutions are both held in check and are released into new forms of (competitive) activity; there are league tables producing a hierarchy of institutions, but so numerous are the performance criteria that, sooner or later, each institution will have its day; and there are implicit both total *and* relative notions of excellence, institutions being measured both against all other institutions and, on other measures, against their own or quite local definitions of purpose.

In the face of such equivocality, it is perhaps unclear that the idea of competition as an ideology has any purchase. After all, ideology implies some particular programme that is being urged forward. If competition in higher education has the ambiguous character suggested here, how can it constitute an ideology? It is possible to have it both ways.

That competition takes different forms and so lacks specificity is a sign of its strength, not of its weakness. That it can have different manifestations shows its adaptability in aid of the 'diversity' in a mass higher education system. As with ideology in general, this ideology has *deeper* holds. Recall the three domains in which I argued that ideology is present: epistemology, communication and ontology. Competition is present in each of these.

Epistemologically, competition works at two levels. Firstly, and in keeping with all ideologies, it has its own inner belief system in which it makes tacit truth claims. Here, truth claims take the form of beliefs that competition 'raises efficiency' or 'increases the responsiveness of universities'. Secondly, competition has, as we might say, *epistemological effects*: it gains its hold when universities are judged through their competitive success. Competition reveals their true nature, or so it is felt.

This competition does not have to be overt; there does not have to be a race for a new source of income (partners in an e-university development, for instance) or for high scores in a national assessment exercise (whether for teaching or for research). The competition can be subtle: simply, the size of the recurrent budget, or the number of research students or the presence – in the UK – of Fellows of the Royal Society or the British Academy. Comparing the performance of institutions against each other becomes a source of validity: through such comparative acts, it is felt that valid accounts of institutions are rendered. It is a particular kind of validity, for this truth-telling speaks of institutions' injections into the world: it is a nice example of Lyotard's performativity. We come to know the world through its competitive performances. The competitive performance becomes the key process through which we are to know our universities. By this competition, so shall ye know them.

Communicatively, this competition engenders watchfulness, inwardness and a refocusing. Watchfulness arises from a concern that other institutions, now become rivals, should not steal an undue advantage in the public domain (in the league tables). Inwardness arises as institutions fear to share with others their plans, perhaps for a new kind of course. A refocusing arises as efforts are turned to orchestrate an institution's resources so as to secure a high profile in particular competitive exercises (such as a national assessment exercise).

The inner discourse comes to be structured by the demands of competition, both particular impending exercises and more generally. There is talk of 'staying ahead', of the demands of national teaching audits or research evaluation exercises and of being disadvantaged. In the Vice-Chancellor's office in the fortnightly planning meetings, a university's comparative performance supplies parameters that frame the discussion. Individuals come to be judged by the value they add in advancing that comparative performance.

Ontologically, competition works, at least in part, to structure academic identities. Whether in research or in the offering of courses, and whether at senior levels in universities or among departmental staff, academics come to be looking over their shoulder at what the 'opposition' might be doing. It will be countered that, at the same time, a feature of the academic life is its propensity to sponsor collaboration across units. Indeed, in a global age, collaboration is perhaps increasing: global alliances of universities form and the internet facilitates cooperation at more local levels, as individuals work together on research, scholarly and even teaching projects. But that countercurrents can be identified does not diminish the presence of ideology. Ideology works its effects precisely in the midst of countercurrents – that is its purpose.

Competition comes to be seen as a legitimate way of structuring a university's activities. Certain individuals may be asked to take on roles to further a university's competitive position. Not only overtly, in the guise, for example, of the marketing manager, part of whose role is to secure forms of competitive advantage, but more subtly, too, we see subjectivities being shaped in part by the ideology of competition. The Registrar's office will come to be imbued with this orientation, conscious of the need to provide responses to course enquiries in ways that match if not surpass the competition; but even academics, in different disciplines and in different roles, will come to engage in activities intent partly on achieving a competitive advantage.

At one time, competition was intrinsic to the workings of the international 'invisible college' and was accompanied by collegial mutual recognition; witness the international community of physicists in the 1930s. Now, competition has emerged with institutional or even national dimensions: competition is needed for institutional survival or even, in a globalized knowledge economy, for national survival. In turn, activities are undertaken and identities are formed around the project of competition. In developing a new kind of course, perhaps appealing to an emerging professional community (in art and design, in museums and galleries, in the media or in the health sector), the course leader will have her eye on other institutions and will be wanting to ensure that all is in place to secure competitive advantage. Identities come partly to be structured by competition, much as there might be resistance towards it.

We can, therefore, talk of *ideological acts*. In an ideological act, the world is seen through a lens that shapes and colours the world. Individuals come partly to acquire their identities through such acts. They are valued by their Head of Department or Dean of Faculty or even by – or especially by – the Vice-Chancellor. New identities are formed around ideology; new spaces appear in which ideology can do its work through academic persons who come to be partly structured by the ideology. Ideological *personae* are formed: sometimes, they are all too visible; at other times, they work surreptitiously and, thereby, even more effectively. Competition on campus *both* sponsors and legitimizes ideological acts and ideological personae.

Conclusion: the arch of ideology

As with ideology in general, the ideology of competition comes bearing reason on its side. The vice-chancellors and the pro-vice-chancellors – now become managers – who speak the language of competition and who see their world at least partly through that concept do have right, *some right*, on their side. After all, this state-induced competition is simply imparting an external shape to a competitive urge that has long been characteristic of academic life.

The difficulties that this ideology presents are the inevitable result of its being an ideology. Whereas the competition inherent in academic life was simply part of an academic life, *qua* ideology, this competition threatens to occlude academic life as such. The criteria of validity within the academic community and its discourses and identity structures: all these are in danger (the word can be used here) of being colonized by the ideology of competition. Just as it wears reason on its sleeve so, too, does ideology work to suffocate all that it encounters. Ideology is able to reach out in this way because it has power on its side; here, state power. Ideology in general and this ideology in particular will sweep up all before it, given half the chance. After all, if the university's epistemologies, modes of communication and identity structures are all potential supplicants to this ideology, there is little of substance left which will escape its gaze.

To say this is not to deny that there may remain space for counter-moves: ideologies meet with resistance on campus as elsewhere; it *is* to note that this ideology has powerful backers inside as well as outside universities. The ideology of competition has hegemonic tendencies. However, it also offers opportunities for development that even have a positive aspect.

We see, then, an ideological patterning beginning to take firmer shape. In the last chapter (on entrepreneurialism), we saw that ideology in higher education has three moments – epistemology, communication and ontology. We have followed that pattern through in this chapter but we have also developed the parallel sense that ideology is potentially *both* pernicious and virtuous. We have, as it were, an ideological spur appearing before us (Figure 6.1). In Figure 6.1, the single vertical line represents an unformed ideology, potentially able to take alternative routes. The two sides of the spur – forming an arch – represent divergent paths down which an ideology

Figure 6.1 The arch of ideology

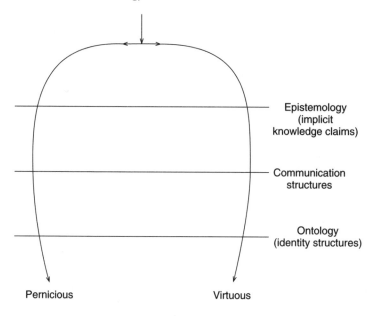

might move. In one direction, an ideology takes on a pernicious character because it not merely challenges but also undermines the traditional self-understandings of the academic world; in the other direction, an ideology takes on a virtuous character, challenging but also strengthening the academic world. In parallel, the two sides of the spur are structured by the three moments of ideology: epistemology, communication and ontology.

Competition is a largely pernicious ideology *as it is being currently framed*. In itself, and kept within proper bounds, competition has its place. It could offer a virtuous countenance to academe. Individuals can even come to constitute themselves as academic persons *partly* through the idea of competition: with good reason, academic subjectivities can take on a competitive aspect. The problem with this competition is that, *qua* ideology, it brooks no half-measures. Of course, it has to find its way through other ideologies in the academic world: it does not have the stage to itself. This ideology has not yet won, has not yet secured the unrivalled position which it would arrogate to itself, but it will keep trying.

This ideology of competition, then, as currently framed, has to be counted as a pernicious ideology. It would, if left to its own devices, come to provide the contours of academic life and, in the process, would distort the main components of that life, in its epistemologies, its communicative patterns and its ontologies. It is an ideology that has to be kept in check.

7

Never Mind the Quality

Introduction

Like competition and entrepreneurialism, quality as an ideology is being levered into higher education primarily by the state. *Qua* ideology, quality is state-sponsored. In the USA, quality as a project is engendered mainly by the market, but the generalization holds for most other countries. Across the world, states have been developing quality systems apace and have been, indeed, looking at each other's emerging systems if not actually borrowing from them.

Like the ideologies of competition and entrepreneurialism, too, the ideology of quality has potential for becoming either pernicious *or* virtuous in the way in which it is realized. *Both* outcomes may even be present at the same time in the same university: we can point to features that are virtuous (for example, faculty investing time and effort in collective self-assessment) and to features that are pernicious (for example, time and effort being invested in evaluation exercises that are disproportionate to their effects). However, it is its pernicious character that should command the major part of our attention and for three reasons.

Firstly, it is to be hoped that efforts invested in improving quality *per se* do have positive educational and academic outcomes; that, after all, is part of their purported purpose. At least those efforts should be neutral in character (if, for example, they are intended to drive up the level of accountability of the system). Secondly, any pernicious potential of those efforts threatens to occlude their virtuous potential. That virtuous potential may be suffocated. Thirdly, if quality *qua* ideology comes bearing not the gift of improvement but a poisoned chalice, its insidious character may not be easy to spot. Again, our attention is justified.

Like entrepreneurialism and competition, to say of quality that it is an ideology is to point to the way in which quality has become a project. All at once, quality has become a means of marshalling resources, a concept that structures academic activities and a source of identity; in short, a way of life.

Again, like entrepreneurialism and competition, quality has some right on its side: it has its virtuous moments; indeed, its virtuous achievements. This, too, is characteristic generally of ideology: it comes wrapped in reason. There are entries to be made, therefore, on both sides of the balance sheet.

The ubiquity of quality

Quality, as an ideology, as a project, envelops higher education. There is hardly a feature of universities that does not fall under its gaze. Not just the main academic activities – research and teaching – but also the supporting activities come in for scrutiny as to their quality. The library and computing services, the registry, the finance office, the staff development unit and the catering services: all are liable to be evaluated on quality grounds, at least by internal review and possibly through external review as well.

In principle, there can be no difficulty with this drive. Irrespective of external agencies or 'stakeholders', institutions will want to assess the quality of their activities and services. But the very ubiquity of this quality interest within institutions and across the higher education sector suggests that an ideology is to hand. A sign of an ideology is its tendency to colonize all before it: nothing should be free of its reach.[1] Yes, in practice, pools of activity may not yet have been embraced by it. A university may seek to ensure that its income-bearing activities should be subject to quality evaluations and it may have set up quality assurance systems for its continuing professional development courses and its conference office, but it may not yet have installed such systems for its consultancy activities. They are likely to come. In reaching out to the community, the university will, if only by *force majeure*, be obliged to ensure that such activities bear the university's stamp and are subjected to its quality audit systems.

The drive for quality has right on its side, even more than competition. Unlike competition, the idea of quality has right explicitly written into it. There are many definitions of quality – expressed in such concepts as 'peer review', 'fitness for purpose', 'customer satisfaction' and 'total quality management' – but the family of concepts of quality shares an interest in doing something well. However, the family of concepts of quality differs over by whom or by which criteria that 'doing something well' is to be judged: it might be against the actor's intentions or against the institution's objectives, or by the actor's peers, or by the voice of the consumer or by third parties such as employers or even against considerations lodged by the state itself. Despite these differences, the family of concepts is united in the belief that quality connotes an interest in doing things well. 'Poor quality' is, therefore, a parasitic concept, which takes its bearing from the tacit qualifier 'high' in front of the term quality in its ordinary usage. Since quality has this inherent interest in doing things well, who can be against it? Not surprisingly, quality has an easier time than others in becoming a project with a head of steam behind it: it can easily gain converts.

That there are, nevertheless, public resistants is, in itself, indicative of the way in which quality has become a social project with questionable dimensions. Quality looks to annex every piece of ground: that is an indication of both its strength and its potential point of weakness. Precisely because it seeks to become ubiquitous, with the project of quality having something to say on every act, every utterance, every process and every procedure within universities, it is liable to generate resistance, irrespective of the actual forms that the ideology takes.

In the ideology of quality, we have a nice example of the tensions between the state and civil society. Being largely state driven, this ideology effaces the space available to the academic community; it even effaces the space available to the academic community to develop a culture of care towards quality. Its ubiquity is not happenstance, not just an unintended consequence of the way that the project is being driven forward, but is central to the ideology. Only by becoming ubiquitous can it realize its inner aim of supplanting the room enjoyed by the academic community to maintain its own form of quality assurance.

Trow (1992) talked of a lack of trust towards the academic community evident in the way in which the state (in the UK) has developed its quality regime. Lack of trust is a kind of shorthand: a more formal description would be that of a disinclination to allow space to the academic community over quality affairs. A corresponding process happens in academic institutions themselves: as managers are forced to become proxies for this state ideology so, in turn, they are charged by the academics, *their* academics, with the question: 'But don't you trust us?' The managers are obliged, by this ideology, to ensure that there are no spaces left within their universities to fall under the gaze of the quality assurance procedures to which this ideology has given rise.

A counter may come in the form of the concept of accountability: in a public service (that is, giving service to a public), and particularly one in receipt of public monies, all are accountable. Students, too, are investing both their trust and their savings or borrowings in their courses. It is right, therefore, that universities should be required to give an account of themselves and demonstrate that the services that they are providing are of sound quality. There can be no escape from this injunction. It follows that quality should be ubiquitous: none should escape the responsibilities inherent in demonstrating the quality of the activities in which they are engaged.

In principle, the argument is sound but it does not go far enough. The first and most important point lies in distinguishing between giving an account of one's own volition, with one's own will, and giving an account because that account has been willed by *an*-other. The empirical point can certainly be put that the academic community was unduly slow in furnishing quality accounts of its own volition. It may be that the academic community is culpable in not developing sufficiently quickly or robustly its own accounts of its quality and that it reaped as it sowed. The imposition of a state-managed system was given a credibility that could have been denied it, but the logical point still stands. Vague talk of accountability fails to make a crucial distinction between an internal will to give an account of one's quality and having that account drawn out by others.

Other points follow. That there should be some systematic means of ensuring that institutions be accountable says nothing about the form of the ensuing procedures. It does not, for example, entail that all institutions should be subject to similar procedures and a similar accounting system. After all, the accounting systems employed for a multinational multiproduct corporation would not be identical to those employed for a small specialist company. The concept of accountability, therefore, is insufficiently specific to justify the totalizing character of quality *qua* ideology.

Outside in

The officers of a national quality agency may be heard to say that they are not interested in producing a compliance culture. With a straight face, they declare that they wish to encourage the development within universities of an institutional culture characterized by a collective will to take quality matters seriously. But quality, as a state-backed project, is *always* likely to produce a compliance culture. It only has to be followed by systems that are uniform across the higher education sector, that yield definite judgements and that allow comparisons to be made across institutions, especially through a simple numerical scoring system, and a compliance culture becomes inevitable. There can be no surprise at such an outcome: it would call for an irrational (not just a non-rational) response on the part of universities were they not to comply with the measures put their way. Not to do so would invite a level of risk that could not be justified. Indeed, to come out well in the inevitable league tables would allow a university to play up its clearly demonstrated virtues. A conspiracy in favour of compliance is born.

Quality, *qua* ideology, is itself *an*-other. It calls upon institutions to give themselves up to a project that stands outside themselves. The codes of practice, the documentation, the self-assessments, the particular components (employability rates, non-completion rates, transferable skills) and the ensuing public report: all these and other elements constitute a system that is independent of individual institutions and to which they are required to yield. That individual measures of this kind may have some right on their side – and they do – does not rebut the general point that this ideology of quality, now become a state apparatus, stands outside institutions and their activities and calls for allegiance. There is placed upon individuals a strong expectation, backed by state sanctions, that they should come to embody this ideology. Not just the systems that it bequeaths, therefore, but quality as an ideology stands over universities itself as *an*-other.

In this process, the outside becomes the inside or, at least, it seeks to do so. It seeks to capture individuals so that they do not just act out the ideology but come to live it. In practice, there is resistance, of different orders in different disciplines and in different institutions. There are those who are appointed as quality officers, both administrators and academics, who are required to take on the ideology at least to some extent. These quality officers may attempt to ride separate horses at once, both getting on the inside of the messages from the state agencies (preferably aided by having some members of staff themselves becoming selected as members of the relevant agencies) *and* also seeking to develop an autonomous culture of quality improvement separate from the culture of quality assurance required by the state.[2] There may even be some distancing from the state ideology while driving it forward so as to achieve the best possible scores.

Bad faith appears here, but from which direction? Is it that the state ideology is used as a pretext for brokering quality assurance improvements that should have been in place all along *or* is it that the rules of the state ideology are simply being adopted faintheartedly so as to produce the best result? The question propels itself but must be resisted. It is the question that the ideology *wants* to be raised for, in its raising, the real work of this ideology is overlooked. What the question fails to notice is that on either reading – playing the game for results framed by the state ideology or playing the game for results framed by the university itself – a system of compliance with *an*-other has been extracted. The other has claimed its victim. The outer has become the inner, surreptitiously and unwittingly.

That there may be spaces for resistance, and that the state agency may be obliged to keep its practices under review, again do not dent the general point. The ideology may not have everything its own way. Ultimately, it may be weakened, especially if universities can combine forces and find powerful friends to lobby for them. As most of the major texts on ideology have noted from Marx onwards, the playing out of an ideology is partly a matter of power. Contemporaneously, with 'quality', that power is exerted (i) financially (through the addition or withdrawal of funds), (ii) discursively (through public and semi-public judgements), (iii) ontologically (in the sequestering of identities as individuals are encouraged, for instance, to become members of panels of 'peers') and (iv) through policy framing. All four are precarious moments of power, a state agency being liable to be tested in each of them.

The worm may turn: the power of the ideology to impose its will may be shown to be weaker than it would *claim* to be. The room for resistance, in a democratic society and in a world in which university autonomy still has a value, may offer a way out. The level of compliance may turn out to be rather thin. Althusser's picture of an all-pervasive and all-powerful ideology may even turn out to be itself a form of mystification.

Due process

What counts as quality can never be neutral: it reflects certain kinds of interest. We could put this generously by saying that behind any idea of quality stands a tacit idea of higher education: an idea of higher education fuels a notion of quality.[3] If higher education is felt to be a matter of producing highly qualified manpower for the labour market, a definition of quality is likely to result that plays up employability as a measure of quality.

But to put matters this way *is* to put them generously. It is to cede the prospect that there is an idea of higher education afoot that is genuinely open to debate and is negotiable. It holds open the sense that the two ideas – of quality and of higher education – are discursively separate. However, where quality has become an ideology, and has taken on life as a social project, no such conceptual separation is present. The account of quality and the implicit framing of higher education take in each other's washing: they form a discursive compact[4] *and* it is a discursive compact that brooks no dissent. Neither element in the pairing is discursively *separately* available. It is taken for granted – in this example – that higher education just is a matter of producing highly qualified manpower *and* that a measure of quality lies in a university's employability levels for its students.

Quality as an ideology, therefore, focuses its attention on dimensions of academic life that are expressions of the ideology. The filling out of the ideology, its realization in practice, not surprisingly takes on the contours of its driving interests. Quality is not neutral. It is not, for example, independent of wider socioeconomic interests. It stands as proxy for those interests which, in turn, it masks. Given an interest in turning higher education into an institution supportive of global economic competitiveness in a changing world, higher education will come to be seen *as* that kind of process. In turn, a measure of its quality will be the extent to which it fosters the kinds of competence that will be felt to be conducive to that end. Against that background, it should hardly cause surprise if a vocabulary of 'key skills' or 'transferable skills' emerges as part of 'quality audits'.[5]

A state-driven quality process will tend to focus attention on aspects of university life that are readily identifiable and preferably measurable. Reliability will be emphasized at the expense of validity. Outcomes will take priority over matters of process. But it may be felt that our preceding observations have opened the way for matters of process to have a hearing. An interest in 'transferable skills' surely points to a concern over matters of educational process. Indeed, the evaluation procedures may include classroom observation of teaching processes. They may even include some attempt to recognize the collective effort that the evaluation process has itself engendered in, for instance, the production of the 'self-assessment document'.[6] Educational processes and even institutional processes may have their day, after all. The charge that quality as an ideology focuses overly on outcomes appears to be exaggerated.

This ideology of quality would wish us to believe just that. We have here a nice example of an ideology at work, in which its real intent is masked. An interest in educational process may be present but it is skin-deep, liable to be put to the service of further interests – for example, in institutional comparisons, institutional exposure and public institutional judgements –

that lie at the centre of this ideology. These latter interests do not sit easily with a genuine interest in educational processes, for *that* interest would lead to intricacy, particularity and even intimacy. Educational processes are not to be caught in simple judgements and characteristically, in the UK, at least, numerical ones at that; they are much more likely to be caught in a careful, discrete and sensitive characterization of an institution's or a department's *particular* qualities and that would be bound to be outwith the limits of the methodology. Educational processes, accordingly, come into the reckoning, but only in so far as they can be dragooned into the service of the instrumental reasoning lying within this ideology.[7]

Due regard cannot be paid to educational processes in this ideology of quality. Indeed, this ideology cannot allow *even itself* to become an educational process. Being intent on judgements, the public accountability of universities and simple 'accessible' comparisons, this ideology must keep itself to itself. It cannot allow dialogical spaces to erupt. Its visitations will be conducted 'courteously', 'professionally' and 'scrupulously', but dialogical engagement cannot be permitted for that would open the prospect of the ideology itself being tested. Why should the ideology run such a risk? Even more than that, to become dialogical in nature would cause it to become precisely, as the embodiment of instrumental reason, that which it is not, namely dialogical.

This ideology is intent only on making pronouncements that have the appearance of judgements. Actually, they are not even judgements, for judgements imply the dispassionate gathering together and hearing of evidence in a cool and calm manner. Here, though, being driven by instrumental and operational reason, time is the enemy of judgement. Decisions have to be reached in a limited time frame: justice cannot be done to the evidence. Impatience is built into this ideology: provided there is an outcome that contributes to the inner intents of institutional comparison and which, at the same time, appears to render institutions transparent and, thereby, accountable, this quality process will have realized *its* purposes. For this ideology, due process is no process at all.

A virtuous quality

Quality has the capacity to be a virtuous ideology. It can be a force for improvement but that virtuousness should not be assumed to be always present. It contains also a pernicious potential, some of which we have seen. Quality becomes pernicious when it becomes a project in its own right, which stands outside activities and agents. When agents are obliged to take account of Quality (with a capital 'Q', as it were), quality imposes itself as an alien force.

Why did quality not become a virtuous ideology of the academic community? How could the situation have arisen in which the state had to step into that ideological void and generate an ideology of its own around quality?

The situation arose because the academic community did not identify with quality as a worthwhile project. This is *not* to say that the academic community did not care about the quality of its activities, but it is to say that the academic community was not able to identify quality as a project around which it would form its identity. Ideology, we may recall, is collective in nature, forms identities and sustains a project. If this is the character of ideology, the academic community could not bring itself to form an ideology around quality because it had other interests – other ideologies, indeed – on which it was more focused.

Ideologies in general generate resistance, and quality as an ideology has found resistance among the academic community. Not only has the academic community resisted a state-propelled version of this ideology but it was also disinclined to develop a project of quality, even on its own terms. When, in the UK, it did show signs of doing so, it did so half-heartedly. In truth, it was never on the cards that it would develop an ideology of its own around quality. From its viewpoint, the ideology of quality, if taken seriously, would have actually impinged on the character of its academic and educational activities.

There is an irony here in the suggestion that the project of quality might be injurious *to* quality, but it has point on its side. It can, for example, be evident in the pedagogical relationship: where that is invaded by the ideology of quality, quality comes to be an intervening variable. It comes to be a moment in its own right which the tutor must, at least, heed. As a result, quality comes to be a point of consideration, intervening in the tutor–student relationship. Things have to be done with an eye to the particular shape that the project of quality has taken on in the locale. The tutor may be required to produce a record of each meeting with the student but its completion may cut across the conversation between the two. The actual conversation may come to a halt while the proforma is filled in. In that writing, a complex and creative interpersonal process is frozen in a two-dimensional form. The quality process intrudes into the pedagogical relationship.

The bending of the pedagogical process to the requirements of the quality procedures may also be evident in assessment methodologies. A proforma may have been developed so that there is both uniformity and transparency in the feedback to students on their assignments from members of a course team. But the sheer act of classifying one's comments under particular headings may constrain the commentary itself. The proforma as a text, after all, presupposes that tutors' comments are classifiable under given headings. Yet, in higher education, where students are reaching out in necessarily idiosyncratic ways in being creative and even original, such predictability and uniformity on the part of tutors will not be a natural or even a professionally valid response. In higher education, quality processes will tend to classify and constrain and, in so doing, run counter to any emancipatory hope of higher education.

It is this otherness, this third-party nature, that characterizes the pernicious potential of quality as an ideology. It presents itself from the outside of activities and their attendant relationships. It asks to be taken seriously in its own right, as if quality were not already an attribute of those activities and relationships. As implied, the academic community can itself be called to account in quality becoming an ideology imposed from without, because it failed to make explicit to interested parties that it had an interest in quality as such and it failed to spell out the character of *its* exemplifications of 'quality' in its activities. Nevertheless, the subsequent imposition of quality as an ideology brings in its train this alienable character.

The challenge to quality 'managers' in institutions is, therefore, severe: to encourage the formation of a *transparent* culture of self-willed caring about quality such that concerns for quality permeate the constitution of academic activities, processes and relationships. Bringing about such a culture *now* may be well-nigh impossible, given the presence of quality as an imposed ideology. Quality is now seen and felt as external, as alien and as separate. Winning over academics to quality so that it becomes a virtuous ideology, internally constituent of and thereby improving of academic activities, and with which academics identify because it springs from their own agendas, is now a formidable task. Only the most astute and adept institutional leaders will be able to bring it off, if at all.

The precariousness of quality

Like all other ideologies on campus, quality has to fight its corner. It will not have everything its own way. Its contenders come not just from the academics, for whom quality invades their collective space, but also from beyond academe. For example, an ideology that we encountered earlier, that of entrepreneurialism, cuts across quality. Entrepreneurialism looks to transcend boundaries: in the process, it is not exactly blind to quality considerations but it is not predisposed towards them either. Its orientation and its drive are elsewhere, towards new ventures, new clients and new knowledge products. Quality considerations, after all, may serve to limit the horizon of innovation. They may slow down the new venture or even rule it out of court altogether. In getting a new course off the ground and securing a cohort of students from a fresh client group, *some* quality considerations may just have to take second place.

To say that quality, as an ideology, has to fight its corner in no way undermines the idea of quality as an ideology. Ideologies have always had to fight their corner. Their success has been, and is, dependent on the power that they can wield. Ideologies seek to conquer the world and, often, they threaten to come close to doing so; but they may not. All too easily, we identify ideology with the possession of power, but ideologies may be weak and may flounder.

In the UK, at present (spring 2002), the quality agenda, as it is being driven forward by the main agency responsible, the Quality Assurance Agency, is having an unaccustomedly hard time. The Agency was intending to move its assessment regime to 'a lighter touch' (lighter than hitherto), but is coming under pressure from both the Government and the Funding Council to move instead to 'a light touch', so that its reviews of institutions are pitched at a level that would generally be felt to be 'light'. A reading of this little altercation is that the state is itself riding competing ideologies – those of enterprise and quality – and that the latter is now giving way to the former. Those among the universities that have been urging the need for 'freedom from bureaucracy' are those that are particularly associated with knowledge production and the knowledge economy will have contributed to this shift in the relative influence of the ideologies.

Ideologies gain their adherents through the perceptions that they induce: ideologies conjure a hinterland of prospects, of a new world. We do not have to term this new world, a là Mannheim (1976), a utopia. An ideology carries a narrative simply of a changed world. Whether the ideology has adherents at any particular time will depend on the sentiment that that narrative evokes. That sentiment, too, may wane: strong today, it may be weak tomorrow. The time of the ideology may pass. Quality may not yet have had its day, but it may be passing. It is more precarious than may be imagined.

The measure of quality

Building on our discussion of quality as an ideology, we are now in a position to refine our general schema: let us, therefore, return to the diagram at the end of the last chapter. In Figure 6.1, we depicted ideology in higher education in the form of a spur, ideology taking – on either side of the spur – a pernicious or a virtuous form. In either pernicious or virtuous form, ideology has to acquire three moments: epistemological, communicative and ontological.

Quality takes on its *epistemological moment* in its evaluative character: outcomes and products – and usually measurable at that – are its epistemological emblems. Activities are not just prized; they are *known*, through their measurable performances. Quality takes on its *communicative moment* in several guises. Pedagogical relationships are contoured by quality considerations, and relationships between academics become bureaucratized and hierarchical (as senior academics become charged with managing quality matters). In addition, communication between institutions and national quality agencies becomes strategic rather than dialogical, as the parties dance around each other, intent each on its own agenda.

Quality takes on its *ontological moment* as actors identify with quality as a project in its own right. Quality managers are appointed, whose *raison d'être* consists in their promoting quality as a project within the university: they become the advance guard in proselytizing the ideology. The officers of the national quality agency, too, have their entire professional identity grounded in the ideology. But others may be enlisted, wittingly or not; ideology may creep over them. Deans and professors may, Janus-like, look two ways, both repudiating the ideology and yet urging their colleagues on and even half coming to believe in the ideology as such.

We observed too that quality, as an ideology, may take either a pernicious or a virtuous turn. In practice, however, both through the desultory character of the academic interest in quality – in demonstrating only reluctantly the character of 'quality' in academic practices and in collaboratively advancing that quality – and through the power of the state and the professional bodies, quality comes to be imposed and the ideology takes a pernicious turn. In our diagram, it runs down the arm of pernicious ideologies.

So far, then, our summary reflections fall in exactly with our earlier schema. All ideologies – in higher education as elsewhere – are sustained by collective interests and depend, therefore, on structures of power. Ideology has had a bad name, normally being felt to be injurious to rational enterprises. In higher education, ideology can certainly take on such a nature, particularly where it is imposed and comes to have an alien character. However, as we have noted, ideology – again in higher education as elsewhere – can also have a virtuous character. There is no reason *in principle* that quality, too, cannot be put to the service of higher education, in improving the quality of the student experience and of academic activities more generally.

This positive aspect, of course, is precisely part of the rhetoric that accompanies the state-imposed ideology. In this way, *this* ideology falls in with the classic Marxian view of ideology, as a social project that attempts to cloak itself in a description that is the opposite of its true character. Its concerns with 'the student experience' and its wish to avoid a 'culture of compliance' are not even skin-deep: they are signs of discursive manipulation, of an attempt to invert reality. But that quality, as it has been usurped by the state and forged into an insidious ideology, becoming an *other*, an alien force, a project standing outside academic activities, in no way rules out the possibility that quality could be a force for good, for collective improvement, for taking seriously the student experience. As with other ideologies, quality can turn – on our diagram – in either direction, taking on either a pernicious or a virtuous character.

Arising out of our reflections in this chapter, then, we are able to refine our general schema. The first refinement arises from the reflection that quality has to fight its corner. It may have the power of the state behind it but, in a pluralistic society, the state will not have matters all its own way. More than that, in a pluralistic society, the state will be a carrier for many and even conflicting ideologies. Quality has, as we noted, to fight its corner against the other state ideology of entrepreneurialism. The energy behind quality and which propels it forward – to whichever arm of our spur – may be blocked, therefore. It may not be possible for the necessary head of steam to be built up; or, having been built up, it may be dampened as other ideologies gain new levels of energy. As a result, a process of *ideological displacement* may be set in train. This process, by which the necessary impetus may be thwarted or diminished, may be represented by a horizontal line at the top of our diagram, prior to the ideology taking shape in one direction or another. Where this happens, the life force that sustains an ideology may die and the ideology, in turn, withers.

The next refinement of our schema arises out of our reflections that, in principle, a pernicious ideology can be turned into a virtuous ideology. Quality can be a force for advancing towards utopian ideas of higher education *and* a means by which the academic community can develop its collective professionalism; entrepreneurialism can be a force for imparting new ideas; markets can challenge those in universities to reflect on their effectiveness in communication; and competition can be a force for imparting new sources of energy. Within a pluralistic society, universities have space of their own. If this allows them to resist ideologies that others seek to impose on them, it also allows them to develop ideologies of their own. The *ideological space* available to universities permits them to deploy ideologies for their own use. That is clear. But recall the distinctions that we made in the last chapter between internal/external ideologies and pernicious/virtuous ideologies. That the academic community is driving forward with an (internal) ideology in no way guarantees that the ideology is virtuous; on the contrary, it may be pernicious.

A conceptual challenge, therefore, arises wherever the presence of ideology is detected on campus and it is this: Does the ideology, despite its pernicious character, have a virtuous potential? This is a conceptual problem, since it poses the challenge as to whether the ideas that constitute the centre of the ideology could *ever* be put to work in support of a positive conception of the university. Identifying and driving forward a positive ideology in turn requires, as a first step, that we actually try to spell out a positive conception of the university.

Two further refinements to our diagram, therefore, become necessary (see Figure 7.1). Firstly, ideologies in higher education are often in the service of unspoken conceptions of the university, *regressive* conceptions in the case of pernicious ideologies and *positive* conceptions in the case of virtuous ideologies. We need, therefore, to symbolize the ends of the ideologies as some conception of the university, regressive and positive conceptions respectively. Secondly, ideologies require institutional energy for their realization. Characteristically, the line of energy runs down the pernicious arm of the spur; and, on our diagram, that line of energy is represented by arrows in that direction. But, in principle at least, new energy could be imparted such that the ideology could take on a virtuous character. The arrows could go in the opposite direction. For that to occur, there needs to be an *ideological turn* in the direction of a positive conception of the university.

It follows that, if progressive ends are to be achieved by universities, especially in an ideologically saturated situation, *positive conceptions of the university have first to be determined* that can, in turn, help in identifying any one university's progressive ends. It is no good assuming that positive conceptions of the university are already organically present and will have their day sooner or later. That is a recipe for disaster: the corrosive ideologies

Figure 7.1 The ideological turn

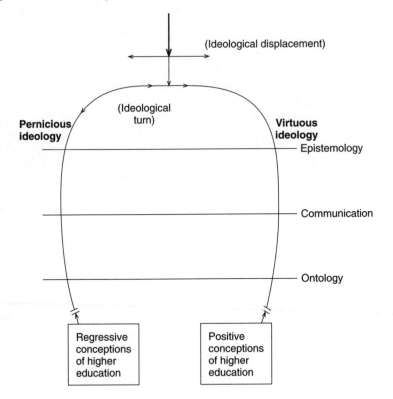

will simply sweep all before them. Realizing progressive ends requires both hard collective thinking and a determination within the leadership of each university to bring off such ends. Achieving an ideological turn is not for the fainthearted. However, the conditions under which such an ideological turn might be brought off await our further explorations.

8

'The Academic Community'

'Community': what community?

'The academic community' makes its presence felt precisely as ideology; it is nothing other than pure ideology. There is no empirical entity that we can point to that resembles an 'academic community'; the phrase contains a huge pretence.

Part of this seemingly outrageous claim, on reflection, will surely command general assent. It would be accepted that the academic world is composed of a multitude of communities. Those communities, too, are well understood themselves to be divided in manifold ways: disciplines and sub-disciplines, closeness to professions, interest in practice as such, interest in students, pedagogical approach and internationalism are only indicative of the fault lines. Indeed, so numerous are the possible sources of classification that probably no singular community is now visible. *All* the sub-communities are complexes, susceptible of manifold allegiances. In turn, individual academics secure their identities in quite different kinds of community *and* in multiple communities. That there is no single 'academic community' is now a commonplace, at least at the level of sentiment if not of expressed thought.

There are now not even boundaries to the academic community. Academics often have their livings to a large extent outside the walls of the university, in setting up free-standing companies, in consultancies and in professional activities. Those who offer or develop their views to wider publics than academic audiences are not simply rehearsing their academic views but are engaging with themselves as 'pure' academics in yielding to alternative discourses. Tacitly, they negotiate with those discourses of the wider world. Staff on part-time contracts are, of course, living in a perpetual state of such multilingualism.

The academic world and the wider world run into each other, if not perhaps as much as some would like. Those who espouse the view that there are, still, two worlds of knowledge usually imply that the dissolution of the boundaries between the two worlds has not gone far enough. There are three critiques of that two-world thesis: (i) the traditional position, which claims that there is only a single world of bona fide knowledge, namely academic knowledge; (ii) the moderate position, which claims that the boundary is much weaker than the two-world thesis pretends, with the two worlds already interpenetrating each other to a considerable degree; and (iii) the more radical position, which claims that, amid postmodernity, there are numerous and proliferating knowledges and that the two-world thesis, far from being a disturbing wake-up call to academe to recognize a form of knowledge radically different from its own, in fact conveys an over-simplified picture of the heterogeneity of knowledges both within academe itself and at large in the contemporary world.[1]

We can dismiss the traditional critique: amid postmodernity, the academic world can no longer claim hegemony over the definitions of knowledge; there will be other claimants. On either of the other two critiques, it is implied that the boundaries are dissolving at a considerable rate, if they have not actually dissolved. The two-world thesis is, we can say, a helpful reminder that there are epistemologies that stand outside the framing of academics, but misleading in implying that there are tight boundaries between these epistemologies (so producing just two modes of knowing). Academic life is itself increasingly one of living in a plurality of epistemologies. However, the key part of our opening statement remains unsupported and, now, even more implausible than ever. Just how can 'the academic community' be an ideology? If the idea of community is itself in trouble, as it is, the notion that 'academic community' can constitute an ideology is surely in even more difficulty.

The invisibility of 'the academic community'

In pointing to 'the academic community' as ideology, the quotation marks are necessary in a way that they are not in respect of entrepreneurialism, competition and quality. Each of those latter three ideologies are movements, espoused by advocates and generating systematic means of carrying them forward. Universities organize themselves so as to encourage entrepreneurialism among their staff, national systems are developed to encourage competition among universities and quality is driven forward by bureaucratic mechanisms internationally, nationally and within individual universities. In those separate infrastructures, individuals gain their identities by espousing the cause and come to believe in the cause. Pro-vice-chancellors are appointed with such projects explicitly written into their portfolios and units are established to drive forward those projects internally. These ideologies are full-blown ideologies, with their public forms of framing, exchange and identities. Our three dimensions of ideology – of truth criteria, of communication and of subjectivities – are evident in and through those three ideologies.

In contrast, the apparatuses of national body, of government white papers and of university personnel and units are more or less invisible in relation to 'the academic community': *it* is hardly present as an explicit project. Some signs are certainly present but in a more *sotto voce* form. In the UK, for instance, a national body represents the interests of all universities. Significantly, though, that body is showing signs of dissolution. Recently, it underwent a transformation, changing from a single entity – the Committee of Vice-Chancellors and Principals – to several bodies: as well as Universities UK, there are now three further bodies representative of the UK regions. At the same time, there are informal groupings of particular universities which recognize each other as like institutions. The presence of these informal groups implies not just difference but also hierarchy; one of the groups, for instance, known as The Russell Group, comprises universities that are recognized to include the leading universities in research.

That such difference reveals itself is hardly surprising in a mass higher education system. Institutions bear a common name – 'university' – but hold different relationships to culture, the economy and the institutions of power (such as the judiciary, the government and the financial centres).[2] From time to time, those universities may find cause to hide their differences to a large extent as the university sector makes its pitch on major issues. For example, in 1997, through the Committee of Vice-Chancellors and Principals, the UK universities produced a composite statement in contributing evidence to a National Committee of Inquiry into Higher Education (CVCP 1997).[3] Such a symbol of unity may be difficult to sustain as the tension between diversity and common interests plays itself out across the higher education sector.

'The academic community', therefore, seems to be failing our criteria: if universities are divided among themselves, if there is hardly anything approaching a substantial apparatus embodying and projecting the academic community, and if there are no obvious identities to be formed around 'the academic community' as a project, how can it be argued that 'the academic community' represents an ideology? Where are the pro-vice-chancellors with 'the academic community' in their portfolios to match those with specific responsibilities for competition, entrepreneurialism and quality written into their contracts? If this is an ideology, it seems strangely invisible.

A hopeful description

The phrase 'the academic community' speaks of a set of collective interests. The character of those interests is far from obvious, both parts of the term – 'academic' and 'community' – being in difficulty. The second term has already been put in question: in a mass higher education system, with institutions networked to the wider society and economy in contrasting ways, the existence of a single *community* has to be in doubt. But the first term in the phrase also gives rise to difficulty, with individuals in universities balking at describing themselves as 'academics' and preferring other terms – teacher, researcher, tutor and even, perhaps, facilitator of learning. This is understandable: in an age in which higher education widens, the category of *academic* is eroded. The separateness from the wider world that the term 'academic' implies has come to attract pejorative connotations: to be 'academic' is to be unhealthily other-worldly.

'The academic community', therefore, stands in double jeopardy. The two terms of 'academic' and 'community' each claim both a separateness *from* an outside world and a unity *within* that cannot easily be upheld. And yet the term retains a resonance that can still be and is drawn upon. Admittedly, part of the explanation of its use is that, so far, alternative expressions have not entered the (English) language with any durability. That state of affairs, however, could be explained negatively: no alternative expression has emerged precisely because no alternative expression is necessary. If the academic community is no more, we do not require an expression with which to refer to it. But that consideration will hardly suffice: the term 'the academic community' *is* still with us and is not infrequently deployed.

It is deployed both from without and from within. Both those positioned in the wider society *and* those in the academic world itself can and do resort to the term. Fictive 'the academic community' may be, but it is a fiction that still has its supporters. The motivations for that support are, though, we may judge, somewhat different.

For those 'outside', the term offers a convenience. It implies that despite internal differences, there remain large unifying features straddling the territory marked out by institutions of higher education. The implied claim goes further: the suggestion is that this is more than a mere collectivity working in its own interests and that the constituent parts are linked in some significant way. But, from an external perspective, the term implies, too, a separateness from the wider society. The boundaries between the academic world and the wider world are still recognizable. 'The academic community', deployed from an external vantage point, tells a double fiction of commonality and separateness. That double fiction is, in turn, doubly useful: the term enables its user both to achieve certain effects on the audience – the 'academic community' *is* of this unified and separate form – and saves that same user from having to consider seriously its inner constituents. Any potentially divisive differences that this 'academic community' may harbour can safely be overlooked.

If, then, in being deployed from the outside, the term 'academic community' emphasizes separateness from the wider world, when used from the inside, the connotations of togetherness are played up. What those connotations might be are, of course, ambiguous. The term 'community' implies a collective identity, a common language and even a common culture. That all of these are in question in a fluid age gives pause in the deployment of the term. The term, however, lives on. There is a hope attached to its usage as well as a possible fading description. 'The academic community' is, above all else, a hopeful description.

A peculiarly academic ideology

The end-of-ideology thesis is another hopeful description *and* is a product of certain academics. It is also, in itself, an instance of ideology: it is a piece of ideological mystification. The end-of-ideology thesis falls in nicely with one of the classic hallmarks of ideology as supplying a veil, in making things appear other than they are and producing an illusion that has an interest structure behind it. It suits various sets of collective purposes to have us believe that ideology is at an end, one of those purposes being that the thesis seems to supply order in a chaotic situation.

That situation is precisely a world in which our cognitive options are multiplying beyond our capacity to comprehend them. The end-of-ideology thesis, under these conditions, serves to offer a handle on a world that threatens to become out-of-cognitive-control. By describing this state of affairs as 'the end of ideology', we buy a form of cognitive peace. Through the end-of-ideology thesis, the world is described and so a form of order is placed upon it. If ideologies help us to live in the world by giving us cognitive frames that allow us to comprehend it, the end-of-ideology thesis is, paradoxically, an ideology *par excellence*. In turn, there are those in academe who further their identities out of the thesis and construct their intellectual communities around its espousal. Epistemology, ontology and communication structures: all the dimensions of ideology that we have picked out in our story so far are to be found in the end-of-ideology thesis.

Those who espouse the end-of-ideology thesis in the academic context might argue that the formation of mass higher education has brought with it both an internal dissolution and a dissolving of the boundaries with the wider world. Higher education has acquired fissiparous tendencies and, in the process, has witnessed internal epistemological and social break-up such that there is no unity. On the other hand, its various constituent parts have forged relationships with the wider society such that there is often mutual interpenetration. The corporate world has come onto campus *and* vice versa: the different forms of academic life have often gone into that world, not just by marketing their wares or pitching their tents – by forming their own companies – but also by negotiating relationships with institutions and organizations.

In this situation, so the argument would presumably run, higher education becomes itself an ideologically free zone. Ideologies, after all, would present solid frames of self-understanding and action precisely at a time when universities need to be able to move across boundaries and space in fluid ways. Universities find themselves in enough difficulty simply in surviving and in responding with positive effect to the vicissitudes that beset them, without signing themselves up to large binding projects of the kind represented by 'ideologies'. The university splits asunder as a single coherent project, its increasing constituents going their own way in forming their separate accommodations to the world around them. Behind adjacent rooms on the corridor develop biographies that may have very little in common.

The end-of-ideology thesis is explicable, therefore, in part at least, precisely as an outcome of the absence of academic community. The university dissolves, becoming so many contrasting projects and identities. There is neither the durability of circumstance nor the commonality of purpose on which ideology can gain an anchorage.

Putting the argument simply, on both philosophical and sociological grounds, ideology finds no anchor within the university. In a postmodern age, in an age of fragility, the foundations for forming large claims of the kind on which ideology rests dissolve (the philosophical thesis); while amid postmodernity or late modernity, the world becomes so fluid, amorphous and individualized that the conditions for ideology to be present, those of commonality and of large counterposed interests, collapse (the sociological thesis).

The counter to the general end-of-ideology thesis being advanced here is simply that, much as ideology might be felt to be at an end, there is a will to ideologize amid human life. Ideology bestows purpose and identity and, therefore, will be needed even more under the conditions of anomie that enabled the end-of-ideology thesis to be plausible. Indeed, the end-of-ideology thesis takes on the character of an ideology, precisely in that it supplies purpose and identity.

We should note that the end-of-ideology thesis is advanced by academics, at least within particular disciplines. In other words, the end-of-ideology thesis supplies purpose and identity *on campus*. Through this ideology, certain academics can proclaim their non-ideological virtues: their non-ideology thesis becomes their ideology. The end-of-ideology thesis as a thesis about the university is a nice example of the way in which academics' stories about themselves project their own interests and even come to cast the world as other than it is. The academics' stories about themselves are not to be trusted.

Community and individualism

We can pursue this argument about self-identity by focusing even more directly on 'the academic community'. We have noted the dual tendency of the contemporary academic world both to fly apart, its constituents taking up different stances within the university and negotiating different postures with the wider world, *and* for academics themselves to be subject to the process of *individualization*.[4] Yet saying that the university has become a site of manifold projects *and* personal trajectories does not destroy the basis on which ideology gains its grip. On the contrary, it offers new spaces for ideology to secure a purchase. Competition, quality and enterprise are only three of the ideologies to find their way onto campus. In turn, 'the academic community' itself serves as a site of ideology, and it does so at both the general and the local level.

At the *general* level, the academic community reveals its ideological character in defending its collective interests or, to put it more accurately, interests that the academic community would wish to portray *as* collective. The academic community may resist *en bloc* the imposition on it of the excesses – as it would suggest they are – of a national quality evaluation framework as it becomes ever more intrusive; it may seek to secure a salary framework in keeping with a collective self-image that draws on a status that it enjoyed half a century ago; and within institutions, it may seek to curb – as it sees it – extreme forms of managerialism with the question 'But don't you trust us?' and its implication that managers are undermining collegiality. In each of these examples, there is resort to a sense of a common set of purposes and interests. Furthermore, there is a tacit claim that university staff share a particular space in which to conduct *their* projects; it is *there*, in particular, that 'the academic community' supposedly resides.

One of these examples, the jibe made by some academics that senior colleagues in their managerial roles are undermining collegiality, is especially interesting for our present purposes for, there, ideology is doubly at work. On the one hand, it pretends to a collectivity that has to be in doubt. On the other hand, the angst over the diminution that the new managers are accused of causing to collegial life is particularly suspect since, all too often, we can reasonably surmise that the 'real' message behind the charge takes the form of 'leave me alone to do my own thing'.

This is an example of an ideology in full flight: an utterance that inveighs against a malign state of affairs by calling up interests that have been damaged, when the utterance itself obscures the real interest at work which is an *inversion* of that portrayed. Here, the real interest is precisely an *individual* interest when a collective interest has been summoned in aid. Indeed, that collective interest has been invented for the purpose of advancing the opposite interest, namely of academics as individuals. Communication, projection, the summoning of collective interests and obscuring the real intent: many of the classic signs of ideology are present here.

We should note, then, that within the academic world, *commonality and collectivism are by no means the same thing*. It is doubtful whether universities have ever fully lived up to their claims to be 'self-critical academic communities', but what is surely apparent is that, left to themselves, as universities break apart ever more, the idea that universities are unitary communities in *any* sense has to be in even more doubt. Yet, as collegiality dissolves and individualism grows, collective interests are to be seen flourishing precisely in the defence of individual interests. X and Y may be engaged in quite different activities (one might be active in leading-edge research and the other might be generating significant consultancy income) but each requires the other, for each contributes something important to the university *qua* enterprise. From *gemeinschaft* to *gesellschaft*: from community formed around similarity to community formed around difference. The valuing of the individual interest supplies the collective currency.

What emerges is that the 'academic community' is an ideology doing double duty. It serves as an emblem of unity when it is in the interests of university staff to pretend – both internally and beyond the university – that there is a collegial unity to their work *and* it obscures, while advancing at the same time, the collective interests of academics as *individuals*. This ideology at best adverts to a fading community, even a community that never was, while promoting the new individualism that is in the collective interest of the academic members of the university.

The truth, the whole truth . . .

Those who research and teach in universities gain their livings through their capacities to live in and through knowledges. Knowledge is their thing; it has to be. And with knowledge comes truth. Nothing fancy need be intended here: those who produce papers for the literature and who assess students will carry at least tacit conceptions of knowledge and truth, *their* conceptions of knowledge and truth, with them in their work. These conceptions *may* be made explicit. Some may even espouse views to the effect that they are not looking for truth (either in their own work or in that of their students) and do not see themselves as working within particular knowledge structures. Such individuals may talk of truth as being 'relative' and knowledge as being 'social' or 'tacit', but such individuals are demonstrating their sophistication in deploying the concepts of knowledge and truth. Their accounts are parasitic upon knowledge and truth having substance.

In saying that we may continue to understand academic life partly through the concepts of knowledge and truth, therefore, all that is intended is to indicate that they stubbornly remain – for now – as helpful concepts even if they have to be both widely *and* inexactly drawn. If we are seriously trying to unravel the general character of university life to a visitor from another planet and to distinguish it from other callings, sooner or later the concepts of knowledge and truth are likely to be found to be helpful.[5]

To say that the concepts of knowledge and truth are significant in the unravelling of university life does not, in itself, conjure the sighting of ideology. Yet ideology is not far from view. Less a matter of expression, ideology here is to be found in the way in which knowledge and truth exemplify a form of life.

Ernest Gellner insistently remarked that our epistemologies were social in character: they expressed forms of life held to be valuable. It was on that account that he was able to place Ayer's logical positivism of *Language, Truth and Logic* in the same company as Snow's identification of *The Two Cultures* (the comparison coming out to the disadvantage of Ayer, the professional philosopher).[6] *Both* implicitly gave high marks to science: both were epistemologies of a society in which science attracted high marks. Gellner was not taking up arms against such epistemologies in themselves; on the contrary, Gellner's *oeuvre* sought to provide, so far as was possible, a justification of the inner beliefs of a science-based society. Strangely, the concept of ideology is only rarely to be found in Gellner's writings, although its fuller treatment would surely have assisted him in his sociological insights into knowledges.[7]

Perhaps Gellner was just too reasonable: his *oeuvre* is suggestive of utter reasonableness, of participating in a transparent conversation.[8] Ideology, however, works its wonders *not* to behold. Ideology has come into academic life *pari passu* with the arrival of the knowledge society. In the knowledge society, by definition, even if it is not yet the case that everyone is his or her own producer of (his or her own) knowledge, the production of knowledge is very widely dispersed. At the same time, knowledge is valued more than ever.

This state of affairs prompts a kind of SWOT analysis of the academic world: what are the Opportunities and Threats that are presented to it and what Strengths and Weaknesses does it have in turn to present to them? The main *threat* is that the universities' forms of knowledge and their tacit truth criteria are going to be challenged, and even ridiculed, by other claimants from the wider (knowledge) society. In turn, *opportunities* arise since society now values knowledge: if they can only find ways of presenting their knowledges, universities can turn formal knowledges into knowledge *wares*, having a (Lyotardian) performativity. The academy's *strength* to move in this direction lies in its *gravitas*: it is used to being taken seriously. It has the power to move and shake. Its *weaknesses* are that it will come to take itself *too* seriously and underestimate the task of selling those knowledge wares in a credulous age. Precisely because it is used to being given a platform, it will underestimate the communicative challenge that lies in wait. Its self-presentation could be found wanting.

Under these circumstances, ideological spaces open. Variously, academics will advance their newly found epistemological interests, often with pecuniary advantage. At other times, academics whose epistemologies are being threatened will find ways of securing new legitimations for them and of identifying new publics. Hardly a discipline seems to be ruled out as the source of authority of media dons. Indeed, some disciplines find suddenly that they have a public for the first time in over a hundred years; or that the making of a public is at least within their grasp. Even philosophers are called up to advance their views in television programmes and other mass media.

Advocacy as such cannot be said to constitute ideology. That shift, the jump to ideology, is made when the non-knowledge components of a communication take priority over the message. In the process, the message is liable to be corrupted. What is advocated is not the truth claims as such but their significance, their *outturn*. The outturn may be in the form of technological products or, as we may call them, human products, namely the academics themselves as they promote themselves. Social and symbolic capital capture the high ground from economic capital.[9] Philosophers even become media personalities.

In these performative processes, knowledges are put to work and are called upon to fulfil extra-epistemological purposes. A sub-discipline, the sociology of knowledge, develops its range in part to map these extra-epistemological dimensions (McCarthy 1996). Knowledge is not what it seems. It comes to count only in so far as it has some kind of pay-off. Knowledge counts as knowledge in so far as it leads to '*action*' (Stehr 2001).

In this milieu, each knowledge becomes its own ideology, asserting itself not just extramurally, outside the university, but also vehemently within it. As each activity in the university is measured, and as the managers develop accounting systems by which to calculate the cost–benefit ratio of each of their activities, so disciplines, far from constituting a community, are turned on each other. Insolvent departments are closed down. For the most part, it is not done explicitly. But ways are found of advancing the interests of each discipline, perhaps by persuading the powers that be to rejig the basis on which the calculations are made for a particular discipline.

Even if he did not use the term 'ideology' in his critical comments on philosophers and others, Nietzsche was perhaps the first to notice the ideological basis of academic life. Academics come to believe their own rhetoric and come to take themselves too seriously. They believe that they *are* authorities.[10] Even in a postmodern age, ideological spaces open for academics to portray themselves as authorities on the end of reason, the dissolution of conceptual and moral foundations and on the end of ideology, even as they acquire identities and livings in the course of making such proclamations. These ideologists advance the truth, but it is hardly the whole truth; and it is certainly not 'nothing but the truth'. Interests, subjectivities and values are being advanced here; and many of those interests, subjectivities and values are not to be described purely through the life of reason. Knowledge and truth live on quite nicely as ideologies.

Remaking the academic community

In tracing ideology in 'the academic community', we have encountered confirmations of our general thesis. Not only does ideology live but, paradoxically, it is called for amid conditions of fluidity, openness and non-foundationalism. In these conditions, exactly the conditions that lead some to proclaim that we are at the end of ideology, a need for ideology arises. Ideology, after all, is a vehicle that brings purpose, identity and a firm comprehension of the world and all of those are just what the contemporary world lacks. Ideology is a means of giving back to the world what it has lost.

'The academic community' is one such ideology. Unlike entrepreneurialism, competition and quality, this ideology is counterfactual in character. It thrives on that which it is not. There is only the barest vestige of a single academic community, if indeed there is even that. 'The academic community' is an expression of hope. But it is also, we saw, a means of obfuscation. The newly emancipated members of universities address the epistemological challenges that come their way in the knowledge society by advancing their own interests in more or less creative ways. No ideology wishes to speak its own name – ideology is always expressed by others, never oneself – but *this* ideology is especially surreptitious. The academic community advances its interests by drawing attention to itself as little as possible and, thereby, hiding the academics' *individualism.*

All ideologies have both pernicious *and* virtuous possibilities. Entrepreneurialism, competition and quality, *in due moderation* and deployed with virtuous ends in collective mind, harbour the capacities to be virtuous in their effects. So, too, with 'the academic community'. For that to happen, however, 'the academic community' with its counterfactual character – and hence the quotation marks – would have to materialize into an academic community as a set of substantial practices (that is, an academic community without the quotation marks). Ways would have to be found of enabling the members of the academic staff of universities to identify with each other, across disciplines, and to work together in the wider interests of both the academy and society.[11] Unless that vision can be realized *to some degree,* unless the academic community can be realized at least in part, we shall continue to be in the presence of 'the academic community' (with the quotation marks) – that is, of a set of disparate interests yielding purposes, projects and personal trajectories that serve narrow interests running against the life of generous reason.

Ideologies, we may say, come in two forms: full frontal, where they are taken forward explicitly as projects, and surreptitious, when the ideology is obscured, the world being presented as that which it is not. In full frontal ideologies, the key terms – such as quality, enterprise and competition – are voiced frequently and come to frame biographies and bureaucratic systems. They become epistemologies in their own right, being ways of knowing the world and supplying the criteria against which other activities are evaluated. Surreptitious ideologies, in contrast, as the term implies, are underhand in their workings. They are characterized by stealth and obfuscation. 'The academic community' is just such a surreptitious ideology, but no less powerful for all that. The academic world finds it in its interests to convey the impression that it *is* a community, when its actual dispositions and, indeed, behaviours are quite to the contrary.

The forces at work conspire to reduce the extent to which academics constitute a community. Those who inhabit universities take up differing identities and do not even necessarily consider themselves to be academics; the disciplines themselves become messy pools of understanding and action such that community breaks down even locally; universities become complex organizations, allowing spaces for differing identities with, for example, some identifying entirely with research and others with teaching; and the development of a managerial capacity injects a vertical challenge to community. So 'academic community', as a term, serves a negative function: to pretend that things are other than they are. If interest structures, discourses and organization conspire to obliterate academic community, it may seem that the only space available to 'the academic community' is that of an insidious ideology that works counterfactually, to defend *particular* rather than community interests. But matters need not be like that. 'The academic community' can be turned from a counterfactual ideology to an expression of a university's being.

'The academic community' can, therefore, be turned into *an academic community*. The ideal can be realized; or, at least, become a definite practical project. For that, though, those in positions of university leadership would have to judge that 'the academic community' was an idea worth realizing *and* to work for it. The pernicious ideology could be turned into a virtuous ideology, but only if effort is put into bringing it about. Especially since the empirical forces are considerable, the counter effort to realize an academic community would also have to be considerable. That effort would have to be felt to be worthwhile. Positive conceptions of academic community need to be framed and turned into strategies that counter, while remaining sensitive to, the separation within contemporary academic life.

Such a counter-culture is not to be achieved by obliterating forms of individualism and separation for that is not a feasible strategy. Instead, this counter-culture is realized by being inserted as an added culture. Community and individualization have to work not hand in hand but alongside each other as parallel tracks. Academic community taken forward as a virtuous ideology is unlikely to displace its more pernicious forms: the two have to come to some accommodation with each other. To return to our evolving diagram (Figure 8.1), the two sides of the spur must remain, in contention with each other: for quite different reasons, neither can vanquish the other.[12]

Conclusion

The realization of universities as academic communities requires new forms of academic leadership, working to bring about process goals rather than operational goals and collective understanding rather than corporate performance. It will only gain something approaching a secure toehold by working through existing conceptions of self-understanding: positive conceptions of the university as an academic community have to be brought to bear on attitudes, values and modes of being – hence the dotted line in Figure 8.1. If corrosive ideologies are primarily ontological in character (a fundamental thesis here), virtuous ideologies will only get off the ground if those attitudes and values are confronted directly by enlightened university leaderships. At times, at least, this will prove to be hard-going, but who said institutional leadership was easy?

As with the others that we have encountered, 'the academic community' is a hybrid ideology: it can take up either a pernicious or a virtuous stance. It can work exactly to reduce the hopes that it stands for – it can reduce the presence of an academic community – or it can be a virtuous ideology offering a set of progressive ways forward for the academy in the twenty-first century. The prospect opens up, therefore, that the positive components of

Figure 8.1   Realizing positive ideologies

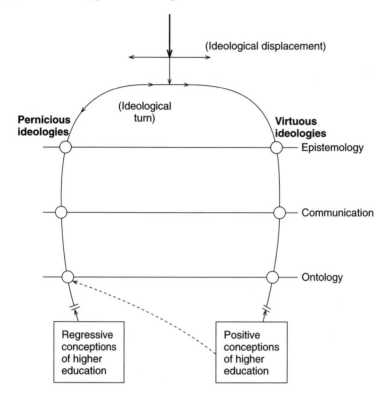

ideologies can be seized upon and offer a glimpse of a way of redeeming the ideals in the idea of the university. Still ahead of us is the investigation of the general conditions of institutional life that might make it possible for virtuous ideologies to become creative and lasting practices in universities and it is that, therefore, that must constitute the main task of Part 3.

Part 3

Virtuous Ideologies

9

Communicating Values

Academic values: non-existent or just invisible?

'Values' is a term that dare not speak its name, at least within the university. Universities are disinclined to admit to the values that they identify with and sustain within themselves. They have their mission statements, their goals and their hopes, but they shrink from declaring the values that might underpin those goals. Why is this? Two extreme possibilities present themselves. Either universities are value-free *or* they are awash with values but disinclined to declare their hand in the matter. The first possibility can be disregarded immediately for no organization, and no group of people interacting and carrying forward projects in a collaborative manner, can be devoid of values. The second possibility, therefore, presses itself forward: that values are embedded in the activities that find expression in universities but are held only tacitly, not being brought out into the open.

The counter may come that the value opposition just offered is misjudged. Universities are hemmed in to such a degree that while they have values embedded in their actions, those values are not theirs: ideologies of the market, competition and quality are so framed by the state and external stakeholders that the room for manoeuvre open to universities is closed off. On this view, the values by which universities operate are coerced upon them. But this argument does not bear weight. Yes, across the world, universities are obliged to fall in with external ideologies that press upon them: their survival depends on such responsiveness. But the *ways* in which they take on those ideologies and the *extent* to which they do so are largely of their own making. In democratic societies, including those where the state has driven forward strategically ideologies that would encourage universities to embrace 'academic capitalism' (Slaughter and Leslie 1997), universities enjoy large pools of space in which to take up value positions of their own.

A more nuanced suggestion may be heard to the effect that the two extreme positions – of value absence and of value-plurality-but-value-silence

– are just that, extreme positions. The university, it may be said, is a broad church permitting of many sects and communities. Consequently, there are many value positions in the university; indeed, that is to be encouraged. A university is open, if not to all possible sets of values then to very many. It is a universe of values as well as of cognitions and theoretical frameworks; different values are even embedded in its disciplines.

The argument may run still further. It may be said that the university is a kind of holding company of value positions. Value positions may be traded, investments may be made in them and a few may even get rich on them. But the university as such, *qua* holding company as it were, is value neutral. It does not, it will not and it dare not declare itself for or against any particular set of values. It offers a ring where the market in values can be played out.[1] However heated the positions become, the university simply holds the ring open. It does not declare its own hand. If it has any values, it keeps them to itself.

This more nuanced position has right on its side but it is disingenuous. That the university is a ring-master, allowing and even encouraging debate between contestants taking up different value positions, itself carries with it certain kinds of value orientations around freedom of speech, engagement and criticality (positions being accorded the respect of a hearing). The university, therefore, can be seen as a setting of layered values: values reside in the particular practices, activities and communities within the university *and* values are embedded in the university *qua* social institution. Values are to be seen in action both in disciplinary seminars *and* in the Vice-Chancellor's management team meetings. But that reflection only underscores the point already made, that the university is a site – potentially, at least – of a multitude of value positions, even if some values speak to the kind of organization in which yet others are nested.

So, then, we are back where we started: the university harbours many sets of values but those value positions are hardly to be voiced as such. 'Values', to repeat, is a term that dare not speak its name on campus. There is a nice paradox at work here. It is *not* simply that the university gives house room to different value positions and yet those separate values are hardly ever paraded as such. That is regrettable, perhaps, but it hardly constitutes a paradox. Rather, the paradox arises from the university gaining its living in part precisely out of its broadmindedness.

Giving house room to conflicting positions – empirical, theoretical, value – is precisely what a university is in business for. *Vive là différence*. This is the motto of the Western university. Not quite all, but pretty well all, can find a place in the university. The university lives through its values. And yet, when it comes to values themselves, even the value orientations inherent in the life of reason – of tolerance, respect for persons and critical dialogue – the university keeps quiet about them. The university, accordingly, censures itself – on its value positions – even when its rhetoric is about freedom of expression. That is the paradox of the university's value positioning.

The paradox goes further. The university is committed to reason *and* its dominant values of tolerance, discursive freedom, respect for persons and critical dialogue – so the university likes to think – have right on their side. If pressed, reasons could be adduced to offer backing for this value framework. There is a rational side even to the university's value position. But, ordinarily, one wouldn't know this precisely because of the university's value paradox: the university rarely stops to try to spell out the reasons that attest to its own values even though the university declares itself on the side of reason. The reasons for the university's own existence are kept out of sight. Unfortunately, out of sight, out of mind. The paradox, therefore, has practical consequences. If the university in the twenty-first century is suffering, as it is, an identity crisis, the university has in part to blame itself. It has simply not carried through its own value framework to its logical conclusion: it has truncated its reason in relation to *itself.*

The university, then, is an especially value-laden institution yet that very matter, a matter in some ways to be celebrated, is kept hidden. It is not spoken about. Silence results. It is a kind of not-in-front-of-the-children silence in which any mention of values brings on sheer embarrassment. The embarrassment is to be seen and felt throughout the campus, whether in the laboratory, the research seminar, the committee meeting or the senior management team meeting in the Vice-Chancellor's room.

Conspiracy of silence

How might we explain this silence? Is it that members of the university have been reading texts on late modernity and have formed the conclusion that values can never be 'grounded', that they lie beyond all reason, and so opt out of value talk?[2] Has there been a wholesale conversion to the idea that values speak of 'grand narratives' which can no longer hold sway, with values only being redeemed through particular and non-communicating forms of life. Values, it may be felt, are simply a means of getting by on a personal basis, a means of sense-making in a chaotic world. Amid 'liquid modernity' (Bauman 2000), values are better understood not as stable pools of meaning but as intersecting swirls of life interpretation. If they ever had them, now values must be understood to have lost any stability and solidity. Any discussion about values, therefore, has to be so much air (hot or otherwise) lacking any referent. There can be nothing outside a value discussion on which any such discussion could find an anchor. Values are not matters over which there can be serious discussion.

If this were the case, if there was found to be a disinclination towards making values explicit on the grounds of the contemporary literature, clearly such reading habits would have been rather narrow. Such academics would not have been reading their Habermas, for example, for whom discussion over values is a rational enterprise, involving the giving and taking of grounds for beliefs and a serious intention to progress argumentatively. But we can put our thought experiment to one side: keeping up with the literature on social theory and philosophy – or at least that part of it in which such scepticism is aired – is the lifestyle of a small, if often noisy, group of academics. For an explanation for the value silence on campus, we have to look elsewhere.

As with most social phenomena on any scale, we see here a situation of *over-determination*. Values are a substrate of academe; for the most part, they are not held in direct focus. Why, then, bring them out into the open? Making progress in academic life is difficult enough, whether in the 'heartlands' of academics' activities (Burton Clark 1998) or in the operational activities pressed forward by those in managerial and leadership positions. Adding value talk, whether to exchanges in the knowledge fields or to those in the practical fields that constitute the university, would simply add a level of complexity that promises no resolution. In any event, the academics have mostly persuaded themselves that the possible influence of values on their disciplinary activities has been largely neutralized: academic methodologies allow exchanges to take place in an antiseptic environment. In parallel, the rise of a professional administrative class to support the operational side of university life has also developed methodologies that wear the icon of *value freedom*: the minutes of committee meetings, the spreadsheets and the numerical tabulations of activities against 'performance indicators' are devices, again, to expunge values from decision making. The rationalism that they represent is a rationalism devoid of value choices.

If the academics and the managers collude to air brush values from their images of academic life, their efforts are supported by an even wider policy framework in which, again, issues are presented as technical issues (how to generate more investment for higher education, how to generate more participants from lower socioeconomic classes, how to ensure that the intellectual products of universities are contributing fully to the 'knowledge economy'). The work of the state's agencies, too, is presented as if their activities – in allocating state monies, in determining initiatives, in conducting quality evaluations – are also purely technical matters. The ends are largely given: all that is at issue are the methodologies and ensuring that both the judged and the judges understand them. That there might be contestable ends serving quite different and even incompatible values – of academic freedom, of the development of professionalism, of control – is simply never admitted. (The 'never' can be used without squeamishness.)

To the state's silence over values in the university's hinterland can be added the silence from the corporate sector. Its interests in using the university's knowledge products for corporate growth and influence and its right to sequester those products, even at the expense of limiting publication in the journals of accounts concerning evaluations, technologies and findings that it has underwritten, are taken for granted. *Its* values, in favour of profit, growth and market share, are not so much assumed as imposed as a *fait accompli*. Value issues are not part of this discourse: 'value freedom' does not really capture the milieu. It is tacitly acknowledged that there is a value base to such corporatism. This is much more a case of an orchestrated *value avoidance.*

The silence in respect of values on campus and in its hinterland, therefore, is – as remarked – *over-determined.* There is a collusion among many parties, within and without the university. There is a conspiracy of silence, endorsed and supported by parties who are otherwise contending against each other. Under these circumstances, a discourse of values cannot gain a hearing.

And what is in it for me?

Values that are characteristic of the university are, we may judge, deep in its academic activities, embedded in its research and teaching. Yet, the university is changing. It is not simply that it is becoming dynamic, demonstrating its capacities to change. It is that this dynamism is now organized and managed. In the process, the university is no longer clear as to its central core; indeed, it can no longer be sure that it has any durable core. Questions do not just emerge but are deliberately posed, in 'awaydays' for a university's managers, as to its key goals for the next ten years: 'nothing is ruled in and nothing is ruled out' in this discourse.

Universities are under pressure to demonstrate their democratic credentials by visibly opening themselves to potential students from poorer backgrounds. In turn, universities – some, at least – acquire a responsibility to develop a service for students in support of their 'academic literacy'. All this generates infrastructure costs. At the same time, overseas students, perhaps paying a particularly high level of fees and conscious of having foregone offers from universities in other countries, seek a return on their investment. Again, they may be able to extract a correspondingly higher level of service from their universities. Consequently, a culture develops in which tutors themselves become sensitive to the economic returns not just from teaching but also from teaching this rather than that student. The pedagogical relationship becomes economicized. 'What is it worth?' comes to rival 'Is it worth it?' Teaching is put under the economic spotlight.

Research looks secure; indeed, there will be calls for more of it, given the increase in research monies in a knowledge-laden economy. But 'research', if not exactly a contested concept, stretches conceptually this way and that. 'Research' comes to embrace consultancies, evaluations for municipal authorities, technology 'transfer' and the production of cultural artefacts and even artistic performances. As the different academic fields are called into the marketplace, both to generate income from whatsoever source and to advance the university's profile, and since the term 'research' commands a high resonance factor among different stakeholders, as many activities as possible come to be labelled in that way. A *first* reading of this state of affairs is that research is becoming conceptually rich, covering so many contrasting activities; a *second* reading is that the concept of research is being thinned such that it no longer counts for anything of substance. In the process, too, the values that inform research both widen and thin to a state of fragility: almost anything goes in this milieu.

A yet *third* reading is possible, however, and one that is captured in the question, 'And what is in it for me?' If modern society is now embarked on a process of individualism (Beck and Beck-Gernsheim 2001; Putnam 2001), the university is hardly likely to stay immune. The disciplines with their forms of collective life have served to ensure that individualism has made its entry into academe only laggardly. But its signs are now assuredly there. If universities devise accounting systems to monitor the performance or productivity of staff, and if those accounting systems are designed to yield data on individuals, academics' collective bonds are bound to be weakened. But this operational disposition in favour of individualism is aided and abetted by changing epistemologies.

Knowledges are having to demonstrate their worth in the world: they leap into the world and become active there. Research projects are designed in partnership with external stakeholders, whether in the policy domain or in the corporate world. Spaces for hybrid identities open: many academics shrink from straddling multiple boundaries but some find it intoxicating. However, the academic entrepreneurialism that effects this boundary-hopping brings an individualism in its wake. There is an apparent paradox here: while knowledge becomes societal in its character, academic life is individualized. The point, though, is that knowledge is becoming societal rather than social: the knowledge society opens up spaces – admittedly fragile – that allow knowledge entrepreneurs in the university to acquire new livings. In this milieu, it is each man and woman for him and herself. They may work in teams but those teams are liable, in any case, to dissolve when the present project is concluded.

For the managers, the manifestation of the *individualization thesis* on campus cuts two ways. On the one hand, the increasing disinclination to associate with university goals and to be loyal to the university as such is a cause of frustration: just how is one to gain academics' motivation and effort towards a new opportunity to develop a university partnership with another organization when there are no obvious personal gains? On the other hand, this new individualization is breathing new sources of energy and motivation that can yet secure new markets and new projects, provided that they are seen to be in individuals' interests. If individuals make the calculation in favour of such a new opportunity, new sources of institutional energy just may be mobilized.

An ethics of the balance sheet

Values, it might be said, are emptied out of the university *or* are undermined. However, the two stories – of emptying and undermining – have different and even contrasting emphases; they could both be right but there are tensions between them.

The image of *emptying out* has, as its context, the age of pragmatism that many would say we now inhabit.[3] It is an age without foundations, an age with a sense that there can be neither an argumentative resolution to large issues nor any worth attaching to the effort. Instead, we can only fall back on our immediate judgements, whether in action or in thought. The image of *undermining* suggests that one set of values for which the university stood has been replaced by another. The institution known as 'university' is in danger of dissolution because the conceptual foundations that served as its underpinning are no more; but those foundations have not simply crumbled away for they have been replaced by others.

In regard to teaching and research, both readings – of emptying out and undermining – are plausible. On the one hand, teaching and research have become such complexes of activities that their value base has become a matter of pragmatic adjustment. The actors hear, even if they do not listen all that attentively to, the mixed voices of their multiple stakeholders, as those stakeholders seek to influence the pedagogic relationship or the character of the research process. Simply getting by is the main concern: ensuring that there are sufficient students and that a goodly proportion of them 'progress' so as to complete satisfactorily or ensuring that another research grant is won somehow, no matter how quickly the report is required or under what conditions. Values are emptied out, as the stakeholders call in their debts. Pragmatism rules.

An alternative reading is that the underlying values are being *undermined*. Interests in promoting knowledge and understanding are being replaced by interests in generating income, personal advancement and sheer survival. The new value structure is one of calculation and of profit and loss understood generally: Is one going to be better off by embarking on this enterprise, this project or this form of engagement? This spirit of calculation is seen at all levels in the university, in the Vice-Chancellor's office, the Registrar's systems, the Finance Officer's spreadsheets, the plans put forward by Heads of Department and the daily lives of teachers and researchers. This is an ethics of the balance sheet.

The bottom line

Universities, accordingly, have become sites of sheer calculation. As we have seen, a key question has become: 'And what is in it for me?' What is in it for me does not have to be anything as sordid as money. In the knowledge society, as universities are shifted laterally into the wider society, many kinds of experience are opened up to the knowledge entrepreneurs: appearing before Parliamentary Select Committees, conducting consultancies for prestigious National Committees of Inquiry, gaining an *entré* to the offices of major corporations, contributing ideas to the architecture of a new building, being interviewed and gaining a public persona in the mass media, and engaging directly with members of relevant professions. Much of this activity is assisted by the new global technologies, but it can also be pursued in person: academics have become *travellers*, both virtual and real.[4] In the process, academic capital is exchanged for social as well as economic capital. It has become fun to be an academic in the knowledge economy.

'What is in it for me?', therefore, can yield many kinds of positive answer. The bottom-line culture is not just, therefore, to be found in the university's Finance Office or in the Vice-Chancellor's suite. All kinds of academics *and* others within the university are making calculations about the enterprises that they take on and the return on their investments; and both 'investments' and 'return' may be calculated in many ways. In addition to monetary gain and intellectual return, experiences may be prized for the personal and even emotional enhancement that they offer. This ethics of the balance sheet may include a measure of *ontological gain*.

There are two processes at work here. On the one hand, a loss of collegiality develops. The academics complain that the managers are undermining collegiality but the academics are also in league, in working to the same end. A corollary to greater individualization on campus among the academics is precisely a reduction in the academics' own collective spirit. On the other hand, the rise of individualization on campus brings with it a wider array of personal dimensions. Academic life has not yet become a site in which its emotional side is particularly evident: managerialism keeps that in check. But it is now a site in which the personal, the experiential and the transactional become more significant: these elements are now present on the balance sheet. And so there is talk of universities conducting ethical audits of themselves and of assessing the extent to which they are healthy organizations. The resistance to examining critically and openly the value basis of universities may be eroding.

This balance sheet, then, turns out to be nicely balanced. On the one hand, less collectivity and more individualization; on the other hand, a widening of the personal dimensions of academic life. The university is a site not just of *knowing* but of *being*. Explicitly, the university takes on heightened ontological dimensions.

If, then, the tendencies to efface collectivism in the university can be kept in check, the university has – rather strangely, perhaps – the possibility to become a fully humane institution. People's feelings count because the university's internal discourse has itself taken an ontological turn. The humanity that always lurked within the university's self-understanding and self-projection, but which was often denied in practice, can now be realized.

A bottom-line culture, then, can have surprising results. The university was always a good place in which to work; now, it can become a good place in which to live. It can become a place, if not of infinite ontological variety – some life forms will not easily find their way onto campus – nevertheless of very considerable ontological variety. The calculative culture ranges to include ontological dimensions and it is unlikely that this tendency, now started in some earnest, will ratchet back. Indeed, we may conjecture that this tendency in favour of the ontological will grow. It will do so because of the wider context of the fluid world in which the university is placed. The boundary between 'work' and 'personal life' dissolves and, in the process, individuals plead for a space to become more fully their individual selves.

That context prompts contrasting considerations. On the one hand, human identity becomes *problematic*. Some believe that we are seeing the dissolution of identity. A better description is in sharp contrast: it is that identity is now a matter of increasing layerings of self-understanding and interpretations of the self by others. Far from the dissolution of identity, strata are laid upon strata as the self moves between settings. On the other hand, identity becomes a matter of *possibility*, of real interest and even of hope and struggle. Amid solid modernity, identity was largely given (in terms of one's economic relations, gender or ethnicity). Amid fluid modernity, the self becomes a pool of ontological possibilities and identity takes on new interest, even as it becomes problematic.

The university is caught in these developments. The university becomes ontologically open. Many kinds of identity are possible. With growing pressures on the budget, the vice-chancellor will find a place for anyone who can make it and who can generate income (and preferably sufficient to cover the institution's overheads). Wheeling and dealing with leading edge technological firms, with professional bodies, with the bureaucrats in charge of international research and development funds or even with national governments in setting up new enterprises in, say, the health or transport fields: the new entrepreneurial openness in turn opens new spaces for new personae on campus.

'Individuals', in this milieu, become sets of sanctioned possible projects and practical frameworks. Any one such individual on campus is but a set of intertwined complexes of concepts, networks, hopes and values; and, within the same 'individual', these frameworks of self-interpretation will pull against each other. Caught in the swirls of these rival frameworks, individuals will be making their calculations as between rival epistemologies and ontologies. Practice/theory; engagement/isolation; individualism/collectivity; institution/discipline; and discipline/client: the dilemmas of thought and action are compounded. Value conflicts proliferate, even if unstated; *and* in the 'one' individual.

The sanctions and the rewards will vary. The pull of the research assessment exercise may just be outweighed by a developmental contract for a national government; or the frisson of conducting a project for a national professional body may outweigh the demands for access to a lecturer's time being voiced ever louder by her students. Where individuals' contracts are increasingly dependent on income generation, there will be ontological and epistemological movement in favour of the short term, the practical and the visible. The quieter, painstaking and often unpaid forms of academic life that served the academic profession as such (external examining, refereeing of manuscripts, engagement with students as persons) are now judged not to warrant the investment. But, perhaps surprisingly, those activities are still conducted. Academics continue to wager on the idea of the academic profession. There remains, despite everything, the possibility of doing some justice on campus to values of collegiality.

Leading values

In the late modern university, the managers' values orient around goals of institutional projection, financial security and comparative advantage. Spaces open such that these goals may be realized in new ways. The university may find itself in the real estate business, the hotel business, enterprises of community welfare and technological businesses connected with its knowledges. Admittedly, the values of the staff become less institutional in character and more individualistic, but this individualism often supports the institutional goals of the managers. Academic staff can be highly costly, but they can also generate several times their own salaries in pursuit of their own interests (Vasagar 2001). The senior management team used to see the employment of new staff as contributing to the costs on the balance sheet; in modern 'entrepreneurial' universities, the financial paradox is that the more staff an institution has, the greater may be the institution's income.

This happy coincidence, of the university's need for new sources of income and the almost natural generation of income on the part of mainly freewheeling individuals, *is* largely coincidental. It turns out that the value structures of institutions both at the managerial level and at the levels of staff have, *as an unintended consequence*, corresponding and even synergistic outcomes. In having the space to develop their own knowledge projects in a fluid world, academics often end up aiding the university's interests in projection, comparative advantage and financial security.

Readings (1997) spoke of 'dissensus' as a way of characterizing the form of the university for the current age.[5] It is a helpful concept and one that carries an inner charge that communication is problematic. But it is important to note that this 'dissensus' is both conceptual and organizational. Conceptually, the university fragments as it interacts with the knowledge society: since the knowledge society is a society of proliferating knowledges (plural), the university becomes 'fissiparous' in character (to use a term of Peter Scott's). But the conceptual mayhem is aided and abetted by the ever looser organization that characterizes the university. Staff are placed on different contracts and are taken on and given the space to engage in different projects, which in turn supply increasingly separate subjectivities. The university's ethical base reflects its growing diversity in its epistemologies, its ontologies and its organizational promptings.

Ethical fragmentation in the university, then, is of two kinds. *Firstly*, the university becomes a site of proliferating values. Individuals take on multiple personae, being perceived as quite different 'persons', depending on their *habitus* in any one situation.[6] An individual may be a project director in one setting but a fairly junior member of a team in another. She may be called upon to judge individuals against bottom-line performance indicators, but be seen by her students actually to engage with them as ends in themselves.

Secondly, and linked to the first point, therefore, the university becomes a site of pragmatic calculation: neither Kant nor Rawls would find himself at home here. Judgements are rarely universalized and individuals – whether managers or staff – seek to maximize differences, whether between themselves and other individuals or as compared with other universities. But Bentham and even Rorty would also find things hard going: decisions are not made in the interests of the greatest number on campus, but neither are they made so as to live out interesting stories as to what campus life might be. MacIntyre and Habermas, too, might be forgiven for feeling some dismay at what they see around them. Universities no longer offer the *universitas* that their separate frameworks implied: neither is the university a self-critical community, nor does it apparently demonstrate its capacity to abide by norms of communicative interaction that extend across all forms of life on campus.

Hobbes, at least, might find this campus life bearing out his analysis. It is becoming a life that is 'nasty, brutish and short': after all, early retirement is increasingly on the cards; even the vice-chancellor grows weary when his office extends into a second decade and looks for an opportunity to find an easier life. Those who follow Machiavelli may just gain personal satisfaction out of the 'fun' of living dangerously and surviving by one's political wits.

If this situation holds sway, there are two conceptual options in front of us. The first is to declare that we are seeing the emergence of a new kind of university, in which community, responsibility and humanity are being disregarded, being displaced by other interests and orientations. The second is to say that we are seeing the dissolution of the university; that the university as a concept that has its origins in mediaeval Europe is now behind us, because the university as a new form of institution concerned with the exploitation of knowledges is emerging.

It seems likely that the second option is a *fait accompli*, the largely inevitable outcome of the kind of fluid world in which the university finds itself, while the first is waiting in the wings: on either account, the common ties that offered a chance of collegiality are seemingly threatened. Is it possible, then, for ethical stances to be sustained in which persons matter and in which communicative processes across the university are upheld? Is such a third way available?

It would be easy to say that, under these conditions, such a third way will be realized if, and only if, the university fulfils its responsibilities; but that option is no option at all, since universities are hardly unitary institutions any more. A yet further option opens up: that, while there are considerable forces that predispose the university towards an ethics of calculability, the associated actions, subjectivities and purposes involve decisions in favour of a dual ethics of communication and being. The spaces that are opening for the university to take on new values are also opening spaces for a leadership that deliberately attends to communicative and community values and for values in which individuals matter. But it follows that, if an ethics of calculability is becoming the dominant ethic, alternative values can only gain a foothold if those in positions of power or influence invest time and effort in articulating and inserting those different values.

Such investment of institutional resources will not, of course, show up on the bottom line – either at the individual or the institutional level – except as a cost. Taking a half-hour or even an hour to talk to a student, engaging in an open meeting, addressing matters of a university's self-image and future positioning and even serving on a committee concerned with teaching enhancement across the university: these may become marginalized activities. Conversation is being marginalized but, given leadership, it can be resurrected. An ideology of calculability cannot be displaced but, alongside it, an ethics of communication can be reinserted. Precisely because the university finds itself caught in a turbulent age, realizing its values of mutual respect, engagement and exploration becomes a feasible project. Humanity can be 'cultivated' (Nussbaum 1997).

Paradoxically, such a counter ethics can be inserted because it can supply positive answers to that key question of calculability: 'And what is in it for me?' An investment of institutional resources in favour of persons and communication can be seen to be in the interests of both individuals and institutions. The mobilization of a university's intellectual resources to meet the demands of discriminating client groups within and without the university will place a premium on communicability. Within the university, there is a will to communicate that the university ignores at its peril, if only for its newer calculative values. The university can yet remind itself that ideas, communication and respect for persons actually matter.

Conclusion: values as ideology

Values of calculability reach deeply into the university's inner life, including its epistemologies, its ontologies and its communicative structures. However, if the university has lurched towards an ethics of calculability, in theory at least it can also turn towards a virtuous value structure that upholds positive hopes of the university's becoming. The university still contains within itself resources for collegiality and communication.

Instituting such a value structure poses two major challenges. Firstly, acts of implementation will be construed as more managerialism, more performativity and more operationalism. The sheer acts of putting in place processes not obviously linked to core activities, such as research and teaching, will be framed as an assault on collegial virtues, even though they may be an attempt to reinstate collegial virtues or, more honestly, to realize collegial virtues where none existed before. Such projects have to be articulated and their rational base has to be made explicit and even argued for.[7] The ideals within such a counter value structure will have to be spelt out.

Table 9.1 Idealogies and Ideologies compared

	Idealogies	*Ideologies*
Communicative structure	• open • dialogical • explicit • reflexive	• closed • deaf • self-assured • imposed
Rational basis	• reasonable • complex • boundary transgressive • imaginative • creative	• taken-for-granted • simple • restricted • judgemental • rule-bound
Ontological basis	• being reinterpreted • generous • compassionate • multimodal	• frozen • limited • self-enclosed • one-dimensional
Values	• universal • supports university • founded on university's conceptual foundations	• parochial • self-interested • judgemental

Secondly, the carrying forward of such a project – of community, dialogue and respect for persons on campus – will face the charge that such implementation is in difficulty. On the preceding analysis, the management of change in the intersecting swirls of cultures, interests, values, epistemologies and identities that constitute a university has to be problematic. How does one manage the intersection of several rivers? The answer is by outflanking the existing currents in ways that utilize those existing currents. New hopes, new purposes and new forms of communication just may gain a hearing if they are introduced in ways that appeal to the university's self-image of a self-critical community, even if such an appeal is counterfactual.

We need a new term for such projects: let us term them, therefore, 'idealogies'. Idealogies are ideologies that are deliberately constructed around the ideals that the university has of itself. They will gain a hearing because the university harbours within itself a will to listen, even as it forecloses on listening. Amid the ideologies that threaten to overwhelm it, the university can find itself again through virtuous ideologies. Such idealogies call for a leadership that can stand apart from the rhythms of the age and can forge alternative sources of *being* in the university. The realization of idealogies, in turn, calls for a sustained effort, for resilience and for organizational nous but, with a fair wind, such counter-ideas can gain a foothold.

Idealogies appeal to the virtuous ideals buried deep in the university's self-understanding, much as it has become in the interests of those on campus to turn to other, undermining, ideologies. They remain, therefore, as ideals: they can never be fully realized amid those undermining ideologies. But if such ideologies can be seriously pursued, especially if they can be instantiated partly through the managerial techniques that allowed the pernicious ideologies to flourish, the university's ideological space can be widened. Ideologies, systematically pursued, therefore offer a kind of ethical value-added. They also indicate that leadership and management may take on a demonstrably virtuous aspect.

10

Engaging Universities

The argument summarised

The Western university has built itself on a project of Reason (with a capital 'R', so to speak) but that project is now dented by assaults from several directions. Universities now find themselves caught up in a complex environment that exceeds the powers of their reason: fluidity, fuzziness and the dissolution of the university's epistemological foundations are just some of the signs of this situation. A particularly insistent form of this assault on the university's well-being lies in the arrival on campus of ideology.

Ideologies are systematically present in universities. They may take silent forms or noisy forms; they can be explicitly on show or they may mask or even invert existing practices. In this last, for instance, the use of the term 'academic community' now turns out to be largely a cloak for individualization on campus (see Chapter 8).

Some argue to the contrary. They proclaim the end of ideology, urging variously that the firm ground on which ideology rested has dissolved, that large claims can gain no purchase and that the world, politically and culturally, is too fluid to support the rhetorical weight of ideologies.[1] Ideology, for those of this persuasion who are interested in higher education, has been emptied out of the university. Grand plans that anchored universities to large projects of the state, whether as a cultural enterprise or simply state hegemony, are no more.[2] Globalization and the internet have put paid to all that.

The argument may be beguiling but that is all. It should not bewitch us. For as long as there are human enterprises, there will be ideologies. Ideologies may not possess the grand sweep that they once enjoyed; now, they are much more identified with discrete locales but are nonetheless powerful for that.[3] There remains, stubbornly, a will to ideologize: collective interests will form, identities will emerge that embody those interests and forms of judgement and beliefs will – to an extent – solidify. All this is found on campus. World claims give way to local commitment.

As the university takes up with the wider society and finds opportunities in society to promote itself *and* as the wider society, not to mention the state, seeks to enlist the university in its projects (with 'offers' that the university can hardly refuse), so ideological spaces open on campus. 'Quality', 'markets', 'entrepreneurialism', 'competition', 'work' and 'skill' are terms that are emblems of ideologies that bear in on the university and to which the university, to a greater or lesser extent, responds. The university will say that it merely complies but, in truth, it usually responds positively. Typically, money talks. New identities are formed, new projects open out (not without their excitement) and new vistas beckon.

The critics who proclaim that we are witnessing the end of ideology are not entirely wrong: they are identifying significant transformations in our grip on the world, our ways of interpreting the world, our sense of the (lessening) significance of language as other forms of representation develop and our sense of our own identity. It follows, too, that if – ideationally, representationally and intersubjectively – we are in an essentially fluid world, the world cannot be contoured by ideologies as it once was. But all that is to say that ideologies have, in theory at least, a problematic time of it. Ideologies make claims about the world and they pretend that those claims rest on stable ground. In a more fluid world, in a world without stable foundations, ideologies' foundations become unstable, but they always *were* unstable. Ideologies have always been pretentious: they presumed and they claimed more than they could redeem. That we live in an essentially fluid world, therefore, is no knock-down demolition of ideologies.

Ideologies live on; and they live on even on campus. Indeed, the university, the great institutional epitome of reason, *harbours more ideologies now than it ever did*. That, for some, will constitute a paradox: in precisely an age when ideology is supposed to be disappearing, the university turns out to be more of an ideological site than it ever was. When the university was a near total institution, when its walls kept both the wider world outside *and* the inmates inside, the university could only have been a site of its own ideologies. But those were weak affairs, for ideology gains its purchase by being a force of tacit resistance to other ideologies. It is with the emergence of the university into the world that ideology has grown apace on campus. New forms of academic life have emerged precisely as the internal and the external have coalesced.

In ideology, there lies if neither fame nor fortune then the prospect of a little local status, as individuals are in turn identified with projects that have backing from one quarter or another. 'Research', 'learning and teaching', 'educational development', 'competition', 'markets', 'equal opportunities' and 'quality': all these and other ideas are taken up as causes that furnish identities, which, in turn, offer good livings to those who reside in them. However, the very presence of multiple ideologies only causes ideologies to grow still further as they contend with each other.

What, then, under these conditions, does it mean to live effectively *with* ideology? Does that imply counterposing one ideology with another? Such a countering act could suggest that ideology is characteristically adversarial, a matter of power blocs squaring up to each other. Certainly, the concept of ideology has had a shady past: it points to claims or projects that ultimately cannot be reasoned through. Ideologies are pernicious, or so it seems. But if higher education can be assailed by pernicious ideologies, it can assuredly be contoured in part by virtuous and possibly utopian projects; even the idea of a virtuous ideology suggests itself.

The idea of a virtuous ideology, especially one that counters a pernicious ideology, certainly invites further questions. Wherein lies its virtue? What legitimacy does it possess that the presenting ideology does not? If ideology as such is ultimately beyond reason, on what grounds might we be persuaded that such a counter-ideology has reasonableness on its side? The answer *has* to be unnerving, in part. If we live in an age that is ultimately without secure foundations, a counter-ideology cannot find a sure basis in pure reason. Under what conditions, then, can an ideology *reasonably* hope to win us over? What form might an ideology take if it is to persuade us as to its virtues? Lurking around the corner is the accusation that 'A virtuous ideology is simply one that I respond to positively; a pernicious ideology is one that I find abhorrent'. All that is present is mere whim, mere prejudice and mere emotional response.

The answer lies, I am suggesting, in a distinction between an ideology and – as I term it – an ide*a*logy. An ide*a*logy is a special kind of ideology. An ide*a*logy is a form of the species of utopian ideology. It is a variant of the utopian ideologies of Mannheimian portrayal in that, while it looks to ushering in a new kind of order, it does so deliberately.[4] The deliberation is of three kinds.

Firstly, the utopian ideal is forged *as* an ideal: the key concepts are worked out and held out but it is understood that in a fluid world, in which higher education is saturated with projects, agendas and, indeed, ideologies, no one ideology can ever be fully brought off. It is *always* utopian. *Only a partial realization may be achieved and this state of affairs is understood and lived with daily.* Secondly, the backers of this ideology do not just live in a kind of Rortian hope but also work actively to orchestrate matters towards it, even if it is never realized. If, however, that were all, its persuasive bite would be limited. There is, therefore, a third element of deliberation at work. Here, the justification for any ide*a*logy of and in higher education lies in its *constitutive progressive programme.*[5] The justification links with the ideas of respect, generosity, understanding and dialogue embedded in the idea of the university.

How are positive ideologies to be distinguished? How do they gain their legitimacy? They do so by becoming virtuous ideologies as such. They reflect the reasonable elements of all ideologies – of community, communication, identity and evaluation – and pursue them doggedly on campus: their legitimacy for doing so derives precisely through these ideas being elements of the idea of the university. Ideologies have reason, some reason at least, on their side: that is how they secure adherents. Ide*a*logies of the university play up these reasonable elements of ideology *and* add to them the specific ideas in the idea of the university – respect, generosity, understanding and dialogue. Ide*a*logies are practical projects: they are ways of realizing on campus the ideals of the university, even in a turbulent, contested and perplexed age.

The links, then, between ideology and the university have both insidious and positive potential. Ideologies can undermine higher education or, by capitalizing on their emancipatory components, *the very components that are intrinsic to the idea of higher education*, can act as progressive forces in favour of higher education. In so doing, they turn themselves into utopian projects[6] – even if never entirely winnable – and unremitting practices; in short, ide*a*logies of the university.

Like ideologies, ide*a*logies supply motivational energy, identity, judgemental criteria and collective human projects. Unlike ideologies, however, ide*a*logies are sets of ideas and practical projects that reflexively attempt to realize the university itself. They try to bring off the better life implicit in the idea of the university and are their own severest critics in the process.

Forms of engagement

The term 'engagement' is currently being picked up in policy debates on higher education.[7] It also offers a further example of the ideological hybridity that we have been exploring. It can become a pernicious ideology, foreclosing the enlightenment potential of the university, or it can become a virtuous ide*a*logy, providing a means of direction and positive development in a fluid world.

We may distinguish four forms of engagement:

1. That form of engagement that is blind and unreflective – we may term this form *non-reflectional.*
2. That form of engagement that is entered into knowingly and where the major intent is *extractional* – that is, where the university enters into projects only in so far as it can extract benefits to itself (for example, it starts up a course on the other side of the world only after and only because the finance officer's spreadsheet has indicated the likelihood of a substantial income stream).
3. That form of engagement that is entered into knowingly and where at least a significant part of the intent lies in the university realizing a sense of itself in the context of imposed standards or expectations (for example, where the university accepts an accountability function within a state-imposed quality framework). Call this an *impositional* form of engagement.
4. That form of engagement that is entered into partly in virtue of a responsibility that the university sees itself as fulfilling *qua* 'university'; call this *realizational.*

These four forms of engagement – non-reflectional, extractional, impositional and realizational – may be separated into two groups, composed of the first three on the one hand and the last on the other. The first three overlap, containing different orders of the operational, the performative and the instrumental. They are examples of engagement as an ideology: universities are now being asked to *engage* with their wider society and they may do so blindly (the decision to engage in a particular project is simply *taken*, hurriedly, at the end of a meeting of the Vice-Chancellor's management team), in a spirit of calculation (will the additional income stream cover the overheads?) or resentfully ('we just have to get through this institutional evaluation').

In practice, these different forms of engagement are intertwined. If engagement implies an intertwining of two or more entities, we have here – in the engagement of the university with the wider society – intertwinings within intertwinings. Transitive/intransitive, reflective/non-reflective, individualistic/collective (does a university strike out on its own or form alliances through which to 'engage'?) and even positive/negative: any one project may exhibit many if not all of these dimensions of engagement.

Engagement, therefore, does not come neatly *boundaried*, in singular form clearly delineated from other, possibly rival, forms of university becoming. Indeed, 'engagement' offers a misleading metaphor. It speaks of hardness and of cogs in machines meshing with each other, in definite predetermined ways, exerting predictable force. But in a world of fluid hopes and identities, metaphors of liquidity are required.[8] There is and there can be no definite design and no neat fit: the decisions taken in the Vice-Chancellor's office or even in the course planning team will intermingle all kinds of possible engagement, some active and some passive, some largely performative ('leave the marketing to the marketing manager') and some much more ideational (a course in citizenship might find a market but it just might even be worthwhile in itself). There is muddiness here as the discursive swirls intermingle.

Engagement in a world of supercomplexity cannot offer us Cartesian 'clear and distinct' ideas. The university is bound to engage and, in the process, will find itself involved in messy transactions. Despite that, it is still possible to pick out certain streams of engagement and even determine to give them greater force.

Engagement as ideology

Engagement is a nice example of one of the theses of this book: the narratives that encircle the university by no means carry equal force. Engagement comes, as we have seen, in various guises, but some of those guises have powerful backers. Additional resources, a heightened profile and new clients for its knowledge services may all come the university's way if it chooses certain forms of engagement; equally, if it declines to engage with engagement, sanctions may follow. It will lose out in the public ratings, its income base will be depressed and it will be marginalized in the policy networks (notably, by the state's department of education) as an institution that is precisely not engaged.

Engagement, therefore, is not just another narrative. The university's narratives are not players on a level playing field. Engagement is becoming a popular idea because so many groups, of different persuasions, can sign up to it. Engagement can take many forms, but some will be promoted more vigorously than others. The big battalions will favour the more performative versions of engagement: the university will be persuaded to structure itself in favour of activities likely to have exchange value in the knowledge economy *and* it will wish to be seen to be complying with external evaluation systems. Spaces for new identities will open: there will be directors of projects that 'reach out' to industry, there will be marketing managers and there will be directors responsible for ensuring that opportunities for establishing new companies are seized, perhaps directly interlinked with the university's local community or region. An agenda of engagement will be pressed forward, but it will be an agenda framed by and in the interests of the powerful of the corporate world. This engagement takes on ideological form and force.

In keeping with the argument of this book, however, if 'engagement' can become an ideology, it can also become an *ideulogy*. It can offer a positive set of images of future university–society relationships which, in turn, supplies motivational energy and sets in train projects, identities and communicative processes that look towards a better university.

Ideology and reflection

Some consider that a defining characteristic of an ideology is that it reveals itself in reflection; if, consequent upon reflection, a project is seen anew and in such a poor light that it comes to be abandoned, then we know – *post facto* – that we were in the presence of an ideology all along.[9] This idea has a certain prima facie plausibility: it is part of the make-up of an ideology that it is not entirely backed by reason. It was also the hope of Critical Theory that, through reflection, ideology would reveal itself and would be dissolved. But a tight connection between reflection-on-ideology and ideology-revelation and even ideology-dissolution cannot work as a criterion of ideology. An ideology may resist reflection; it will come armed with its self-justifying reasons. The question then arises: Are those projects that survive reflection necessarily ideological?

Reasons that may be advanced for a university to 'engage' will be numerous. On reflection, it might seem to a university that is facing certain kinds of engagement with potential clients – whether in the corporate sector or in government – that the price is not worth paying. The 'price' may be material or symbolic: a corporation that has paid for research may bar publication of the findings; equally, a university may judge that it cannot justify its holdings in the shares of tobacco companies. However, in either case, the university may decide that the price *is* worth paying. In short, a process of reflection may have contrasting outcomes: continuation *or* abandonment of a project. Ideology may be present in processes of either kind. It cannot, therefore, be a criterion of the presence of ideology that reflection leads to a project being abandoned.

It may be tempting, therefore, to try the reverse tack and suggest that an ideology reveals itself less by its readiness to dissolve on reflection than by its *persistence*. Its disinclination to lessen in the presence of another narrative is indicative of ideology in the collective midst. Indeed, paradoxical as it may seem, the willingness of a belief system to soften in the face of critique may be a sign of its *reasonableness*, not of its ideological character. Being reasonable, it will be conscious of the precariousness of its own constitution; it will be sensitive to the difficulty of ever grounding absolutely in reason its own purposes. It is reason that is liable to be flaky in the presence of critique, not ideology.

It is in this sense of ideology-as-resistor that the ideologies we have been looking at reveal themselves *as* ideologies. Entrepreneurialism, marketization, competition and quality reveal themselves *as* ideologies not in themselves, not through any inner faults that their associated ideas may possess, but through their persistence, loudness and self-assurance. None of these ideologies will go quietly when faced with their contenders, as they assuredly are. They reveal themselves as ideologies precisely because they remain standing. Little sticks to them and they endure whatever is thrown at them. They so endure because they have a surplus commitment invested in them. Without that surplus commitment, they would soften and wilt in the face of critique, even if they would not dissolve.

In what way is this commitment 'surplus'? It seems to be doing a good job, acting as a protective belt,[10] and ensuring that the belief structure remains stable. It can be said to be 'surplus', since it rides above and beyond all reason.[11] That these ideologies persist as ideologies is testimony to their having a non-rational element even as they come bearing reason. Markets, entrepreneurialism, quality and competition have right on their side; some right, at least. But if that was all that they possessed, their stridency would be tempered by critique. That they keep their sharpness, convinced of their own legitimacy in their hegemonic tendencies, demonstrates that they possess this surplus commitment. This commitment rides above the waves of critique; it brooks no dissent. It hardly engages with resistance because it does not need to do so; it presses on regardless. It takes no prisoners.

And so it is with engagement. Engagement has not just plausibility but also right on its side. Positive reasons can be adduced in favour of engagement and they declare themselves in generally agreeable ways. Universities are worthwhile institutions and there falls on universities, therefore, an obligation to demonstrate that worthwhileness in engaging with the wider society. To pick up one of our earlier distinctions, this demonstration may be subtle; for instance, through the communication of research findings or through the admission of as broad a range of individuals as can benefit from its courses. Equally, the demonstration of the university's 'engagement' may be full frontal, in reaching out and engaging with different publics and in advancing directly the internal goods of the university to different communities.[12]

These, surely, are forms of engagement that would secure a wide consensus of support, both within and beyond the academic community. More contentious, but still with at least plausibility on their side, are further forms of engagement. Since, even under conditions of marketization, universities continue to receive significant investment from the wider society, it is right that they should give an account of themselves to that wider society; and such accountability, if taken on seriously, will call for forms of engagement. Quite separately, a university's engaging with companies in the corporate sector can not only assist with the balance sheet, but also both generate finance that can cross-subsidize departments and activities that would otherwise be difficult to sustain *and* provide academics with additional intellectual capital – not to mention physical plant – that supports and furthers their 'own' research endeavours.

These considerations remind us that ideologies gain their power through securing support and that support is, in turn, dependent upon the prima facie plausibility that attaches to the belief structures lying within them. At least, for an ideology to work as an ideology, it must secure the adherence of many: its central core of beliefs must have some degree of rightness. Ideologies are not just sets of dogmas, to be chanted and internalized. They work by consisting in the first place of propositions to which assent may be given or withheld.

But ideologies are not just sets of plausible beliefs; they are sets of teflon beliefs. Nothing sticks to them – or so they would wish. They survive, come what may. They do so because of the surplus commitment invested in them by their adherents. And so it is with engagement. The multiple projects of engagement have greater or lesser face validity; they secure their adherents who come, in turn, to 'interpellate' those beliefs.[13] These adherents not just come to believe the ideology as their own ideology, but they *live it* through and through. Their being is infused with this surplus investment which, in turn, invests ever more in it. They redeem their own investment by daily living out the ideology. With the world constructed through the ideology, the investment in the ideology – such as that of engagement – is apparently repaid over and over. The ideology of engagement declares itself – for its adherents – as valid, as undeniable and as assuredly profitable. Invest in this ideology of engagement and the future of the university will be secure.

When, therefore, belief structures convert themselves into ideologies and take on this surplus investment, they rebut reflection. They appear to countenance reflection but they do so only in order to see it off. Where the university's senior management team has set itself on a path of engagement, and where that project has become ideological, the project seems incontrovertible. *Of course*, the university has to engage to survive. It has to reach out to the corporate world; it has to develop joint projects; it has to be willing to soften and muddy (both at the same time) its epistemologies as they become more 'Mode 2' in their orientations; and it has to seek customers for its knowledge services wherever they can be found. At least some of this university's Pro-Vice-Chancellors will have written into their own portfolios responsibilities for alliances, enterprise and external income generation; and doubtless, to a significant degree, these individuals will come to internalize the script written for them. The project of engagement steams along, full of energy and fired by those who live it out. It has an obviousness about it: how could things be otherwise?

Undue backing

Engagement, as with all ideologies, becomes an ideology when it stops taking itself overly seriously, when the investment committed to it is no longer in surplus. Then, and only then, the ideology can be seen for what it is, one narrative among others through which we might understand the university. It is both a narrative with powerful backers who would reconstruct the university in their interests *and* a narrative that has some legitimacy in its favour.

The backers of engagement as an ideology are largely from outwith the university; namely, the combined forces of the state and the corporate world amid the global economy. However, to describe the ideology of engagement in this way is triply to mislead. *Firstly*, the typification of 'backers' implies a more or less explicit conspiracy, that of smoke-filled rooms. But ideologies do not require systematic machinations, even if those can help on occasions. Quasi-state agencies may produce consultation papers on topics in and around the theme of engagement, urging universities to take on such an identity (for example, on 'technology transfer'), but such explicitness is an add-on, an ideological superstructure embellishing even larger forces at work in the energized fluidities of late modernity.

Secondly, engagement is being taken up by universities themselves as an internal ideology: they don't need much help from outside. Through engagement, universities fancy their chances at securing additional revenue streams, greater institutional autonomy and enhanced visibility. In addition, for many academics, engagement is a way of advancing their own individual interests. In a fluid world, engagement seems to offer a 'win–win' strategy. Universities are won over to it, independently of any encouragement from extramural forces. *Thirdly*, ideologies find expression in *locales*: they have a fine-grained character, living themselves out in small-scale happenings, in corridor conversations (half-fulfilled on the move) and in phrases in office memoranda and committee minutes. This, too, is how engagement shapes itself *qua* ideology.

The character of ideology does not reveal itself in its having a belief structure (although it has) or in the falsity of that belief structure (to the contrary, there is a truthfulness about it, such as the beliefs that 'engagement' can yield multiple forms of income streams and can secure both intellectual and physical resources that can assist the university). Nor does ideology reveal itself in any manifestly abhorrent character of its outcomes for they may be mixed (engagement can offer a means of enabling the university to assist in realizing an open and learning society just as it can bring closure as new sponsors extract onerous conditions of collaboration). Nor, as we have just seen, does ideology reveal itself in any grand conspiracy and nor does it reside especially in particular kinds of text (such as university mission statements or the policy pronouncements of the state), even though they can add to its weight. Instead, as it has been urged here, ideology reveals itself in its undue persistence.

Ideology persists in the face of critique because it brushes critique aside. The Pro-Vice-Chancellor who wishes to place on the table considerations of counter value structures, of the effects of 'engagement' on other aspects of the university's mission and of the limited opportunities open to some departments to engage on the terms in which engagement is being defined, may simply find that no space is accorded to such reflections. The one institution in society that would proclaim itself through its systematic powers of reflection easily comes to a point where certain kinds of critique are hardly given a hearing.

The idea of 'distorted communication' is recalled to mind, therefore,[14] but it should be seen as a shorthand for a penumbra of elements on campus that indicate the presence of ideology. These elements include the presence of the process of distorted communication itself, a surplus investment in a project, the conferring thereby of an added ideological weight to the project, the undue reluctance to open that project to serious scrutiny and the ensuing persistence of that project.

Such ideological presences on campus have a subtle rightness on their side. They are a means of getting things done. The Habermassian conception of rationality, for all its self-description as a matter of 'communicative *action*', faces the challenge: 'But when does the talking stop?' Where the participants are genuinely wanting to hear all points of view – or as many as possible – and doggedly to pursue all *their* considerations, implications and relationships, the conversation can go on literally without end. So far as I can tell, Habermas gives us no rules for determining how such a conversation can *reasonably* be brought to a close, however temporarily.

In contrast, being so sure of themselves, ideologies have no qualms about action; indeed, the talking is often a sham, just a prelude to getting on with things. Ideologies don't really need to hear counter-views or qualifications: they know that they are right. The state's 'consultation' exercises are all too often conducted with deadlines that permit no serious university-wide debate, with the consultation papers even being published during vacations. Each item on a committee's agenda can have a number of minutes allotted in *advance of the meeting*. Serious debate isn't on the cards, for the principles, orientation and even organizing framework are a *fait accompli*: all that is sought is a tidying up of the administrative detail. But, especially in a university, there has to be a conversation; otherwise, we are not in the presence of a university.

Yet, where ideology has a firm grip, decisions that carry it forward are not far away. The senior management team has a raft of matters before it at its fortnightly meeting. The latest form of engagement, perhaps putting into effect the university's initiative within the Higher Education Reach Out to Business in the Community fund, is decided there and then. Anyway, the Vice-Chancellor's personal assistant has scheduled a stream of commitments for the day; and so on to the next business on the agenda, actions having been determined.

Universities like to see themselves as self-critical communities, but they have not always been good at establishing fora that are genuinely open, inclusive and durable. Of those three terms, it is 'openness' that is somewhat enigmatic, 'inclusivity' and 'durability' being transparent enough concepts. By 'open' here has to be meant a discursive openness such that the big issues of contemporary university life – globalization, quality, accountability, distance learning, alliances, competition, enterprise, consumerism, consultancy, income generation, the relationships between teaching and research, academic identity and so forth – can be carefully addressed.

Each university will have its own take on these large matters, given its own disciplinary make-up and its positioning in the total higher education system of its own country. The nature of the fora in which discursive space can be created for these large matters to be addressed will, therefore, vary. That, indeed, is the key challenge: not in identifying the issues – for they are largely generic and even literally global in nature, affecting every institution of higher education in the world – but in determining appropriate structures, systems and processes by which genuine debate can be developed and sustained over time, such that a university's particular forms of engagement can be collectively worked through.

Engagement as ide*a*logy

It is the process of debate that turns ideologies into ide*a*logies. In the process of debate, ideologies come under a form of discursive control. They are forced to surrender themselves to examination, even against their implicit wishes. As sites of critical reflection, universities – and particularly their leaders – have responsibilities to establish processes of open debate and critical scrutiny such that the dominant working assumptions of a university's policy framework can be subject to continual collective and open review. For that, the Finance Officer's balance sheets and the Planning Officer's projections will turn out to be invaluable: if they can be put to the service of ideologies, they can also be put to the service of ide*a*logies.

Ide*a*logies, however, are not just ideologies *critiqued*. Ide*a*logies are, as the term implies, sets of ideas that contain ideals. They turn what are taken-for-granted working assumptions into explicit and collectively owned ideas.

In the process of open debate, imaginary and even fantastic notions may emerge. Ideologies open up visions of worthwhile possibilities that contend against the ideologies of the age: by definition, therefore, they herald a new future. This, after all, is to be expected in a university, for universities are sites for the production of new ideas. Let universities become, then, *and perhaps for the first time*, sites for the production of collective ideas and even ideals about themselves, and of collective action for themselves, *as* universities.

In a debate over the project of engagement, for example, positive ideas as to engagement with the community, with the wider society and even with the polity would have their expression alongside engagement for economic production. These more positive versions of engagement have a right to be heard, not just as additional ideas of engagement beyond the dominant ideas in present-day policy formation but also as legitimate carriers of the traditional value structure of universities. If universities are institutions for gaining and spreading knowledge and understanding, then ideas of engagement that do duty to these enlightenment axioms have a particular right to be heard. It is in this sense – of doing justice to ideals implicit in the idea of the university – that ideas of engagement that reach out to the wider society, embodying further tacit ideas of citizenship, democracy and inclusion, can be said to be positive ideas. In turn, there would be a necessary process in which universities engaged with that internal value structure of what it is to be a university.[15]

Some of the ideas and certainly some of the emerging proposals for action will embody ideals: they will run counter to the dominant policy-framing, resourcing systems and patterns of academic identity and may even appear to be non-feasible. Such courses of action – action in the community, say – may attract *for now* neither public resources nor internal rewards (academic identity being constructed around public measures, as are embedded in the research assessment exercise, disciplinary networks and teaching quality evaluations). The dominant sentiments of the age may work against the ideals of the university being realized.

Ideologies, therefore, burst out from the confines of the restricted public debates of consultation papers with their predetermined questions and issues. Ideologies do more than remind the university of what it is or even what it might be. Their very production ushers into the university a new process of realizing at a meta-level the university as a critical community. In that process, the nature of the university in the modern world, in all its 'transgressivity' (Nowotny *et al.* 2001), can be raised as an issue for debate and as a platform for the creation of imaginary ideas as to the university's becoming and realization.

Conclusion

As with other ideologies, engagement has various faces and those that it is being encouraged currently to present are but a subset of the faces that might be possible. Forces are at work that would limit the definitions of engagement. Favoured definitions include those of transferring technology, the forming of alliances with the corporate sector, the co-sponsorship of projects with industry and commerce, the development of knowledge services in the form of consultancies, and collaboration with key quasi-national bodies. The balance sheet, however, is more even than might first appear. These forms of engagement bring new sources of commentary, ideas and resources to bear on the university's activities. In the process, the university becomes more accountable to ever wider publics. Its epistemologies may take a turn towards more useful, problem-solving, Mode 2 forms[16] but, again, that can be chalked up as a gain: the university's epistemologies have been overly restricted for too long.

The difficulty with engagement as ideology, as with ideology on campus generally, is three-fold. *Firstly*, the favoured definitions are narrow, being those that support the dominant interests. *Secondly*, they look to sweep all before them and, in turn, decline to examine themselves. The 'reflexive' turn that we are told is characteristic of late modernity has yet to catch up with these aspects of academic life. *Thirdly*, the favoured definitions are taken to have uncontestable virtue on their side. They endure through hardly being subject to reflection. Such critique as raises its head – through two or three queries at Senate – can easily be portrayed as maverick voices, not part of 'the real world'. This ideology, as with its counterparts, has the power of persistence.

A challenge and a responsibility, therefore, that falls on the university's leadership is to construct the conditions of genuine debate and reflection. Not only is there a range of voices that deserves to be heard but also universities typically contain an extraordinary array of intellectual resources that would infuse such debates with expertise. In such a process of deliberate and continuing debate, ideologies can turn into ideologies. Through a process of open communication in which all voices have equal opportunities to be heard, the contemporary accounts of engagement can come in for their due assessment and additional definitions of engagement can be contributed, and yet quite new imaginary ideas, idealistic and even fantastic in their qualities, can emerge. The university contains all kinds of resources for projects of engagement that would be of demonstrable value to the wider society as well as doing justice to the ideals embedded within the idea of the university. Through developing and instantiating ideologies of engagement, the university can realize itself even in an age of supercomplexity.

11

Uniting Research and Teaching

Rival ideologies, if unequal

Seen against the history of an 800-year-old institution, research as a defining part of the university is a comparatively recent arrival: it emerged around 200 years ago, albeit with some difficulty. Within German philosophy of the late eighteenth century, learning and scholarly inquiry constituted a unity: there was no break between them. They were both activities devoted to the realization of 'Spirit'. In England, in the mid-nineteenth century, Newman saw things rather differently. For him, research reflected the presence in the university of non-educational interests, since it had no real interest in the cultivation of the 'philosophical' mind. But the forces against Newman were overwhelming. German idealism was already taking two routes in its practical embodiment: universities were becoming state institutions, supplying cadres that could assist the development of the state, and they were becoming sites of systematic research, particularly in science.

In the twenty-first century, universities look to being players in large-scale scientific research, but it is easy to overlook the latter's uneven emergence. The numbers of students in the humanities in higher education in the UK outstripped those in the sciences until the last quarter of the twentieth century. Until recently, the Oxbridge tradition – and especially the Oxford tradition – was largely a teaching tradition.[1] Even until well after the Second World War, the University of Oxford was predominantly an Arts university. Under those conditions, teaching and research existed comfortably alongside each other in universities. Teaching was, in fact, the dominant activity of the two but it did not shout about it. It did not need to.[2] Universities were largely separate from society and were not yet required to demonstrate their effectiveness in either research or teaching. As such, teaching and research happily co-existed.

Far from being ideologies squaring up to each other, teaching and research were felt to be mutually sustaining. If an ideology is a project that over-asserts itself and that in part because it sees itself as contending against other ideologies, there was no impulse on this reading for either teaching or research to become an ideology. Neither had any reason to assert itself, let alone over-assert itself, for there was no other ideology against which to contend. This ideological void is entirely explicable: until recently, there had been neither reason nor space for the power blocs to form that are a necessary concomitant of ideological presence. There was neither an impulse for ideology formation nor an ear to catch ideological utterances.

The contemporary situation is to the contrary. Research has reached out, has become *the* dominant project in university life around the world. It has taken on new levels of energy through becoming the favoured project of an alliance of forces. The corporate sector sees universities as possessing intellectual resources that can be put to direct effect in its own research and development activities. More long term, the state sees research as a key element in enhancing the nation's position in the know-ledge economy. It also sees, in publication rates and citation indices, indica-tions of an economic return on its investment.[3] It becomes important, therefore, for universities not just to be active in research but also to be seen to be productive in that work. Despite recantations to the contrary, in *this* calculative regime, quantities matter. The volume of researchers per institution, gross and relative amounts of research income generated per head of academic staff and the quantity of publications appearing from any one subject centre: these are characteristic of the indicators at work.

All this plays into the hands of academics-now-as-researchers (or, in some institutions, as would-be-researchers): with a clear conscience, they can take on the mantle of researchers as such. Research, in the process, turns into an ideology, sure of itself, determined to carve out its own resource base and generating new personae. Values, human being and communication structures are framed by research as such.

The emergence of research as an ideology has its counter in the forma-tion of teaching as an ideology. If research threatens to block out the framing of academic life, any interest in teaching has in turn to become an ideology in order to have its voice heard. Teaching has to become a project in its own right: infrastructures, at national and local levels, have to be put in place; journals have to spring up concerned with 'Teaching in Higher Education'; and spaces have to appear for individuals to gain their living from promoting teaching on campus.

Both research and teaching, therefore, become ideologies and rival ideo-logies at that. Research is and has been the dominant ideology; teaching is now becoming an ideology as it seeks to combat research. It knows that it will not displace research and that research will remain dominant: for that very reason, teaching seeks to become a project in its own right. The rise of teaching as an ideology is parasitic on the prior presence of research as an ideology.

Learning as ideology

The arrival of research and teaching as ideologies within higher education is coeval with the twin arrivals of the university in the knowledge economy and of mass higher education.[4] On the one hand, the formation of the university as a vehicle of knowledge production calls for research to become a project as such. On the other hand, the arrival of mass higher education with its heterogeneous intakes and lower unit costs calls for teaching to become a project in its right too.

The twist to the latter development is that teaching is seen as the sponsoring of learning and so the project of teaching is portrayed as one of 'learning and teaching'; and *that* is the order in which the terms are presented.[5] This is a discursive shift that is surely not yet fully understood. In this phrase, we see a pedagogical displacement in which the weight of the pedagogical challenge is shifted from the presentation of a disciplinary culture to an interest in the self-generational capacities of students. No longer largely objects of a pedagogical transaction, grateful recipients of a great tradition, students are now to be subjects in their own self-constitution.[6] If the original meaning of 'student' lay in one who *studied* texts, now it lies in one who studies him or herself. From epistemology to ontology: this is the turn that the curriculum in higher education is undergoing.

We see in this shift the influences at work just noted. Given a heterogeneous intake, with participants having quite different biographies and orientations, many of which – for part-time and mature students – are primarily outside the university, a teaching project hinged on disciplinary initiation makes little sense. In earlier circumstances, attention could justifiably focus on the disciplinary corpus and a curriculum was simply a syllabus of conceptual or even (in some cases) mere propositional components. Here, curriculum construction was understood as barely more than the stringing together of the concepts and theories that formed a syllabus. What was essential? What could be optional? This was a curriculum in its *shopping list* phase.

Under contemporary conditions, however, pedagogical perspectives turn from the inner concerns of academe to considerations of the wider society and the realization of a self adequate to its demands. In this pedagogical shift, the wider world is seen as a world of uncertainty and change and the pedagogical challenge becomes one of sponsoring self-motivational, self-reflexive and self-changing dispositions. In this curriculum, the old notion of the student making something of herself takes on added point: she not just 'makes out' by herself but also makes *herself*.

The emergence of the term 'learning', therefore, signifies large shifts not just in the discursive landscape of higher education but also in its pedagogies and self-understandings. Lecturers now have to take their pedagogical function especially seriously. No longer are they simply carriers of a tradition that they bestow on others; now, they have to *think* about the teaching function, the mode of their pedagogical relationships, their curricular intentions and the manner of the realization of those intentions. None is given. In the process, teaching moves in the conceptual landscape, away from research and towards learning. Learning even becomes an ideology.

Splitting interests

We see, then, research and teaching emerge not just as ideologies but as *rival* ideologies. To say this, as we observed earlier, is to proffer almost a tautology, for ideologies frequently gain both their inspiration and their energy through an oppositional orientation. The point as to this ideological contest, though, is especially potent in the present context.

Although the idea of a university as a place in which teaching and research take place alongside each other is relatively modern, it has its origins in the formation of universities themselves. Well before the birth of research as the systematic attempt to understand the universe empirically, universities understood that they had a responsibility to nurture new understandings. This was to be achieved through the mastery of texts, especially those of the Greeks, and through reflections thereupon. 'And gladly wolde he lerne and gladly wolde he teche':[7] Chaucer's clerk not only understood his twin responsibilities (as scholar and teacher) but saw clearly, too, their order. *His* form of teaching had its point within the understandings developed by his scholarship. Already, the relationship was complex: the two activities were distinct but gained their worth from each other. Teaching, this teaching, was only possible through the scholarship but, and just as crucially, the scholarship gained its point through the clerk's teaching. In itself, it was point*less*.

The universities became the unique embodiment of this dual mission: to gain and nurture new understandings about the world and to teach within the context of the formation of those new understandings. This uniqueness worked at two levels. The first was simply the conjunction of the two activities in the one institution: the university remains, after nearly 1000 years, the supreme institution in which these two activities are pursued alongside each other. The second was that the two activities did not run in parallel, separate from each other, but were organically linked to each other. Each offered the other a kind of *value-added*.

The contemporary conditions of the university are a duality, in and for the knowledge society *and* the massification of higher education. As Nowotny *et al.* (2001) note in their recent book, *Re-Thinking Science*, these two conditions of the university encourage respectively the knowledge production or research function of the university on the one hand, and the social function or teaching function of the university on the other hand.[8] Whatever the force of those who argue for the combination of the two functions – an attempt also to be made here – it should be acknowledged *in the first place* that these two functions have become separate functions, with entirely different structures, forces and interests.

As research and teaching pick up speed as ideologies, and as counter-ideologies at that, so their incipient separateness comes to the fore. The scholarship of the individual mediaeval clerk has turned, in its dominant form, into large-scale collaborative research. In perhaps its most visible form, research in high-energy physics calls for massive physical structures, with papers in the journals bearing perhaps one hundred names or more. Scientists may travel across the globe to access such facilities. Science is globalized research with the characteristics of global corporations: it now enjoys an existence separate from its sponsoring societies. Popper (1975) spoke of a World III knowledge, without a knowing subject; what we have here is a World IV knowledge, a form of knowledge in global space that is independent of location and nation.

Science – certain forms of it at least – is not only globalized but economicized, especially as interconnections develop between universities and the corporate sector.[9] Pharmaceutical companies that are investing hundreds of millions of dollars in research for new drugs consider that they have a right to set restrictions on university scientists that they fund, such that those scientists are not free to access the data that they themselves produce. Economic control goes further, however. 'Scientists are accepting large sums of money to put their names to articles endorsing new medicines that they have not written', the articles having been 'ghost-written' by individuals contracted by the pharmaceutical companies (Boseley 2002: 4). *Both* of Isaiah Berlin's 'two forms of liberty' are here undermined: scientists are prevented from exercising both a *positive* liberty to produce and disseminate their academic ideas (the first example) and a *negative* freedom not to be constrained in those same activities (the second example).[10]

Science, as Paul Feyerabend (1982) remarked, has itself become an ideology, with a determination to drive through its view of the world and to use its own hegemonic powers to realize those ambitions.[11] The scientists, we should note, are themselves – to a significant degree – witting accomplices in the diminution of their own freedoms. They not only sign up to the written word of the pharmaceutical companies but speak it as well, being sponsored to address international conferences: these scientists become (well-paid) spokespersons for those corporations. Both the ontological and the communicative elements of ideology come into play, therefore. But, even more insidiously, this ideology plays out its epistemological effects. Evidence in court cases concerning the effect of a particular drug of a pharmaceutical company may turn out to be based in part on journal papers over which that same company has had a large degree of control. This 'knowledge', as represented in the scientific journals, undergoes a shift, therefore, becoming saturated with economic and corporate interest.[12] The word can no longer be trusted.[13]

Teaching, as we have seen, undergoes its own paradigm shift in which the focus moves to student-as-learner. In this movement, the teacher is projected as a mere adjunct, simply 'facilitating' the process of learning, of enabling the student to develop in herself capacities for self-regeneration in an unknowable world. This ideology is concerned much more with 'learning outcomes' than with the character of any pedagogical process. In this pedagogy, to arrive is infinitely better than to travel. In the 'liberal university', the mind came into view as capable of having a personal hold on a disciplinary tradition. Now, that tradition is to be jettisoned, to be replaced by an interest in the student as a repertoire of skills and dispositions separated from a disciplinary corpus. Teaching is overtaken by a free-floating learning.

We see here how research and teaching split apart. There is little prospect yet of a 'university' concerning itself solely with research on the one hand or with teaching on the other (although there are occasional hints in both directions).[14] There are real prospects, however, that research and teaching will come to be conducted largely as separate activities. The separateness is not just organizational but also connected, as we might say, with different *life-constitutive projects*. On the analysis just offered, research turns into an epistemological enterprise of 'knowledge production', while teaching becomes a much more ontological enterprise, engaged in the promotion of certain kinds of human *being*.

In all this, economic reason infiltrates academe *en generale*. However, whereas in research the presence of economic reason can often be direct (witness the influence of the pharmaceutical companies), in teaching it is indirect and has there a more nuanced effect. It just may be that the 'key skills' that aid 'employability' over a changing lifespan may also impart 'lifeskills': economic reason here may turn out to be a friend of an education for human flourishing. At least, the matter has to be kept open. Corporate interest in research, too, is not an unremittingly black picture, more a dark grey. Opportunities are presented anew, but the position is primarily one of control for immediate economic benefit. The interest of the world of work in teaching, however, may *in the first place* be positive, rebalancing teaching by lessening the weight of the academics' knowledge agendas and raising that of the human qualities called for in a fast-changing world.

We may note an unfortunate quirkiness in these ideological manoeuvrings. So as to secure its own position, teaching attempts – as we have seen – to surround itself with the trappings of a research infrastructure. Even a new phrase appears: 'the scholarship of teaching'. The phrase, culled from the work of Ernest Boyer (1990), encourages a sense that teaching is open to systematic reflection and, in the process, new understandings.[15] But there is an irony at work here. In proclaiming the potential for teaching as a site of research and scholarship, this ideology works tacitly to underline the hegemony of research as the dominant ideology. Teaching can only secure a point of recognition by cloaking itself in the ideology of research. The price of teaching gaining a toehold is its surrender to the ideology against which it contends.

There is a further irony in teaching becoming an ideology. One of the motives of teaching becoming a project in its own right is, presumably, to remind the university that teaching is not just an important activity for the university but was always, from its inception, key to the unity that *was* the university. But, in becoming an ideology, very much with its eyes on research against which it pits itself, teaching now adds to the fragmentation of the university. A force for greater unity now encourages the disunity of the university.

Uniting research and teaching

The unification of research and teaching and, therefore, *of the university itself,* may not now be completely possible. In a fluid age, in which the university is intermeshed in complex ways with society, that kind of grand project may not be feasible. But we should not presume that position to be the case. Lying ahead of us is the task of working out what such a goal might look like: What would it be to realize a unity of teaching and research under contemporary conditions which also takes account of the rival ideologies that are developing?

The particular task in front of us, it will be noted, is not simply a matter of conceptual strategy, as we might put it. It is not a matter of rooting out some concept – such as 'criticality', 'risk-taking', 'enquiry', 'scholarship' or 'learning', to take just some suggestions from the literature – that might serve simply as a bridge between the two sets of activity.[16] What is required, rather, is a set of ideas that will feasibly command allegiance from both the research and the teaching lobbies and that will at least allow the two projects to live in peace with each other. It is not enough to be able to come to see both sets of activities under a single conceptual heading, so to speak. If that were all that was achieved, there would be little change. Ideology, after all, buttresses practices. Unless the practices in question are liable to be changed, we would find ourselves in a situation characterized at best by a changing narrative. The underlying ideological structure, and especially that of research as the dominant ideology, would still carry the day.

Let us focus on the empirical landscape and recall the typification offered a moment ago. It may be assumed that in many multifaculty universities in the contemporary age there are to be found, on the one hand, research units that are organizationally adrift from the teaching endeavour and, on the other hand, some 'self-funding' teaching activities – such as some professional short courses – that are conducted by staff whose research profiles are thin or non-existent and to whom no research resources flow. For the rest of the work of the university, we can say that research and teaching are at least contiguous with each other. Their relationships may be antipathetic but at least there are relationships of *some* kind to be found.[17]

Under these conditions, two sets of questions open up. *Firstly,* what would it mean to bring the independent outliers into the fold such that research units were manifestly seen to be contiguous with teaching and 'teaching-only' activities were accorded proper space alongside the research effort? Would such two movements be susceptible of an overarching description?

Even though they may constitute a small minority of the work of a multifaculty university, such outliers are ideologically significant. They raise as an issue the extent to which universities are serious when they say that research supports teaching and (although less frequently) that teaching supports research. As cases of complete divorce, they vivify any general strategies for unification – ideological and operational – that might be adopted for the university as a whole. If a strategy looks like working in *those* cases, it will probably work for other activities on campus.

Secondly, our ideological and operational strategies will have to be sensitive to the range of contexts that the contemporary university offers. We are faced here with a complex field: undergraduate *and* postgraduate levels of study, disciplines, practices, identities, manifold interactions with the wider world, epistemologies and academic economies, with their separate reward and resourcing structures, all cut across each other. Ideological and operational strategies intended seriously to have effect, therefore, have to be sensitive to the university as a site of extraordinary difference.[18]

Recognizing difference

'Recognizing difference', not 'recognizing differences': the distinction is significant. Our ideological and operational strategies have to be sensitive to difference; they do not, at the outset, have to have a detailed account of all the differences concerning the relationship between research and teaching across the university's disciplines, departments and centres. Our ideological and operational strategies have to understand and to recognize that considerable differences are to be found across the university, but they do not have to be able to describe those differences fully.

I have just used the phrase 'ideological and operational strategies'. In a sense, the 'operational' is redundant: all ideologies are realized in practices. Ideologies are hybrids, speaking to sets of *beliefs* that are embedded in *practices*. But the term 'operational strategies' points up that any attempt to address the research and teaching ideologies as separate, fissiparous and counter to each other will require *definite* operational strategies to be put in place. Indeed, the practices and the ideologies go hand-in-hand. The counter-ideologies will have to be embedded in practices.

Academic life prides itself on its reasonableness but universities are organizations. Being actors in those organizations, university academics will respond to organizational patterns, reward structures, systems and academic and resource structures. Counter-ideologies cannot just rest, therefore, on their own reasonableness. Their effectiveness is not to be assured simply by their being opened to debate. On the contrary, we are here in the presence of *ideological capture*.

Ideologies seek to capture and to colonize, but they do so by imposing difference: activities and their actors are understood as being either on the inside of the ideology or on the outside. The ideologies of research and of learning and teaching are threatening to mark individuals in just this way, either as researchers 'at the cutting edge' or as individuals 'devoted to their teaching'. In this way, they act to break apart the academy. They have become pernicious ideologies, creating difference and being vengeful in relation to those differences.

The differences that these ideologies construct are pernicious, injecting negative energy flows on campus. Wars of attrition develop, with each camp seeking to enhance its position. Internal reward systems are infiltrated so as to reconfigure them in the image of the respective ideology. Certainly, the vice-chancellor and the respective pro-vice-chancellors (for research and for learning and teaching) will assert that research and teaching are complementary and even synergistic. But rhetoric such assertions will remain unless the two ideologies are confronted as such, particularly the ideology of research given its hegemonic position.

In the wake of this ideological battle, therefore, difference lives on campus, but it is an ideological difference that reflects the two warring ideologies and is constructed by them. In this ideological difference, individuals are framed and recognized as either 'one of us' or 'not one of us'. Amidst the emerging ideological differences, the university fragments. Perhaps the university has to fragment in the modern age, but this ideological dispute enhances those fragmentary tendencies.

Challenging links

Given this analysis, our earlier view is confirmed: the task of addressing the tension between research and teaching is no longer a matter of identifying a linking concept – such as 'enquiry', 'scholarship' or 'learning' – that might serve as a unifying banner under which both research and teaching can be placed. All of those ideas *do* have potential mileage in them. Each offers, prima facie, a means of seeing both research and teaching as variants of a single set of academic practices. As such, they seem to provide, perhaps, a means of dissolving research and teaching as counter-ideologies. However, *that* strategy of securing a conceptual and practical link between teaching and research is flawed.

Firstly, the strategy of conceptual and practical linkage too easily conveys a sense of seamless continuity and neglects the substantial differences between research and teaching. Questions as to the relationship between research and teaching derive precisely from their non-identity.[19] *Secondly*, the linking strategy fails to attend seriously to the ideological character of the terrain before us. Academic identities, projects and communicative networks that gain their point from their distinctiveness are not going to be dissolved easily through proclamations of linkage.

Thirdly, the linking strategy tends to treat both research and teaching as if they were unitary activities and took common forms across academe. It neglects the point that research and teaching are both complexes of activities *and* that they take differing forms across disciplines and institutions: laboratory-based teaching as against text-based teaching; small-group classes as compared with very large groups; empirical research involving large teams costing very large sums provided by external agencies in contrast to the work of the individual scholar; and the production of a research paper with a hundred names on it as against a major single-authored book: these are different enterprises, all with their own rules and demands.

Accordingly, the linking strategy downplays both natural difference across academe and ideological difference. The former (institutional) neglect arises logically from a strategy of linkage: it presupposes sharedness and underestimates the extent to which universities and knowledges have become complexes. Each entity in a complex will be connected with other entities but they may be predominantly entities of the *same* kind: research activities may be related to other research activities rather than to teaching activities. The latter (ideological) neglect betrays a political weakness: it overlooks the force of teaching and research *as* insidious ideologies in having a negative impact upon each other.

Academic difference as ideology

As ideologies, then, research and teaching work insidiously to construct difference. Pools of difference emerge in non-communicating networks, identities and projects. The ontologies of research and teaching split *and* become antagonistic towards each other; they even derive their presence and their force from the other: each ideology is not the other. Under these conditions, linking strategies are bound to be inadequate to the ideological challenge. Instead, a strategy suggests itself that is founded *on* difference. This strategy we may term simply a strategy of *academic difference.* This strategy begins from the recognition that there are a multitude of legitimate academic identities and, therefore, a multitude of legitimate relationships – as well as illegitimate ones – between teaching and research.

At a stroke, therefore, through this concept of academic difference, the linking strategy – which has been with us for 200 years, although stepped up considerably of late – can be abandoned. Instead of trying to see research and teaching as two facets of a unity, with all the forms of closure that such a strategy brings, justice can now be done to the different forms that research and teaching take and to the consequent variety of their *due* relationships.

The objections to such a strategy of difference will be several. Firstly, it may be objected that the idea of difference as a characterization of the relationships between research and teaching undermines any sense of a unity within the university. *However*, there is no alternative *and* there is unity through difference. The unity is neither an epistemological nor an ontological unity but is a *communicative* unity. It is a unity in the praxis of the university. It is a unity in which individuals and groups respect the identities of each other as legitimate in their thoughts and actions and engage with each other accordingly. At present, with research and teaching squaring up to each other, this is often not the case. A unity through difference offers a hope of doing justice to the notion of 'academic community' (see Chapter 8). Community is easy enough to realize when the members of a university are manifestly signing up to common agendas; the challenge of realizing community arises amid manifest difference.

A second objection to the idea of academic difference as a conceptual strategy for dissolving the research–teaching ideological battle could be the charge that, despite its title of '*academic* difference', there is little that is academic about it. All that it offers is a plea for difference and, in so doing, it abandons the university to whatever shape it may take and whatever activities that might set up under its umbrella. Simply put, the notion of academic difference has no substance.

There is some validity to this objection. The doctrine of academic difference does not lay down the law as to the character of academic activities. It leaves open the relative weights of research and teaching and their relationships. However, the idea of academic difference taken forward as a project does not present a *carte blanche*; some arrangements are off-limits. It is not enough to allow research and teaching under the one roof and then to allow any kind of relationship between them: *antagonistic relationships are ruled out*. This has practical and even managerial point. A doctrine of academic difference rules out reward structures that favour one activity (say, research) over another. The doctrine obliges universities to look at their promotions procedures and their systems for accounting for academic work so as to ensure that certain academic activities (say, teaching) are not unduly disincentivized. The concept of academic difference, therefore, has practical force. It acts as a critical standard by which policies and practices can be severely tested. Academic difference does not serve as a licence for academic hegemony.

A yet third objection to the idea of academic difference could be that it is self-defeating. The argument of this book is that universities are invaded by pernicious ideologies that are undermining the Western idea of the university but that it is possible to identify, in contrast, virtuous ideologies that can do justice to that lingering idea and insert a practical space for its survival. The idea of academic difference, so it might be said, offers at best a way of dissolving the ideologies of research and teaching and, thereby, their corrosive competitive force. Its price is that it demonstrates that the way forward for the contemporary university is to divest itself so far as practicable of all ideology. The notion of academic difference demonstrates a weakness in the whole argumentative strategy of this book.

The contrary is the case. The idea of academic difference can constitute the basis of a virtuous ideology – or ide*a*logy, as I have termed it. In changing from idea into ide*a*logy, academic difference becomes a project, even if a utopian project, willing a particular kind of university. It would be a university in which it is recognized that the weightings of, and the relationships between, teaching and research may differ validly across departments and even individuals *within* departments. Ruled out is the possibility that either activity can be ignored or be accorded mere lip service. Ruled out, too, are institutional policies and practices that give high marks to one activity and low marks or even '*nul point*' to the other activity. Institutional newsletters that celebrate research successes and are largely silent in respect of teaching would be outlawed.

In becoming an ide*a*logy, what is required is that this idea of academic difference be taken up by individuals and be expressed in working relationships. As an ideology, albeit a virtuous ide*a*logy, academic difference will vivify individuals and their interactions with each other. Through academic difference becoming an ide*a*logy, universities can become *more* than the sum of their parts for it can help to develop positive academic relationships. For that to come about, however, academic difference has to become part of the conscious strategy of an institution's leadership: drive, imagination, political nous, unflagging energy and courage are called for in confronting the dominant academic power blocs and taking forward this agenda.

Conclusion: living together, effectively

The twentieth century saw the university change from a site in which teaching and research stood in a reasonably comfortable relationship with each other to one in which they became mutually antagonistic. Firstly, research became an ideology seeking to become the pre-eminent activity and to supply the dominant set of values in universities. Secondly, and in response to this research hegemony, teaching – now become learning and teaching in a context of mass higher education – is fast becoming a counter-ideology.

In the process, research and teaching, far from offering a unity to the university, are now threatening to tear it apart. As ideologies, they do not just square up to each other but are actually securing their identity and their practical force from each other. *Neither is the other.* In this combative process, they become pernicious ideologies, undermining the unity of the university.

A strategy built around the concept of academic difference offers a fruitful way forward. In the first place, it can dissipate the intensity of research and teaching as mutually conflicting ideologies. Secondly, by respecting difference universally across the university, research and teaching can come into a relationship of mutual peace. Lastly, in such a milieu, new and productive relationships between research and teaching might develop. Antagonistic relationships between research and teaching can be replaced by positive and mutually enhancing relationships. For example, criteria that have to be satisfied for the title of 'professor' can be drawn up such that they allow different kinds of academic identity legitimately to be valued and recognized.

We are entitled to call such a counter-strategy an ide*a*logy. It contains a set of beliefs as to the desirability of the university-as-a-unity and seeks to carry forward that ideal in a practical project. It can have wider policy implications, for example, in providing a means of evaluating claimants for the title of 'university': such claimants would have to demonstrate not only that both research and teaching were present but also that they were not mutually antagonistic. Pursued seriously, the emergence even of positive relationships would be a likely occurrence. For that to happen, academic difference would have to be taken on board by each university's leadership. Tight boundaries in academic identities and academic practices would have to be dissolved. Research strategies and learning and teaching strategies would have to be developed as a combined project.

An ideology of academic difference cannot be brought off by neutral stances. Professors cannot simply isolate themselves from teaching, saying that they respect it, or even worse be permitted to 'buy themselves out of teaching'. Rather, they will demonstrate their recognition of difference by positively supporting teaching. Heads of department will actively have to show their support for a wide range of academic identities across their staff. Reward structures will have to be developed that encourage teaching as well as research and which disincentivize the construction of individual identities around a narrow set of activities.

Academic difference, then, has the capacity to become a virtuous ideology that adds both academic and educational value and vitality to universities. Difference can contend against homogeneity. It is a means of living effectively and fruitfully within the contemporary university. It is also a means of enabling research and teaching to live alongside each other, if not in positive relationships then at least in relationships of mutual respect. The bringing off of such an ideology of academic difference, providing for research and teaching to live in a benign relationship with each other, will place considerable but not insuperable challenges on academic leadership.

12

Reasonable Universities

Introduction

We return to our starting point. To what extent can the idea of reason attach to universities today? In this chapter, I want to address this question directly by pressing further my proposal that virtuous ideologies – ide*a*logies, as I term them – can be developed which represent 'the ideal of the university' (Wolff 1997). Universities retain space in which to move under their own direction, even if that space is diminishing and even if there are no sure footholds. Accordingly, that space can be put to use in the construction of virtuous ide*a*logies.

The task of constructing such ide*a*logies is, as we have seen, triply challenging. *Firstly*, it faces the challenge of its own internal coherence. Ideologies are characteristically both less and more than they first appear: there are limits to their reasonableness, just as they overreach themselves. *Secondly*, that we live in an age of postmodernity threatens to undermine the legitimacy of *any* large project. An age without secure foundations on the one hand and proliferating frameworks on the other hand places severe challenges in the way of any attempt to work out a progressive project. Just how *can* the virtuousness of any strategy be made secure? *Lastly*, contemporary universities are complex and even chaotic institutions.[1] Can ideas as to the purposes of 'the university' ever be more than high-blown rhetoric? Could any such idea be *operationalized*?

In this last chapter, I want to answer these challenges to my argument by bringing together four ideas. For the first idea, I turn to a concept promoted recently by Stephen Toulmin (2001), that of *reasonableness*. My second, third and fourth ideas are *academic generosity*, *institutional adroitness* and universities as *institutions that might learn*. I believe that in these four ideas taken together, we can find a firm but flexible conceptual structure which will generate a virtuous project that will enable 'universities' to prosper in the fluidity of the twenty-first century.

Institutional reasonableness

'Institutional reasonableness' rather than, say, 'institutional reason': the first phrase is spacious, allowing for reason to be expressed as forms of local life within universities. But, more than that, the first phrase allows for different *modes* of reason. It allows for the university having become a characteristically complex institution: as such, reason can and will find manifold forms of expression in the nooks and crannies of the university. The ideas that there is a single form of 'university reason' and that reason is deployed for common purposes within the university have to be set aside. Reason in universities is multifaceted, as are its forms of academic life.

These points deserve some infilling. We can expect that as the academic world engages more with the wider world, its ways of knowing and its self-understandings will become more open, more nuanced, more subtle and, yes, more complex. The highest marks having formerly been placed on purity, general theory and abstraction within bounded disciplines, universities are now obliged to straddle boundaries and to become epistemologically more generous, embracing case studies, action research, action learning, uncertainty and practical arguments.

As those new forms of knowing press their claims, so the academy is obliged to make its tacit presuppositions on these matters explicit, to engage in debate both internally and with its new client groups, and ultimately to widen its conception of valid forms of reason. In any event, its client groups – such as mature students and part-time students working in professional settings – will understandably press hard for the criteria against which they are being assessed to be spelt out: the traditional criteria set within formal forms of reason just may not seem adequate to them.

It may take time, but we can anticipate that the academy will engage in university-wide pondering over its taken-for-granted presuppositions. Working parties will be set up to examine, for example, the nature of the PhD, as that is called into question. Is a PhD a unitary text? Could it be a series of case studies? Is it a solitary endeavour? To what extent can it derive from and be situated in practical endeavours? Might argumentation within a PhD text include practical arguments, where the standards of evaluation lie much more in their practical efficacy as distinct from their formal 'truth'-carrying properties? Should the development of 'key skills' be assessed as part of a PhD? Should there be tests for a candidate's 'stewardship' of her or his discipline? Once embarked on a course of collective self-reflection, there will be no end to such questions. The academy is becoming a set of fluidities, flowing in and through the wider society, and vice versa, and those currents will not be stilled.

For the academy, then, a conversation about reason itself is inevitable, reluctant as it may be to engage in such a process. The conversation will not be easy. To put it formally, the university will find itself having to become reflexive about its own knowledge activities. Quite different value positions will be revealed; the debate may become quite heated.

Clark Kerr pointed out back in the 1960s that universities were *multiversities*, being composed of many different communities having little mutual comprehension. At least, then, literally and metaphorically, we could *locate* universities. In contrast, in the *networked academies* of the twenty-first century, their boundaries are yielding and their conceptual underpinnings are dissolving in the quicksands, or so it may seem. It is not that reason is no more. To the contrary, the university is being asked to become so epistemologically generous that there seems to be no limit to the forms of reason that it might embrace.

In the universities of the twenty-first century, then, Grand Reason – the sense that the university stood for Reason, knew what it was, and was able to nurture it as a project having universal value – has dissolved.[2] The university has become less certain of its own certainties, less sure of its own universality. The idea of universal reason has given way to multiple forms of reason, and with it arises the self-understanding by the university that the forms of reason that it harbours are but a selection of the forms of reason and knowing found in contemporary society.

This *has* to be the case. In the knowledge society, the production of knowledge is distributed across society. In the process, what counts as knowledge becomes drawn in ways entirely outside the control of universities. Multinational corporations do not just produce and manage their own knowledge: the idea of corporate knowledge points to power and control over the definitions of knowledge itself that are beyond the power and control of universities.[3] At a quite different level, individuals seek out 'alternative therapies', which may lack a foundation in systematic bodies of knowledge. Such individuals show their preferences for experience over experiment and, in so doing, also run up the flag for knowledges beyond those on offer in the universities.[4]

The will to reason, accordingly, *has* to give way to a will in favour of reasonableness. 'Reason' within the academy becomes simply those forms of life held to be valid at a moment in time. Forms of life proliferate, each embodying its own orientation to reason and its own style of engaging. The idea of Reason as a universal description of the university gives way to an acknowledgement of different forms of life, each with its own point. Whereas Reason assumes that forms of academic life can and should be confined according to a single description, reasonableness acknowledges valid difference. Reason is totalitarian; reasonableness is generous.

Academic generosity

Deep down, the academy knows all this. It knows that it is but one player – or, at best, a particular set of players – in the knowledge game. As such, the university is obliged to become more modest, less noisy and more generous to alternative ways of understanding the world.

Generosity is not given in any sense on campus; rather the reverse. Ernest Gellner once remarked that collective hostility is often most marked in relation to one's neighbours. Neighbours' circumstances, language, customs and frameworks can appear to offer sufficient links to justify judgements. In contrast, a group in a quite different situation may seem exotic: it is so far removed from one's comprehension that judgements cannot gain a purchase. This, surely, is the case in academic life. The most virulent hostilities break out between those whose territory overlaps: the sociologists are unable to engage productively with the philosophers; the experimental psychologists feel that they inhabit a different world from that of the developmental psychologists; those in business studies who offer critiques of the business world have little respect for their colleagues who advance frameworks that are likely to assist corporations; and the philosophers are sometimes hardly able to engage productively even among themselves.[5]

This particular feature of academic tribalism, in which charity most defi nitely does *not* begin at home, can doubtless be explained sociologically. One theory would be that it is the result of a situation in which formal knowledge production has been mainly driven forward by the academics themselves. Under such conditions, the gaze of academics is turned in on themselves, their being largely unconcerned with the wider world. Their internal fights are a sign of external impotence. For some in the academy, it is as if the academic world *is* the world and they have only themselves for epistemological company and, thereby, epistemological warfare. It is no coincidence that the examples cited are drawn largely from the humanities and the social sciences. It is in those disciplines that there is relatively little direct 'engagement' with the wider society.

Another story is less prosaic: it is that the conditions of academic life increasingly favour competition between the disciplines. The ideologies both of the market and of corporatism have found their way onto the campus (see Chapter 5). Departments, now as cost centres, compete to outscore each other on the university's internal accounting systems and performance indicators. Those that do not perform adequately are liable to face the cry of 'Off with their heads!'

Under such conditions, academic generosity may even be receding.[6] Resource, effort and emotional energy will have to be expended if aca demic generosity is to constitute a feature of academic life. Attention will need to be paid to both 'process and structure' (Becher and Kogan 1992): resourcing strategies, incentives and accountability structures on the one hand, and situations created in which 'colleagues' are obliged to take account of each other – such as in cross-disciplinary projects or over issues of university-wide concern – on the other hand. Inevitably, some academics will dismiss as mere 'managerialism' any such attempt to remind academics of their collective accountability to each other. Ironically, this response often dresses itself up as the true defender of academic values when, in practice, through its disinclination seriously to confront new practices and ideas, it corrodes them.

I have been running together two ideas, those of academic generosity and reasonableness. These two notions come nicely together in the following reflection: in recognizing the reasonableness of others' forms of life, values and ways of knowing, the members of the academy develop their mutual generosity. I add two further considerations.

Firstly, if this reflection is accorded the status of a principle of academic life, it holds as a universal. It affects all units, departments and activities. It affects the university horizontally and vertically. It affects all ideas, frameworks and strategies. *Secondly,* the ideas of academic generosity and reasonableness are reflexive. *If* they are sincerely held, they carry through into the self-beliefs and practices of those who espouse them. Principles such as these cannot be adopted half-heartedly. 'I believe in academic generosity and reasonableness but not in regard to my own beliefs and practices' is not a coherent position.

In other words, academic generosity and reasonableness bear upon universities *as* universities. In a fluid world, in which universities have to make themselves amid societal and global callings, *generosity* and *reasonableness* emerge as ideologies, virtuous projects that can maintain universities as universities. In a world of uncertainty, multiplicity and challenge, these two ideas constitute the makings of a strategy, conceptual and practical all at once, that might outwit the corrosive ideologies now present within the university. Never completely realizable, nor ever completely justifiable,[7] they become utopian projects for doing some justice to the idea of the university amid the conceptual and practical conditions of the twenty-first century.

Progressive ideologies

In this recursive character of academic generosity and reasonableness, we see how the idea of a virtuous ideology gains a purchase. In being adopted, ideologies develop positive institutional energy. They have an internally compelling character. They act as hooks that capture and promote goodwill. They literally add value to the academic community that forms a university; indeed, they help to form and sustain just such a community. The will to engage, communicate and even collaborate that is presently threatening to dissolve but yet lingers on is given an infrastructural strengthening which enables it to flourish.

The virtue of these ideas as educational projects for the university has a dual character. *On the one hand,* academic generosity and reasonableness advance the ideal of a university as a tolerant, interactive community, providing space for new academic pursuits and ideas.[8] The idea of a university, resting not so much in Reason but more in communicative processes of different kinds, is given new vigour. Even in an age of fluidity and fragility, in which large ideas are suspect, we can hold on to academic generosity and reasonableness as universal ideals for the university. But, as academic generosity and reasonableness are not given, they have to be developed as a deliberate strategy, watched with vigilance by academic leaders and, where necessary, defended with energy against the internal and external forces that would undermine them.

On the other hand, academic generosity and reasonableness offer a hope of outwitting the pernicious ideologies on campus. Since they have many of the formal properties of those corrosive ideologies – collective beliefs, forward-looking projects, implicit forms of evaluation of activities, and being carriers of academic identities – they can be construed as ideologies in themselves. Being held seriously and being part of a culture, they even contain within themselves points of resistance: they resist intolerance, domination, a refusal to listen and epistemological blindness and are inclined to treat sceptically apparently strange forms of academic life (as represented in terms such as 'quality', 'management', 'competition' and 'markets'). So far, in their *formal* properties, they coincide with pernicious ideologies.

It is in their substantive properties and their effects that such ideologies part company with ideologies. Because they promote tolerance, even tolerance towards the key ideas contained in the corrosive ideologies, the ideas (here) of academic generosity and reasonableness have the makings of virtuous ideologies. They are ideologies – of a kind – but they have positive effects, which even take forward the ideals of the university in a turbulent and querulous age. They are ideologies of the university as such.

Complexity revisited

A research unit may be formed with a certain kind of zeal: not only will it have implications for the university's technical systems but it will also have repercussions on the university's discursive character. It will usher in new thinking, new ideas and new concepts and these may generate tensions with some of those already present. Perhaps the new centre is funded by a certain private donor or perhaps its research programme focuses on a particular religious order: its establishment will not be ideationally neutral but will have discursive effects. It will add concepts, ideas and frameworks, both substantively and through its sheer presence, and some of those may generate conceptual and human turbulence and, quite possibly, resistance.

Seen in this context, it is hardly surprising that contemporary reflections on universities as complex organizations have also invoked the concept of chaos.[9] The complexities that beset universities are so considerable that they are beyond management in any straightforward sense. This managerial challenge, this organizational elusiveness, is more than that the university is a characteristically turbulent environment, in which its systems are so interwoven that the effects of a change cannot be predicted. It is also that the unpredictability of a university contains further complexities of its own. And yet, there lies embedded, too, in the idea of chaos, the sense that some order, some pattern or some security may be detected amid the characteristic randomness.

Complexity is itself a complex matter. In our earlier discussion, we distinguished between complexities on campus that are bound up with systems, structures and resources on the one hand, from those that are bound up with ideas, frameworks and understandings on the other hand. The first set of complexities relates, we may say, to the *hard-wiring* of a university as an organization. The second set of complexities relates to the *conceptual tissue* of the university. Both sets of complexities have a repercussive quality: their entities rebound on each other in myriad ways, making the effects of any movement difficult to forecast. However, this unpredictability takes different forms across the two forms of complexity.

In principle, *hard-wiring* complexities could be unravelled. Systems could be made to work more efficiently, structures could be made more explicit and more adequate to external audit and new income streams could be generated. With hard-wiring complexities, given enough time and resource, difficulties can be *dissolved*. In contrast, with *soft-tissue* complexities, typically no such resolution is to hand. What is at issue here are conceptual difficulties, different ways of looking at the world and contrasting value systems which do not yield to any resolution. In these circumstances, all that we have (as both Isaiah Berlin and Jürgen Habermas, in their different ways, have pointed out) is the toleration of difference through conversation.

It is this second form of complexity that warrants the term *supercomplexity*. This is a form of complexity that is associated with our hold on the world itself, on who we are and on how we understand ourselves and each other. It is a form of complexity that acknowledges from the outset that there may be no clear resolution of differences, no unravelling of complexities and no unifying of frameworks. A world of supercomplexity is a world both of ideological undermining and of ideological overload. It is a fragile world and an intricate world. It is a world in which the assaults on one's frameworks for comprehending the world come thick and fast and in which none of those frameworks can be secured with any authority.[10]

Both forms of complexity are, at once, both noisy and silent. Having more students than can fit into a lecture hall, the escape of a virulent bacterium from a laboratory and the collapse of a computer system: these are rather noisy varieties of *system complexity*, shouting their presence. On the other hand, some forms of system complexity are rather more subtle, announcing themselves only when they have degenerated to a gross state. *Ideological complexity*, too, may be quiet or noisy. Often, differences of view are simply not even aired on campus, let alone addressed. At the same time, differences may erupt into hostile outpourings, as rival viewpoints – say, over rules for student access, minorities on campus or funding by tobacco industries – shout their positions.

There is, however, a fundamental difference in regard to the noisiness–silence index of these two forms of complexity. In relation to hard-wiring complexity, noise and silence take on a metaphorical character whereas, in soft-tissue complexity, noise and silence have a *facticity*. We can explain this difference in the following way.

Hard-wiring complexity is connected primarily to *instrumental reason* whereas ideological complexity is connected to *communicative reason*. These two forms of reason generate silence and noise of quite different orders. In instrumental reason, other than the crash of a beam as a result of faulty building maintenance, the noise and the silence have an allegorical character. With communicative reason, one can be silent or noisy in communicating with one's neighbours down the corridor in a particularly direct manner: even the silence can be deafening.

Institutional adroitness

I suggested in Chapter 1 that management is the art of the possible whereas leadership is the art of the impossible. But these reflections on complexity offer qualifications to this generalization. *Management* becomes a matter of producing positive effects amid hard-wiring complexity whereas *leadership* becomes a matter of making progress amid soft-tissue or ideological complexity. Hard-wiring complexities offer a chance of resolving difficulties (management information systems could be improved, new income streams could be identified and decision-making structures could be streamlined). The pursuit of such managerial achievements calls for high-level skills of foresight, drive and priority setting; such skills are not to be downplayed. Soft-tissue complexities, however, yield no resolution, only (at best) continuing debate, conversation and a relentless willingness to engage.

In the face of soft-tissue complexities (or supercomplexity), leadership is a matter of opening new frames of understanding and imagining. It is the glimpsing of a new world, a new idea of the university, and the creation of discursive spaces in which such new ideas can be debated even by rival factions on campus. It is the challenge of bringing the warring parties together. *This* is the art of the impossible, an art that calls often for the capacity to persuade disputants to engage purposively with each other, even under new descriptions of their activities. This is a task of engaging with human being as such: in the university's committee rooms, the body language often speaks louder than the spoken language itself.

From all of this, the idea of *institutional adroitness* suggests itself. Institutional adroitness is present when a university has formed the capacity for discursive tolerance which allows ideological complexities to be addressed in a purposive manner. In the presence of institutional adroitness, campus ideologies are softened. They continue to exist but their cutting edge is blunted: all voices have a hearing but none has an *undue* hearing. Such a university arms itself with utopian ideologies that supply counter but progressive forms of institutional energy.

One strategy for the softening of rival frameworks (in the conceptual wiring of the university) is the insertion of new possibilities for the future of the university. The university rides above its factions by focusing its collective imaginations on ideas for the university's positioning and advancement in the years to come. Strategic review – a process in which many universities engage from time to time – has, therefore, to become a permanent way of life for the university. Through strategic review, particular agendas are disempowered if not altogether displaced.

Strategic review, on the analysis here, cannot be a matter of the Vice-Chancellor's senior management team – with or without the usual suspects added – acting in closed session. The point is less one of people 'inclusivity' (to use a modish term) but is more one of *ideological inclusivity*. Unless the conversation is opened out to the whole university, the full range of ideals and hopes for the university will not have a hearing. In turn, such a 'strategic review' would be likely to confine itself to a greater or lesser continuation of the university's present activities rather than entertaining imaginative and even fantastic ideas as to what it might become. Of course, the different views of the university-in-the-future will chafe with each other. Unless, however, that conceptual debate is not just entertained but also actively fostered, the university will end in surrendering itself to the dominant ideologies that beset it.

For the twenty-first century university, pragmatism is essential but it is not enough: it is a necessary but insufficient condition of the university's flourishing. Pragmatism can easily turn into a live-and-let-live philosophy. Or, amid the huge challenges of managing complexity, it can focus too easily on the here-and-now and become bewitched by the myriad of presenting challenges. *This* pragmatism can too easily lead to a 'let's-keep-it-simple' philosophy (see Chapter 2). At best, pragmatism will offer some temporary salvation for the managers. What it does not offer is a guide to would-be university leaders.[11]

A *will towards institutional adroitness*, accordingly, is a virtuous ideology. It is a project that attempts to live out some of the progressive hopes embedded in the idea of the university itself. It is an ide*a*logy.

Two kinds of fantasy

Corrosive ideologies, we should recall, do not just emanate outwith the university. Some are generated by factions within the academic community. Firstly, research became an ideology and then, partly as a counter-reaction, has arisen an ideology focused on learning and teaching as such. Not only are these ideologies attempting to construct the university in their own image but they are also squaring up to each other.[12] In this process, negative institutional energies are created, academic identities are framed under one heading or another and efforts are spent on outmanoeuvring the opposition. Other ideologies have a hybrid character. Entrepreneurialism and quality may have their origins beyond the academy, but they have been taken up with alacrity by some universities such that they have their own undue momentum now written into them.

To repeat, these ideologies have *some* virtue in them. It is in their seeking to colonize all before them that the trouble starts: they have *undue* momentum written into them. Left to their own devices, corrosive ideologies such as these would destroy universities, and in two senses. *Firstly*, they would reduce the capacity of a university as a forum for open debate. It is in the nature of ideologies that they seek to impose their viewpoint, a viewpoint that is characteristically an *ego*centric viewpoint. Their inner message is 'Be like us'; or even, 'You are either with us or against us'. Those who stand for a wider set of interests, values and academic *being* are seen as wearing quite other hats. Ideologies cannot themselves deal either with complexity or with generosity. Ideologically saturated universities are sites of non-communication.

Secondly, universities are presented continually with both opportunities and challenges. Many of these – opportunities *and* challenges – are generated by the universities themselves. Their inner complexities mesh with complexities in the wider world. If universities are to develop maximally rational strategies in such circumstances, cool heads are required. The intensity, noisiness and sheer belligerence of ideologies on campus are likely to serve only to heat up the temperature.

Paradoxically, a necessary condition for turning mere change into rational progress is the development of imaginary qualities. Circled by fantastic visions in the wider society, a university needs to develop capacities for generating its own fantasies of a collective kind; and these latter visions – or fantasies – are of two forms. On the one hand, universities may collectively develop fantasies about themselves that derive, in part, from the ideals embedded in the idea of the university – of community, reasonableness, communication and the value of ideas. On the other hand, other fantasies may derive from a university's sense of its particular position – present and future – amidst the complexities of the twenty-first century in which it is intertwined.

Doubtless, most universities can lumber on: their very complexity allows for pockets of entrepreneurialism of all kinds within themselves (in relation to research, teaching and consultancy). But unless universities can develop collective imaginary capacities, the ideologies that attack them from within will continue to wreak their havoc. Universities' capacities for renewal will have been sabotaged.

Universities that learn

The idea of universities as institutions that learn is not a new idea but I am not sure that it has been properly developed, given the challenges that we have sketched out.[13] We have already encountered most of its elements. They include:

- a process of strategic review that takes the form of a continuing *collective conversation* as to a university's positioning and purposes and that actively encourages the formation of visions of its future;

- a collective identification of the values and principles that inform the university's decision making;
- a determination to combat and to neutralize the ideologies on campus.

This may appear to be a benign and a straightforward programme. In fact, it is a huge programme calling for unrelenting effort, courage from institutional leaders, a capacity for imaginary thinking, the injection of fora for transdisciplinary conversations, and a determined drive to bring together those individuals representative of different ideologies and capacities – at both a personal and a collective level – so as to handle multiple agendas and to work in different dimensions at once (including capacities to work in different time horizons, both backwards and forwards). It calls, therefore, for the deliberate injection of dialogical reason alongside a university's instrumental reason.[14]

It may be that some universities are on their way to realizing such an ambitious programme of institutional self-learning, but full-blown learning universities of this kind are probably not yet thick on the ground. It is easy to understand why this should be. The kind of programme for institutional self-learning just sketched out calls for resources to be invested of a personal, collective and systemic character. It calls for an unrelenting effort to bring together individuals who would otherwise simply not speak to each other. It calls for management information to be not only produced but also disseminated widely in user-friendly form. It calls for forms of communication to be imaginatively exploited – in different media – so that individuals can contribute to a continuing conversation.

When a senior management team is faced with a continual stream of pressing mega-challenges – over the establishment of a new medical school, a new contract with a multinational organization or an amalgamation with another institution – the investment of time, resources and effort into developing the university into this kind of self-learning organization may well seem to be a diversion from the tasks in hand. It will not be clear that there will be a positive 'pay-off'.

Unless, however, a university does proceed along this path of continual institutional and, therefore, collective self-learning, it will fail to prosper as it might in the fluid world that it faces. The ideologies that beset it will continue to wield their destructive force. The university will be less than the sum of its parts. Unless, too, universities move in this direction, an even greater loss looms. What is in front of universities is none other than the loss of the idea of the university.

Four institutional languages

Four languages – *all legitimate* – are available to describe the moves that I am pointing to; and each of these four languages contains its own form of rationality. *Firstly*, there is a systems language, which focuses on the formation within each university of organizational self-steering mechanisms. Without such mechanisms, there is no chance of bringing the corrosive ideologies of academe under rational control. *Secondly*, there is a communicative language, through which the university can be described as reclaiming itself as an academic community in which individuals are encouraged to engage and in which claims over the university's mission can be developed, aired and contested. *Thirdly*, there is a language of *being*, through which the university reminds itself that it has real live individuals within it (even if they are, to some extent, carriers of ideologies). In this language, the university becomes a space for re-forming human and academic being. It offers a way of recasting academic identity so that individuality is endorsed but also widened, such that individuals feel themselves to be part of a greater whole. It is a language that offers a human face to universities. *Lastly*, there is a poetic language of imagination, stories, fantasies and visions[15] and, as described, these visions can look both back to the conceptual archaeology of the idea of the university *and* to the present complexities in which the university is caught.

These four are not just 'languages of description'[16] but speak to forms of *organizational rationality*, containing projects of critique *and* of hope, of dissolution *and* of reconstruction. These rationalities – instrumental, dialogical, ontological and poetic – are not rival but are complementary. Universities that are intent on learning about themselves will have an eye to the systems dimension; for example, management information systems are crucial. They will also not neglect the interactive dimension: heads of department might be brought together to examine their own ideas of the university in the context of their own institution. Such universities, too, will ensure that they are human places, for their members need to feel that their own humanity is recognized if they are to participate in the collective fora of universities as learning institutions.

Conclusion

Academic generosity, institutional reasonableness, institutional adroitness and institutional self-learning: these four dimensions supply ingredients to combat corrosive ideologies on campus. They do more than this, however. They can inject positive educational energies.[17] They enable universities to retain something of their historic and universal mission as places of collective and rational communication. And they inject a suppleness – discursive and organizational – that enables universities to work out their own forms of engagement with the wider world.

In the contemporary world, universities are beset by ideologies that have a corrosive force. But universities have considerable inner capacities for self-development, renewal and collective determination. Paradoxically, spaces may actually be opening for collective engagement, if only universities would seize them. The very complexities that threaten fragmentation and dissolution at the same time open up spaces and opportunities for universities to realize themselves in new ways *as universities*. There remains a will to sort things out together, which enlightened leaderships are drawing on to the advantage of the university.

A new idea of the university may be glimpsed here, one that is at once imaginary and fantastic, is collective and self-learning and is principled and rational. It is built upon a set of ideologies which, while ultimately beyond all reason, enable the university to offer its own contribution to the making of a better world. A darker prospect is also in front of universities, namely that they succumb to the ideologies that beset them, that they become a battlefield for the playing out of the interests of the large battalions. Reasonableness, collective self-learning and humanity on the one hand or dogma, blind assurance and inhumanity on the other hand: which is it to be?

Prospects

The possibility of the university

We started our journey with a question: Is the university possible? Our conclusion has to be that it is. The conclusion is unequivocal but brings its own uncertainties. The conclusion, to repeat, is merely that the university is possible: that is all.

Among those who comment on the nature of the academy, there are many who do so in an apparently pessimistic frame of mind. Those who write in this way tend to have their livings in cultural studies, the humanities and the social sciences. For these critics, the university is 'in ruins' or is in crisis or is imperilled. The imperilled state characteristically turns out to be some form of an alleged fall from grace: the university is not what it was, as compared with a time long ago when the idea of the university seemed manifest. The fall in question is a conceptual fall, a fall away from an idea of the university.[1]

In contrast, there are those who complain about the state of the university in a practical sense. The dominant critique points to a shortfall in resources, alleging that the university cannot achieve what it should unless it can count on a higher level of investment. A subsidiary critique alleges that the host state is not allowing universities their due autonomies to be fully entrepreneurial in generating their own finances. Those who make up this camp are two factions: university vice-chancellors or rectors and professors in the sciences. For them, the shortfall in resources is preventing the university from being all that it can in terms of its manifest accomplishments.

The architecture of this 'debate' over the university is clear enough. Those who hold to an idea of the university live in the past; those who are concerned with its material character live in the present or even in the future. Yet, both camps are united as critics of the university, seeing the university falling short of what it might be.[2]

This book can be read as a critique of both of these camps of pessimists. On the one hand, I have urged, against those who see the university as having fallen short of past ideas of the university, that there are grounds for optimism. The university of the twenty-first century has spaces to realize itself in ways that may yet do justice to the ideals locked within the idea of the university, even against the ideologies that now engulf it. On the other hand, I have indicated that simply to plead for resources and autonomy is a recipe for a narrow set of accomplishments on the part of the university. The university will fall short of what it could be and in two interconnected ways. Large ideals that could inject some direction and positive momentum will be neglected *and* the ground will be opened up for corrosive ideologies. Either way, the pessimists of both camps demonstrate a lack of both vision and courage.

The university remains an extraordinary institution. A higher education system that educates upwards of forty per cent of a population cannot be what it was when it educated, say, less than fifteen per cent. It can be much *more*. Its scale, its reach into society, the intermingling of its knowledges with those of the wider world and the wider forms of human being that it promotes are already enabling it to be much more. But it can be even more still.

To say, then, that the university is possible is both to say much and to say rather little. It is to say that it is still possible to do justice to the ideals embedded in the idea of the university. Precisely at the moment when the situation seems bleakest, when ideologies develop and are taken up on campus such that those ideals – of open communication, of inquiry having universal validity and of the virtues of tolerance and generosity – are put in question, so opportunities arise for those ideals to be realized in new ways and which have greater impact than ever before. So, to say that the university is possible is to say a great deal, but it is also to say rather little because it reminds us that those ideals are present only thinly just now. Yet they *are* present, even if thinly. The pessimists condemn not just themselves but all those who listen to them.

Insecurity

The fragility of the world is rendered transparent for all to see on a daily basis. This is a world in which the university is implicated and on three counts. *Firstly*, materially, this world *is* a world of uncertainty. The university never knows quite what will come off in its various exchanges with the world; it has to hedge its bets. It tries a range of different ventures, such as e-learning, in setting up companies aimed at 'technology transfer', in establishing outposts in other countries and in other forms of engagement. *Secondly*, the university lives in a world of cognitive uncertainty, a world that is partly of the university's own making. In a world of uncertainty, the university compounds our uncertainty by continuing to add new frames of understanding that offer both comprehension and perplexity. That, indeed, is what it is paid to do.

Thirdly, uncertainty is a context in which the human dimension of universities comes into play. Typically, universities are institutions in which several thousand people have their livings to a greater or lesser extent. Even those who form part of universities on a short-term basis – both students and staff – may feel that their lives have been transformed by their association with a university. Universities also have the capacity to reach out to others through the writings, research and other activities of staff. This capacity to get under the skin, to have *ontological effects,* is only occasionally noted in despatches – it is almost as if it is not something to mention in polite company – but it is significant nonetheless. This ontological capacity, as we have seen, may even be growing: the university's interactions with the wider world both let in ideologies of the world and encourage the flowering of multiple identities on campus.

The university, therefore, becomes an arena for multiple forms of human being.[3] What is humanly possible and even desirable becomes problematic. If there is a reluctance for individuals to look each other in the face on campus, it may be due to a lack of *inter*personal recognition. Are there *any* connections between this person and me as we pass each other by on the path between buildings or sit next to each other in the committee room? The university of the twenty-first century sets in train an infinite variety of humanness and so spawns *ontological uncertainty.*

The ideological transformation of the university is part of this situation. Ideology promises security, but the presence of multiple ideologies on campus compounds the university's uncertainties. How can the university act amid such *ideological presences?* Is there a way through that will enable the university to act reasonably? Is it possible for the university *to be* reasonable in a world seemingly short on reason? Can even reason itself be grounded, be made secure, at a time of unease, of insecurity, of a milieu in which sure foundations are not available?

The story here has been a story of the university as a university in a time of fragility and ideological presence. It takes on the challenges of both fragility and ideology by suggesting that the liberal virtues inherent in the idea of the university can yet be taken up as a definite project. Indeed, *only in this way, by the ideals of the university becoming a definite project, will it be possible to sustain universities as 'universities'.* Inquiry sustained by tolerance, generosity and mutual understanding can still have its day and, in the process, quieten – though never completely neutralize – the ideological presences to hand.

Recovering the liberal university in this way is not just a matter of calling up long-lost ideas of the university; rather, it calls for an imaginative and radical reconstruction of the university. The idea of *re*covery, indeed, looks forward as much as it looks back, re-making the university anew.[4] A new kind of university can be born, keen to learn about itself as it searches for original forms of reaching out and connecting with the wider society. This university is a university forever in the making and it requires strong and determined leadership and management if it is to be brought off.

The answer, then, to a question that we posed at the start of our journey – What is a university? – is that the university in the twenty-first century turns out to be a particular kind of discursive space, a generous space that provides for the development of various kinds of human being *and* for their mutual engagement. In its becoming such a generous space, the university neutralizes any ideology that has found houseroom within it. It also, at the same time, takes forward, as positive ideologies, the virtuous ideals implicit in the ideals of the university.

Why should this project itself not be termed an ideology? How, too, can this project escape its own insecurities? This project cannot be said to constitute an ideology as such precisely because it is aware of its own insecurities. The project sketched here, in seeking to do justice to the ideals of the university, can never be completely assured of itself. It can only be reasonably assured of itself. Its justification comes through institutional processes that seek to develop a reflexive university. Often, writers turn to critical friends to offer helpful critical comment on an enterprise. Correspondingly, a challenge in front of universities is that of developing *a culture of critical friendship*, in which their activities and values are a subject for critical commentary. Of course, in an ideologized university, those processes are always liable to be hijacked.

In an insecure age, the liberal university can never be made secure, either conceptually or materially. What will give it a chance of being realized is relentless endeavour, calling for unceasing vigilance and vigour. Talk of the liberal university in an insecure world can only make some kind of sense if it is taken on consciously as a continuing project, one that is built on an awareness of its continuing precariousness. The liberal university, therefore, has to be remade daily with an eye to the future as much as on the past.

The devil still has all the best tunes?

Even if the argument offered here wins assent *as* an argument, it may be said to be wanting as a political strategy. Strong on theory but weak on practice may be the judgement. Precisely because the picture painted shows ideologies in universities to have considerable strength, being backed by powerful forces, it may be doubted that the counter-proposals are going to have much effect. What, after all, do the counter-proposals here amount to? The ideas invoked, it will be recalled, include those of academic difference, academic *community*, academic generosity and collective self-scrutiny. These ideas, it may be said, may echo ideas embedded in the conceptual archaeology of the Western idea of the university, but they constitute a thin agenda with which to confront the ideological forces now present in universities.

If the analysis is correct, it undermines the strategy being suggested. In an age without sure foundations, there can be no substantive form of life that claims our allegiance *tout court* and no secure goal that any particular university might set for itself. There can only be, at best, a determination to realize universities as communities and as places of multiple being and that, in turn, cannot offer an effective counter to the power of ideologies. It is precisely because the liberal virtues of the idea of the university yield a weak programme that ideologies have been able to gain such a powerful presence on campus. The devil will continue to have the best tunes.

That, however, is a precipitately pessimistic reading. To adapt Gandhi's commentary on being asked what he thought of Western democracy, that it would be a good idea, we can say something similar of the Western university: *it may be that it has never been tried.*

There is good reason as to why this perhaps surprising state of affairs may be held to be the case. Until recently, the university could just be itself, in relative independence of the wider society. Now, as we have noted, the university has become intermeshed with the wider society: it has been enjoined to do so and it finds it in its interests to be so. A language of engagement – of competition, markets, entrepreneurialism, enterprise and networks – develops. Individual academics find it in their interests to place their curriculum vitae on the Internet (a barely understood practice in the private sector) and are encouraged to do so by their universities. In turn, two things happen: on the one hand, the networked university fragments as its knowledges grow and its staff acquire disparate identities; on the other hand, its multiple forms of engagement inspire ideological takeover *and* the university's discursive spaces are placed in jeopardy. The idea of the university, therefore, has both point and challenge that it has not previously possessed.

The suggestion, therefore, that ideologies on campus must have their day cannot be left unchallenged. If converted into a programme of collective imagining, engagement and will, the idea of the university offers the prospect of withstanding ideologies. New tunes may be composed, with interesting parts for all the players. Harmony will not always be present; indeed, contrasting tonal rules will sometimes be adopted. There will, though, be a collective effort that encourages improvisation. Ideologies will still be present as themes but, in this collective effort, they will not be allowed to become strident. 'Allowed', here, is intentional in character: in this programme, there would be a will to diminish the overbearing force of ideologies; *and* it is – as we might term it – a *descriptive futurible*, giving us a description of a realizable future in which the space for ideologies will be closed off. To answer one of our opening questions (Chapter 1), the devil will come to have neither the best tunes, nor the most forceful nor the most sustained. The devil's voice cannot be silenced but it can be quietened.

Institutional energy

Ideologies are quietened by new counter-energies being released on campus. As with 'recovery', 'release', too, has a dual structure. It speaks of virtuous energies having previously been thwarted and of creative efforts that may weaken pernicious ideologies. The acts of releasing virtuous energies have, therefore, an end and a beginning all at once: they end barriers to institutional and personal growth and they begin the spreading of institutional energy.

Institutional energy is latent in universities, and it is ready to be harnessed in favour of the most virtuous elements of universities. A will to realize the university is *there*, already on campus. For the most part, it is not orchestrated as such. A responsibility to the ideas of the university does not typically figure in the job descriptions for new vice-chancellors and, indeed, vice-chancellors might be forgiven for considering that such an enterprise was pretentious. But there are positive signs, some of them at the level of rhetoric but some indicative of substantial practices.

In their submissions to governments engaged in national reviews, universities will call in aid ideals of the university *and* make claims to the effect that those ideals are being upheld. In their evidence to the 1997 national review in the UK, the vice-chancellors signed up to a collective statement that included reference to the idea of higher education as emancipation (CVCP 1997). In their annual reports (usually, in the UK, glossy publications for wide audiences), individual universities will attest to their being places of debate, of openness and of inclusiveness, and they will claim to be places in which ideas ferment and persons can flourish. Less in evidence, however, is that these features of university life are being pursued as institutional strategies.

Where individual universities or departments are facing quality assessments by external agencies, especially where those exercises include visitations by panels, academic staff not just work together but also frequently engage with each other in working through their ideas for academic practices. Under circumstances of a common perceived threat, the notions of 'academic community' and 'self-critical community' are often realized in practice. What is in evidence in these circumstances – times of angst and psychological disturbance – is the flowering of institutional energy. Under conditions of a common challenge, what are largely individual identities take on an institutional aspect as energy is released towards collective ends.

Corresponding responses can be seen in other circumstances of common challenge, such as when it is suddenly discovered that a university's financial situation is grave and that major responses are required. Creative and collective institutional energy can be mobilized there too. Unfortunately, the situation may be so serious that conditions either of collective helplessness *or* of anarchic in-fighting may result, as it is realized that considerable proportions of the university's activities will have to be ended.

Again, more positively, many universities are embarked on a process of strategic review: Where might a university aim to be in, say, ten years' time? What might be its key priorities? Are there activities in which it could be active but is not as yet? These can be opportunities to engage the whole university in a collective endeavour but that collective engagement has to be worked at. It cannot just be a matter of putting a notice in the fortnightly newsletter or even holding occasional open meetings at which 'all staff are welcome'. Workshops have to be organized and on separate topics; email discussion groups encouraged and even set up; themes identified around which staff can come together from different departments in multi-disciplinary conversations; individuals across the staff – academic and administrative – given responsibilities for taking explorations forward; and task groups charged with definite tasks (such as examining contrasting scenarios), with external 'critical friends' being engaged to assist and even provoke those efforts.

Institutional energy is not just 'there' to be mobilized: it has to be *re*-created and sustained continually. If individuals feel that their taking a wider view of the interests of the university matters, so the prospects expand for them to widen their own identity to embrace their institution itself. They are also likely to be willing to engage with others, to hear others' points of view, to 'brainstorm' towards creative and collective solutions to problems, and to work on tasks and even carry out 'research' in producing intelligence for that collective effort.

A challenge that those in leadership positions face is that different groups within the university will be more or less inclined to be drawn into such collective exercises. Those with professorial titles may feel no 'need' to engage; there is little at risk for them. Equally, administrative staff or researchers on short-term contracts may feel disenchanted and disinclined to engage. Different tacks may be required with the different groups. The professors just may respond to an overture to clarify their ideas of the university, especially if they feel that it is possible to project their own departmental and disciplinary viewpoint.

Institutional cheerfulness

Universities are not necessarily institutions that justify the name 'university'. The virtuous ideals under the surface of the term – of generosity, openness, self-critique, reasonableness, tolerance and imagination – all too often remain latent. The university is still possible but it has to be fought for, day in and day out. Unless that struggle is engaged, unless those ideals can be given substance as progressive working ideologies, universities will become battlefields for the playing out of competing and corrosive ideologies.

Talk of battles, struggle and fighting might suggest dourness and solemnity. But matters need not be like that. Ideologies take themselves too seriously: they can be deflated, in turn, by optimism, buoyancy and cheerfulness. This is what we see on the best of campuses. The cheerfulness of their leaders inspires energy and commitment from others to the project of the university itself. A university, as a result, becomes 'a good place to be at'.

Universities are not, in the first place, sites of knowing but of being. The knowing comes, if at all, through the being. Commitment to hard, sustained work calling for critical engagement with others – whether in teaching, research or consultancy – requires a sense of well-being. If this is so for the activities that lie within the horizon, still more is it the case for projects, activities and challenges not yet envisaged. Universities have to be places of high levels of energy sustained over time, their projects often lasting for years and often through collaborations being forged across individuals who, at the outset of a project, do not even know each other's names. Energy is more likely to be imparted by an institutional climate of cheerfulness; the renewed energy, in turn, helps to generate the institution's cheerfulness.

It is hardly surprising if institutional leaders feel that there is little about which to be cheerful. Units of resource are driven down by states reluctant to 'invest' in higher education, quality evaluation regimes are idiosyncratic in their judgements, the markets for the university's services are unpredictable and the management systems are themselves so complex that they often exceed the current capacity to comprehend, let alone institute, those new systems.[5] In addition, universities are beset by ideologies that threaten to reduce the capacity of universities to be 'universities'. The apparent dourness in the vice-chancellor's countenance may not be a matter of the particular personality in question, but be more a matter of the apparent intractability, as it might seem, of the university's challenges.

Increasingly, among the attributes of vice-chancellors being sought by search committees are leadership 'qualities' as distinct from leadership 'skills'. There is, rightly, a sense that leading a university in the twenty-first century calls for considerable personal qualities and the dispositions of will and fortitude, as well as capacities to identify major challenges, to create visions of possible futures and to take staff forward in wrestling with those possible futures. Seen in this way, leadership on campus is a matter of promoting change in human being while living out the ideals of the university. For that, engagement with and between human beings is necessary, but in a spirit of realistic optimism.

Such a conception of university leadership is not just a matter that is focused on the vice-chancellor. In the complex environments that universities have become, a senior lecturer may be asked to take on, or may find herself taking on, a leadership role for a challenging task. In the distributed university, leadership is itself distributed. It just may be, too, that the young senior lecturer has not only energy for human engagement but also optimism and a hope for better things.

As remarked, however, cheerfulness inspires energy which, in turn, generates more cheerfulness. At times, hospitals are places of pure being, in which emotional pain overtakes physical pain in its urgency. But universities too are, in their own way, unique places of *being*, as places of engagement between human beings. Human beings in universities engage over ideas but they also, perforce, engage with each other: in themselves, ideas are inert and do not engage with other ideas. Universities are necessarily places of *complexity-in-being*. They can offer, therefore, perhaps unmatched forms of humanness. That humanness, however, can be impaired by ideologies, for they are characteristically divisive: you are either with us or against us.

Cheerfulness sustains the university's humanness.[6] Yet the smile in the corridor offers much more. It is a statement in favour of the ideals of the university, in favour of tolerance, reasonableness, generosity and a will to go on. It is, in its own way, a rebuke to the ideologists who would wreck the university and condemn it to narrow, intolerant and factional interests. This is certainly not enough to rescue the university but it is, at least, a start.

Appendix 1: Glossary of key terms

The location in the text of each of these terms can be found in the Index.

Commitment-in-being: the kind of commitment that infuses being such that the being comes in part to be constituted by the commitment. Hopes, projects and values are filled out by this commitment.

Complexity-in-being: the kind of being that is saturated by complexity such that the complexity is *in* the being. This is a key, if largely unnoticed, part of contemporary organizational life, in which the being is held in a state of continuing tension as it grapples with the challenges of complexity and is, therefore, never still. It is compounded by the presence of *supercomplexity* and the never-ending sets of dilemmas that that situation presents.

Conservative ideologies: ideologies that preserve existing traditions and/or power structures and that, therefore, are resistant to transformatory projects.

Discursive compact: where, under conditions of ideological contamination, two potentially separate discourses (such as those around 'higher education' and 'quality') are brought together such that each is framed partly in terms of the other. For example, 'quality' may be framed such that it is assessed by certain performance indicators and they, in turn, come to be the measure of higher education itself. The quality tail wags the higher education dog.

Ideologies: forms of ideology that deliberately pick up the virtuous ideals embedded in human institutions, such as 'the university', and which are yet reflexive and, therefore, conscious of their own precariousness.

Ideological acts: acts that are contoured by ideologies such that, in the practices that those acts comprise, the world is seen through those ideologies. The deep purpose of the act – whether more or less masked – is to further the ideology.

Ideological capture: the attempt on the part of ideologies to convert all to their way of thinking and being. Under such conditions, possible converts are seen in black-and-white terms: 'You are either for us or against us'. Such a process of capture would, therefore, suffocate other picturing of the world and modes of being by, for instance, foreclosing on debate that keeps options open.

Ideological displacement: the shift that an ideology may undergo where it is thwarted: under such circumstances, a would-be ideology may simply be blocked off and be dissipated *or* be superseded by a more powerful ideology. For example, the ideology of 'quality' may have to give way to the ideology of 'entrepreneurialism' (cf. *Ideological turn*).

Ideological overload: a situation characterized by multiple and competing and even proliferating ideologies such that they together seem to crowd out the available discursive space, so reducing the chance of dialogical 'reasonable' debate. It is a situation not just of hot air but of discursive power being wielded to corrosive effect.

Ideological presences: the presence of multiple ideologies in a locale, evident in identities, ways of framing the world and discourses. This nearness, in all its variegated complexity, has both disturbing and perplexing characteristics, since the ideologies press themselves forward but perhaps in opposed directions.

Ideological space: the space available to institutions and actors to take up or, at least, negotiate their own stances in relation to the presenting ideologies.

Ideological structure: the configuration of ideologies that bears upon a particular locale and which finds its bearers, interpreters and advocates within that locale. 'Structure' here is a metaphor, since the ideologies present in a locale may well contest each other, setting up messy and disputatious relationships.

Ideological turn: the possibility that an ideology may be deflected, locally at least, so that it changes something of its character, whether in its ontological, epistemological or discursive elements (cf. *Ideological displacement*). Through the application of virtuous ideals applicable to a locale, there is the potential for a pernicious ideology to take an ideological turn in favour of a virtuous aspect.

Institutional adroitness: the situation in which an institution – such as a university – forms the capacity for discursive tolerance, which allows the presenting complexities to be purposefully addressed.

Institutional energy: that energy – often latent only – to which institutions as such can give a life force, an energy that inspired and inspiring institutional leadership can do much to enhance.

Institutional identity: the identity that is specific to an institution in virtue of its positioning in relation to epistemologies, markets, the state and other academic institutions. The four moments are in a dynamic relationship with each other, their intersections producing a particular but uncatchable internal composition.

Institutional stress: a condition in which an institution is beset by major challenges which it is failing to address. Characteristically, where contending ideologies – for example, 'research' and 'learning and teaching' – are left to pitch against each other in an unexamined and corrosive manner, institutional stress will result. More generally, conditions of undue complexity and *supercomplexity* would also bring on institutional stress.

Life-constitutive projects: projects taken on with such commitment that, for those actors, they come to constitute at least a significant part of life itself, playing a part in constructing their being. (Whether particular projects should be construed as positive or nugatory would be a further matter.)

Necessary others: those actors whose presence, by virtue of their roles, is logically necessary to a particular act or process.

Non-necessary others: actors whose presence is not logically necessary to a particular act or process.

Ontological diffusion: the spreading of an identity structure, for example, across an institution. An ideology, for instance, works in just this way, by permeating identities.

Ontological effects: ideologies may have epistemological, ontological or communicative effects: of these, it is their ontological effects that are the most significant. It is through their ontological effects that ideologies generate energy and, thereby, come to be taken forward in the micro-practices of institutional life.

Ontological gain: the enhancement of ways of being in a locale or setting. *Virtuous ideologies*, for example, are virtuous partly through their achieving such ontological gain.

Ontological overloading: an identity structure that is over-freighted, especially with an ideology. Actors bearing such an identity place themselves at the centre of their worlds, acting out their ideological fantasies which they attempt to project onto all around them.

Ontological uncertainty: a locale in which a range of different and even competing identity structures have their home. Under such conditions, what it is to be human is open, challenging and even exciting.

Pernicious ideologies: those ideologies that diminish human life, whether by downvaluing forms of human being, by exerting non-consensual power or by constraining ways of understanding the world (cf. *Virtuous ideologies*).

Societal *Bildung*: the growth of understanding across a society, incorporating a generosity towards different value systems and traditions: such understanding has a developmental character, since it can be accomplished on ever higher levels and in wider senses, providing a societal wisdom.

Supercomplexity: the presence of proliferating and competing frameworks of comprehension, many of which present as unreasonable ideologies, a situation that yields no definite resolution.

Surplus commitment: a degree of commitment that is more than is required to make progress in any situation so filling out the space for commitment and, in the process, producing a lack of reflexivity and an overbearing character (cf. *Undue commitment*).

Transforming ideologies: ideologies that have the potential to transform the settings in which they have a natural application.

Undue commitment: a degree of commitment that blocks off counter-views and, thereby, diminishes not just reason in that locale but also human being itself (cf. *Surplus commitment*).

Virtuous ideologies: those ideologies that have the capacity to enhance the locales in which they secure themselves. They have virtue on their side precisely by being reflexive in a way that *pernicious ideologies* are not (cf. Ideologies).

Appendix 2: Twenty-seven examples of complexity in universities

1. Sheer size (perhaps upwards of 20,000 students and several thousands of academic and support staff).
2. Range of disciplines (overlapping and intersecting).
3. Structures (departments – perhaps over forty – faculties, units and centres, with units and centres sometimes sitting uneasily in relation to the more formal faculty/departmental structure).
4. Courses (say, several hundred, themselves long and short, and full-time and part-time). Modular systems may be evident, particularly at undergraduate levels, generating thousands of units or modules.
5. Heterogeneity among the students, including nationality, ethnicity and religion.
6. Alliances and collaborations (with other educational institutions and with other organizations in the public and the private sectors).
7. Geography (immediate city, region, own country and global reach).
8. Physical presences (bodily presences, networks, virtual realities, distributed activities, work and learning at a distance).
9. Ethical base (plurality of value systems).
10. Epistemologies (propositional, action-based, interpersonal).
11. Ontologies (array of academic and personal identities).
12. Modes of communication.
13. Systems (technical and human, formal and informal).
14. Missions (plurality of missions even in the one institution).
15. Structures (governance; decision making; executive).
16. External accountabilities (research quality, teaching quality, safety regulations, accreditation by professional bodies).
17. Frameworks (formal and tacit, internal to disciplines, societal, individual and collective).
18. Political environment (local, regional, national, state, inter-governmental).
19. Conceptual and ideational (competing discourses and their key concepts).
20. Financial (multiple income streams, with different costing bases and net outturns).
21. Opportunity structure.
22. Human resources.
23. Technical and physical resources.
24. Management information systems.

25. Estates.
26. Support services (which may be 'outsourced').
27. Strategic options and priorities (and the extent to which they are explicit and shared).

Notes

Acknowledgements (p. ix)

1. W.R. ('Roy') Niblett, CBE (1906–) is Emeritus Professor of Higher Education at the Institute of Education, University of London, being the holder of the first such chair in the UK, 1968–73. Among achievements worthy of several lives, he is co-founder and the Life Vice-President of the UK's Society for Research into Higher Education and founder of the Higher Education Foundation.

Introduction (pp. 1–8)

1. I am not sure whether Jürgen Habermas has actually used this term, but I take it that this is his conception of his philosophy. See, for instance, the Postscript to *Knowledge and Human Interests* (1978) and his interviews with Peter Dews, *Habermas: Autonomy and Solidarity* (1986), e.g. pp. 52–3.
2. We may recall that, for Habermas, the 'ideal speech situation' has always itself been an idealization. See Habermas (1995: 46–7) and Roderick (1986: 78–9).
3. The literature, both classic texts and secondary overviews, on the idea of ideology is considerable. Helpful commentaries include Plamenatz (1970), Larrain (1979, 1994), Thompson (1985, 1996), Eagleton (1991), McClennan (1995), Hawkes (1996) and van Dijk (1998). Raymond Williams' overviews in his (1977 and 1988) chapters on Ideology retain value since, *inter alia*, they bring out the slipperiness of the concept. McClennan (1995), indeed, begins his book by observing that 'Ideology is the most elusive concept in the whole of social science' (p. 1). Eagleton (1991) graphically demonstrates the point by listing sixteen definitions of ideology 'currently in circulation' (p. 1), 'not all of [which]', as he observes, 'are compatible with one another' (p. 2).
4. We should note that Foucault seemed to equivocate on the usefulness of the concept of ideology. In his *The Archaeology of Knowledge* (1974), while careful to identify its useful meaning, Foucault is fully prepared to allot a role to 'ideology', provided that we understand that 'the question of ideology that is asked of science . . . is the question of its existence as a discursive practice and of its functioning among other practices' (p. 185).
5. Perhaps the most significant of the international networks of universities is Universitas 21, a network of 18 universities across 10 countries (website: http://

www.universitas.edu.au). This network is not simply 'academic' in character but is looking to capitalize on its market potential by forming alliances with organizations in the private sector. See Maslen's (2000) article in the *Times Higher Education Supplement*.
6. See my book *Realizing the University in an age of supercomplexity* (Barnett 2000).

Chapter 1   The Ends of Reason (pp. 12–23)

1. The uncovering of those differences at a micro level began in earnest only recently following Tony Becher's pioneering work (Becher 1989; Trowler 1998; Becher and Trowler 2001).
2. J.K. Galbraith (1969), *The New Industrial Estate*, p. 372.
3. So producing an 'epistemological wobble', as Peter Scott (1997c) so delightfully puts it in his paper on 'The changing role of the university in the production of new knowledge'.
4. So far as I can see, Stehr's conception of a 'knowledge society' turns on the idea that knowledge is used across society and becomes a resource to individuals widely in society. The further point that knowledge is actually produced across society comes through much more evidently in Gibbons *et al.* (1994).
5. On the opposition between Critical Theory, especially as advanced by Habermas, and postmodernism, especially as advanced by Foucault, see Samantha Ashenden and David Owen (eds) (1999) *Foucault versus Habermas: Recasting the Dialogue between Genealogy and Critical Theory*, and David Couzens Hoy and Thomas McCarthy (1995) *Critical Theory*.
6. Another way of putting the point is to say that we have entered an age of fragility; it is, however, a peculiar fragility, one characterized even more by a state of conceptual fragility (as distinct from an ecological, economic or social fragility). On the idea of 'fragility', see Barnett (2000) and Stehr (2001).
7. A key term deployed by Nowotny *et al.* (2001) in their recent book is 'transgressivity' (p. 21), the argument being that there is, crucially, an epistemological interweaving between universities and the wider society.
8. Cf. Luntley (1995), who boldly develops a thesis to the effect that, despite there being a plurality of interpretations or 'explanatory frameworks' of the world, there remains 'such a thing as simple truth and simple knowledge' and even that 'there is a common language or point of view' (pp. 140–1). Rationality is 'something we share with the Azande' and 'we share an awful lot with the Azande' (p. 133).
9. Another indication of managed silences is the low proportion of women in senior positions in universities. See *Times Higher Education Supplement*, 25 November 2001.
10. M. Oakeshott (1989: 24). See also Kenneth Minogue's (1973) trenchant exposition of *The Concept of a University*, in which he argues for a separation of the university from society through their having separate knowledge interests.
11. See, for instance, Rorty's *Contingency, Irony and Solidarity* (1989) and *Philosophy and Social Hope* (1999).
12. Cf. 'The pressure on universities in recent years . . . has been tremendous but it has not yet caused them to think in any fundamental way about their new function in society' (Niblett 1974: 2). Professor Niblett held what was almost certainly the first chair of higher education in the UK (at the Institute of Education, University of London, 1968–73) and has recently written a personal memoir of his life and thought: *Life, Education, Discovery* (2001).

13. The title of one USA-based journal is *Educational Advancement.*
14. The phrase, 'grand narratives', is Lyotard's. See his book on *The Postmodern Condition* (1984), but see also his qualifying note (1992). On decisionistic rationality, see Habermas (1976).
15. Anthony Giddens (1995: 32): 'The self becomes a *reflexive project'* (emphasis in the original). See also Beck *et al.* (1995) *Reflexive Modernization.*
16. Gunther Kress and T. van Leeuwen (2001) *Multimodal Discourse: The Modes and Media of Contemporary Communication*; G. Myerson (2001) *Heidegger, Habermas and the Mobile Phone.*
17. The phrase '*A Runaway World?*' was originally deployed by Edmund Leach in his 1967 Reith Lectures (Leach 1968) and then taken up again by Tony Giddens in his own Reith Lectures two decades later.
18. I am not sure whether he says anything precisely like this, but I think that this is implicit in Michel de Certeau's (1988) work on *The Practice of Everyday Life.*
19. Stehr (2001) offers the contrasting thesis, that it is the production of high-level skills in individuals – especially by universities – that produces in turn forms of work in which those capabilities can find expression.
20. See the 'Benchmarking' statement produced by UK historians for the national quality assurance exercise (QAA 2000). It should be noted, however, that the group declined fully to play the hand dealt for it by the UK's Quality Assurance Agency (QAA) and ran into much flak from the QAA as a result.
21. John Henry Newman's (1976) *The Idea of a University*, Discourse V.
22. For instance, Rorty's *Consequences of Pragmatism* ([1982] 2001) and his *Philosophy and Social Hope* (1999).

Chapter 2   A Complex World (pp. 26–36)

1. In his *The New Constellation* (1991), Richard Bernstein – following Jay on Adorno and Benjamin – develops a concept of 'constellation' as 'a juxtaposed rather than integrated cluster of changing elements that resist reduction to a common denominator, essential core, or generative first principle' (p. 8; p. 42; p. 309). Both 'reconciliation' and 'rupture' are 'irreducible elements' in the constellation that Bernstein urges, a constellation that is sympathetic both to modernity and to postmodernity.
2. For example, Eve *et al.* (1997), Cilliers (1998), Rescher (1998) and Marion (1999), although Rescher, to my mind at least, indicates more fully the complexity of complexity.
3. '. . . to the extent to which human beings can be said to possess powers, these mainly derive from their complex interconnections over time and across space . . . Indeed, the role of the human may be exceptionally limited and impossible to identify separately from their interconnectedness with these other elements' (John Urry 1998: 'Contemporary transformations of time and space', pp. 14–15).
4. On globalization and higher education, see, for example, Jan Currie and Janice Newson (eds) (1998) *Universities and Globalization*; Peter Scott (ed.) (1998a) *The Globalization of Higher Education*; and chapter 8 of Gerard Delanty's (2001) *Challenging Knowledge.* Andy Green's (1992) *Education, Globalization and the Nation State* has the larger canvas of education as such. A larger canvas still is offered by Tony Giddens (1999) in his Reith Lectures, *Runaway World.* Indispensable is *Empire* (2000) by Michael Hardt and Antonio Negri, which we may regard as an

extended essay on and a reinterpretation of 'globalization': '. . . Empire . . . is a *decentered* and *deterritorializing* apparatus . . . that progressively incorporates the entire global realm . . . [This] transformation of the modern imperialist geography of the globe and the realization of the world market signal a passage within the capitalist mode of production' (pp. xii–xiii, original emphases).

5. See Nowotny (1994) for an incisive examination of this general matter.
6. See, for example, John Daniel's (1998) *Mega-Universities and Knowledge Media.*
7. See Ernest Gellner's (1964) *Thought and Change,* to which he added a footnote, 'Recollection in anxiety: thought and change revisited' in his *Culture, Identity and Politics* (1987).
8. See A.T. Nuyen on 'Lyotard and Rorty on the role of the professor', in M. Peters (ed.) (1995); Malcolm Tight's (2002) paper on 'What does it mean to be a professor?'.
9. See my book, *Realizing the University in an age of supercomplexity* (Barnett 2000). However, the discussion here overtakes the account of supercomplexity provided there. I am now persuaded as to the multitextual character of supercomplexity; accordingly, anything approaching an adequate account has to be as much sociological as it is conceptual in character and, thereby, a matter for the sociologists as much as for the philosophers.
10. See Shirley Fisher (1994) *Stress in Academic Life: The Mental Assembly Line.*
11. As Alistair MacIntyre (1990) implies in his *Three Rival Versions of Moral Enquiry.*

Chapter 3   The States of Higher Education (pp. 38–48)

1. See the introductory chapter by Michael Peters (1999) on 'Disciplinarity and the emergence of cultural studies' in his edited volume, *After the Disciplines.* In the context of Peters' overview of the matter, rather than 'discipline', a neologism such as 'ill-discipline' comes to mind.
2. Any serious exploration of the latter idea would have to grapple with the complex but important idea of *Bildung,* on which concept see Gadamer (1985: 10–18) *Truth and Method;* Rorty (1980: 358–64) *Philosophy and the Mirror of Nature;* Rothblatt (1997: 24–6) *The Modern University and its Discontents.*
3. G. Neave (1998) 'The evaluative state', *European Journal of Education,* 33(1): 265–84.
4. See David Watson's (2000) *Managing Strategy,* which, *inter alia,* indicates the range, intensity and volume of the many challenges facing universities in developing a coherent institutional strategy. A key axiom in effectively bringing off such a challenge lies in the notion of steadiness: 'A much underrated institutional value is that of "steadiness", of identifying and nurturing a set of core commitments while seeking to adapt them where necessary' (p. 63).
5. On chaos, see Cutright's (2001) volume on *Chaos Theory and Higher Education.* On pandemonium, see Burrell's (1997) *Pandemonium: Towards a Retro-Organization Theory.*
6. I owe the point about the university as a moral institution, especially to its being made forcibly to me, to Alison Phipps.
7. On corporate universities, see Peter Jarvis (2001) *Universities and Corporate Universities: The Higher Learning Industry in Global Society.*
8. The key passages in MacIntyre's (1985) *After Virtue: A Study in Moral Theory* that are particularly relevant, where the concepts of 'practices', 'internal goods' and 'virtues' are set out, are to be found in pages 184–94. Responding to the possible

charge that the 'traditions' which such 'practices' form do not easily admit change, MacIntyre suggests that 'an institution – a university, say, . . . will be partly . . . constituted by a continuous argument as to what a university is . . . Traditions, when vital, embody continuities of conflict' (p. 222). What I am not sure that MacIntyre entertains, however, is a situation in which the defining concepts of an institution themselves include those such as critique, argument, reflection, openness and rigour. Under those circumstances, it may be that such an institution, which we may term a 'university', has the seeds of its own disintegration embedded in its conceptual archaeology.

9. This hope, however, was fulfilled in England more often in the breach than in the observance – as distinct from Scotland: 'Enlightened thought . . . united in criticizing the ancient English universities' (Roy Porter 2000: *Enlightenment*, p. 347).

10. For Downie, this is a 'tuistic' relationship.

11. The sub-title draws on the title of Will Hutton's (1995) *The State We're In*. Hutton has rather little to say about higher education as such, but does imply that the state – in the UK, at least – is having a constraining effect on the sector: the state's concerns for efficiency, performance review and income generation on the part of universities have driven up competition, marketization, entrepreneurialism and universities as production units but without any obvious benefits for quality and effectiveness; on the contrary, the outcomes may be counterproductive (see pp. 216 *et seq.*).

12. For Althusser (1971: 152), 'the ideological State apparatus which has been installed in the *dominant* position . . . is the *educational ideological apparatus*' (original emphases). Notably, it is 'the system of the different public and private "Schools"' that is cited by Althusser in his specification of the educational Ideological Apparatus (p. 143): universities, as such, do not appear. Their omission, presumably, allowed Althusser to avoid the question: Was he part of an Ideological State Apparatus, including his own essay on the topic? The key section on Althusser's idea of 'interpellation' is to be found in pp. 170–5 of that text.

13. On the matter of trust as such, two apparently quite different treatments are those of Fukuyama (1995), in his survey of trust as a key element in the generation of prosperity, and Hollis (1998), in his philosophical exegesis of the concept of trust, especially its relationship to the concept of reason. The two texts, however, despite their considerable differences (not only in their length), perhaps are united in a sense that trust is reasonable. I will leave the ambiguities of that last phrase hanging, but there is an important theme here, surely, that may assist any reconceptualization of the university in an age of fragility.

14. A point caught nicely in a front-page article in the *Times Higher Education Supplement* of 21 September 2001, entitled 'Russell elite go for jugular of ailing QAA' (Baty 2001). The article points to the resignation of the Chief Executive of the Quality Assurance Agency, a consultation paper from the QAA proposing major reforms of its evaluation procedures and continued resistance from a group of the UK's leading universities.

15. For details on the UK Government's Foresight Programme, see its website (listed in the bibliography).

Chapter 4   The End of Ideology? (pp. 50–60)

1. Some treatments of postmodernism that are relevant to this work include: (on postmodernism in general) J.-F. Lyotard (1984) *The Postmodern Condition: A*

Report on Knowledge; Herbert Simons and Michael Billig (eds) (1994) *After Postmodernism: Reconstructing Ideology Critique* (especially the contribution by S. Deertz on 'The new politics of the workplace: ideology and other unobtrusive controls');
(on postmodernism and education) Michael Peters (ed.) (1995) *Education and the Postmodern Condition*; Nigel Blake *et al.* (1998a) *Thinking Again: Education after Postmodernism*; P. Dhillon and P. Standish (eds) (2000) *Lyotard: Just Education*; (on postmodernism and higher education) Anthony Smith and Frank Webster (eds) (1997) *The Postmodern University?* (especially Peter Scott's contribution 'The postmodern university?'); Frank Webster (2001) 'The postmodern university?'.

2. We may note, however, that Bell has – in the 2000 edition of that book – recanted to some extent, such that history, in the form of a search for national identity, has 'resumed'. We may also note that Habermas had earlier endorsed the 'end of ideology' thesis in his magnum opus, *The Theory of Communicative Action* (1989), his argument being, if I understand him, that with the separation of discursive spheres, on which ideology trades, having become threatened through the colonization of the life-world by the purposive-rational systems world, ideology loses its anchorage. See Volume 2 (1989), especially pp. 352–5: '. . . as the rationality differential between the profane realm of action and a definitively disenchanted culture gets leveled out, the latter will lose the properties that made it capable of taking on ideological functions. Of course, this state of affairs – which Daniel Bell had proclaimed as "The End of Ideology" . . .' (p. 353).

3. The phrase 'broad sunlit uplands' was used by Winston Churchill in some of his speeches in the Second World War; for example, his speech to the UK's House of Commons, following the recovery of the British expeditionary forces from Dunkirk, June 1940 (Churchill 1963: 43). There is, we may note, a particular point of contact between this reference and the theme of this book itself, namely that Churchill was quite clear that his – and the world's – opponent at this time was as much the ideology of Nazism as it was Hitler.

4. For example, Peter Scott's article in the London *Guardian*, 5 March 2002, although we should note that Scott is far from sanguine on the matter but is urging that 'We need . . . more ideology'.

5. On the history of the institutional birth of 'ideology' through the work of Antoine Destutt de Tracy and the argument with Bonaparte, see, for example, Larrain (1979: 6–8), Eagleton (1991: 66–70) and McClennan (1995: 5–9).

6. 'If in all ideology men and their circumstances appear upside-down as in a *camera obscura*, this phenomenon arises . . . from their historical life-process'. 'The ideas of the ruling class are in every epoch the ruling ideas, i.e., the class which is the ruling material force of society is at the same time its ruling *intellectual* force' (Marx and Engels 1977: 47 and 64, respectively) (emphases as in the original).

7. Two exceptions are chapter 7, 'The ideological imitation: the dangers of a little learning', of Kenneth Minogue's (1973) *The Concept of a University* and Gerald Collier's (1982) paper on 'Ideological influences in higher education'.

8. For a brilliant exposition of ideology as a rational enterprise, see Alvin Gouldner's (1976) *The Dialectic of Ideology and Technology*.

9. In an incisive examination of the claims of Critical Theory, Raymond Geuss (1981) rightly – to my mind – makes much play of the concept of interests. For

Geuss, Critical Theory distinguishes between those interests that are rational – which are also 'real' or 'true' or 'objective' (p. 48) – and those that are not. *If* such a sharp distinction is central to Critical Theory, then it seems to me misguided, at least in the context of the more local and ontological infused ideological settings characteristic of the fluid world of the twenty-first century. Rather than distinguishing between different *kinds* of interest, it may be that we may gain more understanding of ideology by distinguishing the *intensity* of their interests. An ideology announces itself through the presence of an interest being pressed unduly and, thereby, uncharitably.

10. '... in which domination and ideology both arise under conditions of distorted communication...' (Habermas' essay on 'Technology and science as "ideology"' in his *Toward a Rational Society*, 1972). For an application of Habermas' notion of 'systematically distorted communication', with its sense of different kinds of speech acts, see Robert Young (1989) *A Critical Theory of Education: Habermas and our Children's Future*, pp. 106–9.

11. There is a nice irony at work here, namely that our supremely rational and research-led professors do not bother themselves overmuch with the indications as to the ways in which, *de facto*, the role of the professor and the criteria by which the title is conferred (in European models of higher education) are broadening to allow mixes of strength in scholarship, research, teaching, academic leadership and organizational leadership. Admittedly, the published research on the matter is presently thin but there is some, e.g. Malcolm Tight's (2002) article on 'What does it mean to be a professor?'.

12. '... ideologies "ideally" reflect the goals and the interests of the group, and do so optimally when these interests are coherently translated into a set of basic beliefs shared within the group' (van Dijk 1998: 94).

13. S. Zizek (1999) *The Sublime Object of Ideology*: 'The fundamental level of ideology... is not of an illusion masking the real state of things but that of an (unconscious) fantasy structuring our social reality itself' (p. 33).

14. While van Dijk (1998) quite fairly presents his theory of ideology as 'multidisciplinary', one of its strengths lies in its clarifying the epistemological elements of ideologies: 'ideologies essentially control group specific *judgements* about what is good and bad and also about what is true or false *for us*' (p. 116, emphases in original). This statement, however, should be put in the context of a later statement: 'ideologies are not primarily about what is true or false, but about how people represent their beliefs about themselves and about the world, truthfully or not... In other words,... we need a pragmatics of use of ideology rather than a semantics of truth' (p. 130).

15. Althusser (1971: 173): '*all ideology hails or interpellates concrete individuals as concrete subjects*' (emphasis in original).

16. Ibid.

17. '... I don't see who could be more of an anti-structuralist than myself' (Foucault 1984: 55). 'The problem does not consist in ... truth but in seeing historically how effects of truth are produced within discourses which are in themselves neither true nor false' (p. 60). The interview from which these quotations are taken is also to be found in *Power/Knowledge* (Foucault 1980: 109–33). What is surely striking about this comment of Foucault's is that his rejection of ideology in its reliance on 'truth' actually leads him to a position that itself relies on 'truth': how, otherwise, are 'effects of truth' to be determined unless, *a fortiori*, we are able in the first place to establish what counts as truth?

18. For such a reverential view, see R. Jones (1990: 93), which nevertheless offers a helpful analysis of the implications of Foucault's 'genealogical' approach for educational practices.
19. '... ideologies as such, that is, socially shared beliefs of a specific type' (van Dijk 1998: 26).
20. For an authoritative and exhaustive account of and a particular argument in relation to 'voluntary servitude', see Rosen (1996).
21. This sense of the facticity of such collective perceptions may conjure up Gramsci's concept of 'hegemony', through which Gramsci pointed to the apparent necessity in ideologies. However, 'the key category in the writings of ... Antonio Gramsci is not ideology but hegemony' (Eagleton 1991: 112). This is because 'hegemony ... *includes* ideology, but is not reducible to it' (ibid.).
22. '... in bad faith it is from myself that I am hiding the truth' (Sartre, undated: *Being and Nothingness*, p. 49).
23. I derive many of the points in this paragraph about stories and reasons and their interrelationships from my reading of Rorty.
24. See, for instance, Mary Henkel's (2000) *Academic Identities and Policy Change in Higher Education*.
25. Sometimes, the back-stabbing isn't even as refined as *back*-stabbing: it can be face-to-face, even over the crumpets in an Oxbridge don's room. See David Edmonds and John Eidinow (2001) *Wittgenstein's Poker: The Story of a Ten-Minute Argument between Two Great Philosophers*.
26. The idea that concepts are not limited to describing the world but may call up alternative worlds through which the present world may be questioned and held to account, and thereby shown to fall short of the present world's own concepts, was implicit within Critical Theory, although it was often just implicit. 'Through reflection and critique, it can become aware of its own limitations; that is, that it fails by its own standards. [So] the truths to be drawn out are primarily negations' (David Held 1980: *Introduction to Critical Theory*, p. 185). But, 'A true dialectics, Adorno argued, was "the attempt to see the new in the old instead of seeing the old in the new"' (Martin Jay 1996: *The Dialectical Imagination*, p. 69). Probably Marcuse emphasized the creative role that Critical Theory could and should play most of all: 'Critical Theory must contain a strongly imaginative, even utopian strain, which transcends the present limits of reality: "Without fantasy, all philosophical knowledge remains in the grip of the present or the past"' (ibid., pp. 77–8).

Chapter 5 'The Entrepreneurial University' (pp. 65–76)

1. On risk, see Ulrich Beck (1992) *Risk Society*; Jane Franklin (ed.) (1998) *The Politics of Risk Society*; Nico Stehr (2001) *The Fragility of Modern Societies: Knowledge and Risk in the Information Age*. Perhaps I could be allowed to comment that, while there are two large stories in Beck's book – around risk and individualization – and while the two are brought together to some extent, for example, in the notion of 'an individualization of social risks' (p. 100), I am not sure that the idea of personal risk in the sense of ontological risk is fully developed in that volume.
2. Although this formulation might be held to imply that the concepts of performativity and belonging are distinct if not polar opposites – and an argument could be made along those lines – they are actually interwoven. See Vikki Bell (ed.) (1999) *Performativity and Belonging*.

3. 'The services offered by the total screen have radically changed our relationship to reality. From now on, man has a place but the place has no claim on him . . . Now everything is now, and the word *here* means virtually nothing . . . Man is no longer indigenous . . . he is global'. But this is 'a globalization of me' (Alain Finkielkraut 2001: *In the Name of Humanity*, pp. 105 and 109). In other words, the *uni*-versalism for which the wars of the twentieth century were fought are becoming the *me*-ism of the twenty-first century.

4. On the creation of entrepreneurial universities, see Burton Clark's (1998) analysis, *Creating Entrepreneurial Universities: Organizational Pathways of Transformation*.

5. Oakeshott's view, in other words. See Oakeshott (1989) *The Voice of Liberal Learning*.

6. Cf. M. Jacob and T. Hellstrom (eds) (2000) *The Future of Knowledge Production in the Academy*. Although the book does not examine consultancy as a form of knowledge production as such, what it does tacitly indicate is the increasing messiness of knowledge production in the wake of university–business transactions and that we probably do not possess an adequate vocabulary to describe the range and character of the new knowledges.

7. In his chapter on 'Mochlos: or, the conflict of the faculties', Derrida (1992) raises precisely this matter of the 'responsibility' of the university in the contemporary age (and whether it makes sense even to ask the question) but, to my mind at least, fails to give us any kind of satisfactory answer to his own question.

8. See Stehr (2001) for a distinction between risk and uncertainty.

9. If it is possible – for Schopenhauer (1819), at least – to describe '*The World as Will and Idea*', then surely we can speak of the university in this way? cf. 'In ideology the real relation is . . . invested in the imaginary relation, a relation that *expresses a will* . . . , a hope or a nostalgia, rather than describing a reality' (Louis Althusser 1969: *For Marx*, p. 234) (emphases in original).

10. For an insight into the impossibilities of computing in advance the consequences of an organization embracing the information technology revolution, see Manuel Castells' (1999) analysis of 'Flows, networks, and identities: a critical theory of the informational society'.

11. In a national exercise within the UK to assess the comparative resources expended on research and teaching (the 'transparency review'), it has proved notoriously difficult to obtain robust data, not least because of the difficulties of attributing activities to the separate headings: if I have a thought, do I place it under 'research' or 'teaching'? Perhaps it depends on the circumstances in which I have that thought.

12. For explorations of connections between knowledge, space, identity, power and learning, see Paechter *et al.* (eds) (2000a) *Learning, Space and Identity* and Paechter *et al.* (eds) (2000b) *Knowledge, Power and Learning*.

13. As Cardinal Newman (1976 edition) understood it, in *The Idea of a University*.

14. On academic futures, see Michael Thorne's (1999) collection on visions of *Universities in the Future*. What, for me, is striking about that collection is that, in its focusing on matters of the use of technologies, on globalization, on 'new learning paradigms' and even on 'new epistemologies', there is a large silence in respect of the internal life of universities and what it might be to live and work in 'universities of the future'. This matters even for an operationalist view of the academic universe. What, after all, are the ontological requirements of achieving the 'foresights' offered by contemporary commentators?

15. For a wide-ranging examination of the discursive influences of 'marketization', albeit in the particularly challenging environment of South Africa with all its ambiguities, see Eve Bertelsen's (1998) paper on 'The real transformation: the marketisation of higher education'.

16. For some relevant texts on constructivism, see John Searle (1995) *The Construction of Social Reality*; Irving Velody and Robin Williams (eds) (1998) *The Politics of Constructivism*; David Nightingale and John Cromby (eds) (1999) *Social Constructionist Psychology*.

17. The idea of 'validity conditions' I derive from Jürgen Habermas (where, at least, we find the term 'validity claims'). See, for instance, his *Communication and the Evolution of Society* (1979), e.g. p. 2 *et seq*, p. 28, pp. 118–19; and *The Theory of Communicative Action* (1991), especially Vol. 1, pp. 301–9.

18. On mode 2 knowledge, see Gibbons *et al.* (1994); Nowotny *et al.* (2001).

19. See the (2000) article by Pat Leon in the *Times Higher Education Supplement*, 'Risk is now an option'.

20. 'The immunizing power of ideologies, which stifle the demands for justification raised by discursive examination, goes back to blockages in communication' (Jürgen Habermas 1996: *Theory and Practice*, p. 12).

21. Cf. John Tribe (2002) 'The philosophic practitioner', who offers a conception of a curriculum that confronts the corporate tendencies, at least in the field of tourism studies.

22. A literature on the character of 'academic life' and 'academics' has developed apace over the past decade or so but, in this particular connection of the widening or even disappearing category of 'the academic', see Oliver Fulton's (1996) chapter 'Which academic profession are you in?'; Nixon *et al.* (1998) 'What Does it Mean to be an Academic?'; Peter Taylor (1999) *Making Sense of Academic Life*; Malcolm Tight (ed.) (2000) *Academic Work and Life: What it is to be an Academic, and how this is Changing*.

23. For an account of the way in which the 'neo-conservative ideology' has been having just this constraining impact in higher education in the USA, see Stanley Aronowitz and Henry Giroux (1986), *Education Under Siege*, chapter 8.

24. We may judge that much of the self-doubt in the humanities arises from understandable nervousness about their role and place in a technological and scientistic age. Such crises of the humanities may seem new but they are not, for they stretch back for over 100 years. Recent volumes that examine the matter from a contemporary viewpoint include the Michael Bérubé and Cary Nelson (1995) collection; Ellie Chambers' (2001) collection; and the (2001) collection edited by Roberto Di Napoli, Loredana Polezzi and Annie King (see note 27).

25. This sentence draws on Carl Rapp's (1998) *Fleeing the Universal: The Critique of Post-Rational Criticism*.

26. For a balanced analysis of the marketized university that indicates both the undue resistance in the academic community and significant challenges that marketization presents, see Ian Reid's (1996) *Higher Education or Higher Education for Hire?*

27. For a contribution towards explicating fuzzy boundaries and identities in the humanities, see Di Napoli *et al.* (eds) (2001) *Reflections on Modern Languages and the Humanities*. The ontological challenges and possibilities that fuzziness presents are nicely captured in Alison Phipps' concluding chapter, 'Busy foundries in modern languages and the humanities' (ibid., pp. 185–92).

28. On the potential virtues of sour grapes, indeed for an ethics of sour grapes, see Ernest Gellner's (1964) *Thought and Change*, pp. 110–13.
29. On the design and development of 'entrepreneurial universities', see Burton Clark's (1998) analysis.
30. Cf. D.S. Preston (2001) 'Managerialism and the post-enlightenment crisis of the British university', *Educational Philosophy and Theory*, 33(3&4): 343–64.

Chapter 6   Anything You Can Do (pp. 78–85)

1. The term 'practical logic' is also employed by Pierre Bourdieu (1998) in his *Practical Reason* (p. 132). We may note that the practical logic to which I refer here in the text – that of the state's audit processes in higher education – is having the effect of effacing the 'freedom from urgency, from necessity' that Bourdieu sees as structuring the surface conditions of 'the scholastic posture' (p. 129). Perhaps, therefore, there is a deep intention buried within the processes of public audit precisely of bringing the academic world to address the practical logic of the wider world. Audit, in other words, may be helping the academic world to become more worldly by denying it its own space and obliging it, thereby, to live in the wider world.
2. On benchmarking in higher education, see Smith *et al.* (1999) *Benchmarking and Threshold Standards in Higher Education.*
3. There were even examples of acrimonious priority disputes in the eighteenth century: 'The Astronomer Royal, John Flamsteed, would have liked to run up the stairs of the Royal Society to punch Newton's nose, but gout prevented him' (Michael White 2002: *Rivals: Conflict as the Fuel of Science*, p. 23). The quotation comes from a chapter that focuses on the rivalry between Newton and Leibniz.
4. Cf. Nigel Blake (1995) 'Truth, identity and community in the university', *Curriculum Studies*, October, pp. 263–81.
5. If only because they characteristically depend on language and understanding: 'And [that which] no one else understands but which I "*appear to understand*" might be called a "private language"' (Ludwig Wittgenstein 1978: *Philosophical Investigations*, p. 94, para. 269) (emphasis and quotation marks in original).
6. See Simon Marginson and Mark Considine (2000) *The Enterprise University: Power, Governance and Reinvention in Australia.*
7. For example, 'Diversity in higher education: has it been and gone?', professorial lecture by Dr Roger Brown, Goldsmiths College, University of London, 11 March 1999.

Chapter 7   Never Mind the Quality (pp. 91–6)

1. The idea of 'colonization' I take from the work of Jürgen Habermas: see, for instance, Vol. 2 of *The Theory of Communicative Action*, where Habermas (1989) develops a thesis as to the colonization of the life-world by systems rationality. A summary of that analysis is to be found on p. 356.
2. See the chapters on 'Evaluation of higher education in Europe' by John Brennan and on 'Academic responses to quality reforms in higher education: England and Sweden compared' by Marianne Bauer and Mary Henkel, both in Mary Henkel and Brenda Little (eds) (1999) *Changing Relationships between Higher Education and the State.*

3. See my (1992) book on *Improving Higher Education: Total Quality Care* for an elaboration of this point.
4. We may note that the term 'compact' was one of the more significant terms of the Dearing Report, the report of a UK national committee of inquiry into higher education (NCIHE 1997), although much underplayed in the commentaries. For an attempt to redress the balance, see Gokulsing and DaCosta (2000) *A Compact for Higher Education.*
5. In turn, a 'literature' develops *on* so-called 'key skills' or 'transferable skills' that attempts to offer operational strategies for their instantiation within institutions. See, for example, Bennett *et al.* (2000) *Skills Development in Higher Education and Employment;* and Stephen Fallows and Christine Steven (eds) (2000) *Integrating Key Skills in Higher Education: Employability, Transferable Skills and Learning for Life.*
6. A feature of the quality systems in the UK has, for some years, been the provision by institutions of a self-assessment document in which they are expected to offer a frank and incisive critical self-scrutiny. Given that that self-scrutiny then becomes part of the 'evidence' on which public judgements are made, it is hardly surprising if those self-assessment documents are composed with an eye on their propensity for success as against the self-development that they might have offered. It is hardly surprising, too, that some multifaculty universities have sought to ensure that those self-assessment documents are subject to the control of a central 'coordinating' office.
7. It will be evident, therefore, that in making these cautionary comments on the extent to which considerations of process are at the heart of contemporary evaluation processes, I am implicitly suggesting caution, too, with the dominant analytical state-of-affairs on this matter. Cf. John Brennan (1999) who, in a chapter on 'Evaluation of higher education in Europe', in summarizing the so-called 'general model' of quality assessment in Europe, states that 'It is an approach which places its emphasis upon *educational process*' (original emphasis).

Chapter 8 'The Academic Community' (pp. 104–14)

1. For the most influential recent statement of the two-world thesis, see Gibbons *et al.* (1994) together with its further elaboration in Nowotny *et al.* (2001).
2. Surely, it is Peter Scott who, more than anyone, has helped us understand the nature of mass higher education. Among many works of his on the topic, see his *The Meanings of Mass Higher Education* (1995); 'The crisis of knowledge and the massification of higher education' (1997a) and 'Massification, internationalization and globalization' (1998b). What I carry away from these writings (and others of Peter Scott's) is a heightened sense of the increasingly intricate nature of higher education, epistemologically, culturally and politically, both at the local level within institutions and across the system. If I might be allowed to say so, it is the ontological and communicative dimensions that, in particular, would assist in filling out the analysis even further.
3. We should note, even if with some surprise, that in that statement, the vice-chancellors collectively even felt able to enunciate a view of higher education as 'emancipation' (CVCP 1997). Unfortunately, they didn't tell us what they meant by that suggestion.
4. For a general description of the individualization thesis, see Beck and Beck-Gernsheim (2001).

5. For quite different treatments of this thesis, see Christopher Norris (1996) *Reclaiming Truth* and Alvin Goldman (1999) *Knowledge in a Social World.*
6. In his *Thought and Change* (Gellner 1964): 'Of the two formulations [of the relation between that which is science and that which is not], Snow's seems to me by far the superior' (p. 209). For more explicit examinations of epistemologies as social, see Frederick Schmitt (1994) *Socializing Epistemology* and Randall Collins (2000) *The Sociology of Philosophies.*
7. Although it was certainly evident: for instance, Gellner's article 'Notes toward a theory of ideology' in his *Spectacles and Predicaments* (1991a). A key consideration that Gellner offers in those notes is about the double-think inherent in ideologies: they claim to know the world *tout court* but are brought up sharp against other ideologies and then are forced to defend their corner, thereby falling back on external criteria of judgement and truthfulness: 'they are bi-lingual ... [entertaining] diplomatic–conceptual relations with other worlds ... Inter-ideological detente inevitably involves double-think ... arguing in favour of [certain principles] presupposes that there are more authoritative principles' ('An ethic of cognition', in same volume, p. 172).
8. Indeed, see Gellner's (1992) *Reason and Culture* for a characteristically trenchant but nicely judged defence of reason as such: 'Rationality is our destiny ... Yet it is true that we were bound to fail' (p. 159).
9. A point that Pierre Bourdieu has done much to help us appreciate. See within his writings, for instance, his essay 'The economy of symbolic goods' in *Practical Reason* (1998), his essay 'Symbolic violence and political struggles' in *Pascalian Meditations* (1999a) and his 'scattered remarks' (1999b: 336–8). We may note that, in the second of those, Bourdieu seems to imply that, for him, the concept of symbolic capital is more powerful than that of ideology. He observes that 'If I have little by little come to shun the use of the word "ideology", that is ... above all because, by evoking the order of ideas ... it inclines one to forget one of the most powerful mechanisms of the maintenance of the symbolic order, the *twofold naturalization* which results from the inscription of the social in things and in bodies ... with the resulting effects of symbolic violence' (Bourdieu 1999a: 181). I would just want to add, if I may, that ideas, too, are social in character and that they come often to be reflected themselves in 'things and bodies' (as we have been observing in this book): I am not persuaded, therefore, as to the sharp distinction that Bourdieu seems to want to be making between the ideological and the social.
10. 'What makes one regard philosophers half mistrustfully and half mockingly is not that one again and again detects how innocent they are ... in short their childishness and childlikedness – but that they display altogether insufficient honesty, while making a mighty and virtuous noise as soon as the problem of truthfulness is even remotely touched on ... what happens ... is that a prejudice ... is defended by them with reasons sought after the event' (Nietzsche 1988: *Beyond Good and Evil*, p. 18).
11. Cf. '*Communitas* is the word [Victor] Turner uses for the sense of being united in an experience of liminality for those who are part of its social force' (Alison Phipps 2001: 189).
12. Virtuous ideologies can never see off pernicious ideologies: the backers of pernicious ideologies are too powerful for that. At the same time, pernicious ideologies can never be permitted to see off virtuous ideologies for that spells,

at least, the end of the university. The first 'can' points to an empirical situation; the second 'can' points to a moral imperative.

Chapter 9   Communicating Values (pp. 120–30)

1. For a generally positive philosophical treatment of neutrality in the university, see Montefiore (ed.) (1975) *Neutrality and Impartiality: The University and Political Commitment.*
2. For an attempt to recover a basis for values in the wake of postmodernism, see the collection edited by Judith Squires (1994) *Principled Positions: Postmodernism and the Rediscovery of Value.*
3. The age of pragmatism that I have in mind here is largely the one that Richard Rorty describes in his writings, but we should note that Rorty by no means has such descriptions all his own way. For example, Hilary Putnam's (1995) account of *Pragmatism* is deliberately drawn out partly in contradistinction to the relativism in Richard Rorty's variety of pragmatism.
4. Although it has nothing to say about education as such, Paul Virilio's (1994) *The Lost Dimension* both captures the character of the kinds of academic travel that are now part of this age of more or less instantaneous communication and hints at the significance of the losses involved.
5. 'The University's ruins offer us an institution in which the incomplete and interminable nature of the pedagogic relation can remind us that "thinking together" is a dissensual process' (Bill Readings 1997: *The University in Ruins,* p. 192).
6. To use a term of Bourdieu's. See, among his many explorations of this idea, *In Other Words* (1990b).
7. On *Virtue Ethics,* see the (2000) volume of that title edited by Roger Crisp and Michael Slote.

Chapter 10   Engaging Universities (pp. 133–45)

1. In addition to the works identified earlier (on the end of ideology), see also Gerard Delanty's (2002) chapter, 'Meaning and social transformations: ideology in a post-ideological age'.
2. This sentence is prompted, in part, by Readings' (1997) book, *The University in Ruins.*
3. 'Underpinning . . . practices [in university departments] are values, attitudes and ideologies that are partly developed and communicated *locally*' (Paul Trowler and Peter Knight 2002: 'Exploring the implementation gap: theory and practices in change interventions' p. 146) (emphasis added).
4. It may be said that Mannheim's utopias contain their own form of deliberation: so they do. A utopia can hardly be worked up and carried forward as a project without some form of deliberation. But the deliberation that I have in mind here, and that is characteristic of ide*a*logies, is a deliberation in relation to *ideas as such.* If they are to be brought off as practical projects, ide*a*logies must take up and develop theoretically the ideas embedded as ideals in a concept such as 'university', must work on them and find ways of giving those virtuous ideas practical form. The utopian element in ide*a*logies, therefore, is to be won partly as a conceptual and practical craft with its own multiple forms of deliberateness.

On Mannheim's distinction between ideology and utopia, see his classic text, *Ideology and Utopia* (1936: 173–84). It is worth noting, too, that, for Mannheim, it was the forward-looking, energizing and transforming character of utopias that elevated them in importance above ideologies: 'whereas the decline of ideology represents a crisis only for certain strata ... The disappearance of utopia brings about a static state of affairs in which man himself becomes no more than a thing' (p. 236).

5. The idea of a constitutive progressive programme is prompted, in part, by Imre Lakatos' idea of a 'progressive research programme' in his 'Falsification and the methodology of scientific research programmes' in *Criticism and the Growth of Knowledge* (1977: 91–196), which he edited with Alan Musgrave. I am not sure whether the phrase actually appears in Lakatos' long essay but the term is implied, for example on p. 118, where he suggests that 'a series of theories is *theoretically progressive* (*or "constitutes a theoretically progressive problem-shift"*) if each new theory has some excess empirical content over its predecessor' and that we may call 'a problem shift *progressive* if it is both theoretically and empirically progressive' (emphases in original). In the present context of virtuous ide*a*logies for the university, we may say that an ideology may be considered virtuous if it makes probable both conceptually and practically an increasing realization of the ideals of the university. Under such conditions, we are then in the presence of an ide*a*logy of and for the university.

6. For polarized treatments of the idea of utopia, see (for a positive view) David Halpin (2003) *Hope and Education: The Role of the Utopian Imagination*; see also (for a sceptical view) Russel Jacoby (1999) *The End of Utopia: Politics and Culture in an Age of Apathy*.

7. For example, ACU (Association of Commonwealth Universities) (2001) *Engagement as a Core Value for the University: A Consultation Document*; H. Newby (2001) *From Solitude to Engagement: The University in the New Millennium.*

8. I would like to take this opportunity to say that, in the writing of this book, it was Zygmunt Bauman's (2000) *Liquid Modernity* that helped me most to grasp something of the fluid character of the present age and, thereby, helped me to understand much of the social context within which the story of this book is set. However, I should add that the idea of ideology does not, I think, appear between the covers of Bauman's book and I have no reason to believe that Professor Bauman would endorse any of what appears between *these* covers.

9. For example, Edward Harcourt (2000) *Morality, Reflection and Ideology*: 'to the extent that a moral belief or practice fails to survive when reflectively understood – to the extent, that is, that its survival requires that it not be understood ... – the belief or practice would stand revealed as a piece of ideology' (p. 3).

10. The notion of a 'protective belt' I steal from Lakatos (op. cit., note 5, pp. 133–5), for I put it to a use for which it was not intended.

11. Doubtless, my notion of surplus commitment in this context carries some trace of Marcuse's idea of surplus repression: see his *Eros and Civilization* (1972: 42).

12. On 'internal goods', see MacIntyre (1985); also op.cit., note 5, chapter 3.

13. On 'interpellation', see Althusser (1971); also op.cit., note 5, chapter 3.

14. On Habermas' notion of 'distorted communication', see Habermas (1972); also op.cit., note 9, chapter 4.

15. MacIntyre equivocates, I think, on the possibilities for such a debate. On the one hand, '... universities are places where conceptions of and standards of

rational justifications are elaborated, put to work . . . , *and themselves rationally evaluated*, so that only from the university can the wider society learn how to conduct its own debates, practical or theoretical, in a rationally defensible way. But that claim itself can be . . . justifiably advanced only when and insofar as the university is a place where rival and antagonistic views of rational justification . . . are afforded the opportunity . . . to conduct their intellectual and moral warfare. It is precisely because universities have not been such places' (Alistair MacIntyre 1990: *Three Rival Versions of Moral Enquiry*, p. 222). On the other hand, 'Happily, however, possibilities seem recently to be opening up within the university system which may afford new points of entry for radical dialogue and new opportunities for recasting older genres, so that they may allow new antagonisms to emerge' (p. 221). I confess that I do not follow, from the text, what these 'new points of entry' are for MacIntyre. Nevertheless, my argument here is that there are good grounds, indeed, for believing that new opportunities for the recovery of dialogical spaces may in fact be presenting themselves in an age of fluidity.

16. Cf. Moti Gokulsing and Cornell DaCosta (1997) *Usable Knowledges as the Goal of University Education*. The contributions address several themes that have engaged us here (including markets, performativity, the role of the state, postmodernity, quality and institutional change).

Chapter 11 Uniting Research and Teaching (pp. 146–54)

1. The tutorial, while understood as characteristic of Oxbridge, was essentially a pedagogy for the humanities in Oxford. See Ted Tapper and David Palfreyman (2000) *Oxford and the Decline of the Collegiate Tradition*, especially chapter 5, neatly entitled 'The tutorial system: the jewel in the crown'; and David Palfreyman (2001) *The Oxford Tutorial: 'Thanks, you taught me how to think'*.

    We may note that the Oxbridge tutorial system has not always enjoyed robust health. Indeed, in the late seventeenth and eighteenth centuries, the system pretty well collapsed as the senior Fellows sought to line their own pockets by taking to themselves increasing numbers of students, such that the student : tutor ratio rose 'from about six pupils per tutor to fifty or more'. 'Discipline also collapsed at the same time . . . after the mid-1660s, the practice of whipping students ceased in both universities' (Lawrence Stone 1983: 'Social control and intellectual excellence: Oxbridge and Edinburgh 1560–1983', p. 16 in N. Phillipson (ed.) *Universities, Society and the Future*.

2. Even as late as 1989, only 20 per cent of university staff claimed to be 'heavily oriented to research as distinct from teaching' (A.H. Halsey 1992: 191).

3. '. . . the UK carries out 4.7 per cent of the world's research, it has 7.6 per cent of the world's scientific publications, and over 9 per cent of the citations of scientific papers'. Speech given by Rt. Hon. Estelle Morris, MP, UK's Secretary of State for Education and Skills, 22 October 2001.

4. This sentence bears the trace of Habermas' comment that 'Ideologies are coeval with the critique of ideology'; 'Technology and science as "ideology"' in his *Toward a Rational Society* (1972: 99). The substantive connection, if there is one, seems to me to lie in the sense that the presence of ideology is dependent on the co-presence of large discursive spaces in society, indeed of the kind furnished by a literate society. Higher education, accordingly, we may say, both partakes of ideology and contributes to ideology at the same time.

5. The promotion of 'learning' before and above 'teaching' was possibly the most influential and, yet, among the least noticed consequences of the (NCIHE 1997) report of the UK's Committee of Inquiry into Higher Education (the Dearing Report). This insistence is reflected, for example, in the requirement placed by the Higher Education Funding Council for England on institutions each to produce its 'learning and teaching strategy'; the formation of the Institute for Learning and Teaching; and the establishment of the Learning and Teaching Support Network. The order of the terms 'learning' and 'teaching' is clearly not coincidental.

6. Perhaps it was F.R. Leavis (1948) who first coined the phrase 'The Great Tradition'. Leavis' 'Great Tradition', we may recall, was a particularly limited 'tradition', containing just five members (Austen, Eliot, James, Conrad and Lawrence) and we may ask, surely, whether five of anything can constitute a 'tradition', great or otherwise. The signal recent attempt to defend the idea of a great tradition or 'canon' in higher education as such is probably that of Allan Bloom in his *The Closing of the American Mind* (1987) and, for all the doubts one may properly entertain over that volume, it actually contains indications of a large and generous 'canon'. Indeed, perhaps it was its very scale and implicit demand that was unsettling for some of an 'inclusive' frame of mind.

7. l.308, General Prologue, Geoffrey Chaucer, *The Canterbury Tales* (edited by F.N. Robinson 1957).

8. Although we should note that Nowotny *et al.* (2001) observe that, in some sense, the two functions – 'the social and scientific functions of the university' – are also conflating 'if a wider Mode-2 definition of knowledge is accepted' (p. 82).

9. On economic reason, and for a critique thereof, see Andre Gorz (1989) *Critique of Economic Reason*. For Gorz, education has become a form of 'rape' (pp. 176–7) in which 'we find ourselves [required] to fit in to a predetermined model'. The alternative vision that Gorz offers is, I sense, an education that maximizes 'existential autonomy' (p. 98) and which promotes human qualities of 'generosity' in which 'each person regards the other *unconditionally* as an absolute end' (p. 167). Teaching itself should be characterized by 'this type of relationship' (p. 167). Schools 'need to give priority to developing irreplaceable human capabilities such as manual, artistic, emotional, relational and moral capabilities, and the need to ask unforeseen questions, to search for a meaning' (p. 240). I am not sure, however, that Gorz presses his own analysis far enough. For the most part, Gorz's 'existential autonomy' is to be found outside the economic sphere, but then the subject is rendered an object precisely in the economic sphere against which Gorz takes such umbrage. What, therefore, I think is missing from Gorz's account is an adequate indication as to the challenges and accomplishments (e.g. of ontological engagement) that are necessary if existential autonomy is to be achieved in the world of work itself.

10. Isaiah Berlin, 'Two concepts of liberty' in *Four Essays on Liberty* (1979 edition). Anyone who, like me, has struggled over the years trying to understand *precisely* the distinction(s) that Berlin was making between his two concepts may find helpful his clarification of the matter in the (2000) volume on *The Power of Ideas* (pp. 15–18): I certainly did.

11. 'Science does not excel because of its method for there is no method; and it does not excel because of its results; we know what science does, we have not the faintest idea whether other traditions could not do much better. So we must find out . . . The maturity I am speaking about can only be acquired by frequent

contacts with different points of view . . . This is why . . . the *slow* erosion of the authority of science and of other pushy institutions . . . is to be preferred . . .'. Chapter 10 on 'Science is only one Ideology among many and should be separated from the State just as Religion is now separated from the State', Paul Feyerabend (1982) *Science in a Free Society*.

12. In this economicizing and politicizing of knowledge, the boundaries between science and technology become ever less distinct as science is put to use. See David Dickson (1988) *The New Politics of Science*; Andrew Feenberg and Alistair Hannay (1995) *Technology and the Politics of Knowledge*; John Pickstone (2000) *Ways of Knowing: A New History of Science, Technology and Medicine*, especially chapters 7 and 8. In the process, issues are heightened over (a) the status of science, (b) its governance and (c) its character within the research process and knowledge production process more broadly. See, respectively, for example: (a) Steve Fuller's (1993) *Philosophy of Science and its Discontents*; and (b) his (2000) *The Governance of Science* and Joseph Rouse ([1987] 1994) *Knowledge and Power*; and (c) Nowotny *et al.* (2001) *Re-Thinking Science*.

13. For Gellner, the key word indeed seems to be that of science: 'its superiority . . . is not open to doubt', a characteristic claim about science but taken from his *Plough, Sword and Book* (1991b), p. 200. What I have never been able to fathom is the paradox surely embedded in Gellner's writings that in their wit, generosity, breadth, cross-cultural sympathy, historical perspective, kindliness and sheer humanity, they speak to human qualities and values that science can never in itself give us and which, therefore, demonstrate the limitations of science and, thereby, threaten to undermine a central plank of his whole *oeuvre*. How Gellner might have responded to this friendly observation, we shall sadly never know.

14. There is a variety of the so-called 'corporate universities' that focuses entirely on (profit-making) educational services and has no truck with 'research'. An analysis of the educational legitimacy of corporate universities is to be found in Peter Jarvis' (2001) *Universities and Corporate Universities*.

15. Ernest Boyer (1990) *Scholarship Reconsidered: Priorities of the Professoriate*.

16. For various kinds of linking arguments, principally though not only around the five concepts that I mention, see Stephen Rowland's paper on 'Relationships between teaching and research' (1996) and his *The Enquiring University Teacher* (2000) (which embraces 'criticality', 'risk-taking' and 'enquiry'); on learning itself, see Angela Brew and David Boud's article on 'Teaching and research: establishing the vital link with learning' (1995); on 'scholarship', see Ernest Boyer (op.cit., note 15) and Peter Taylor (1999) *Making Sense of Academic Life*. In his paper on 'Research and teaching: conditions for a positive link', Lewis Elton (2001) looks to the link in specific kinds of pedagogical process.

It should be noted that, in doubting the feasibility of linking strategies as a means of bringing research and teaching into a more effective relationship with each other, I am not doubting that there are common features worth bringing out. Indeed, I would offer yet two other linking concepts of my own: 'open-endedness' and 'doubt'. All I am doing is querying whether such a strategy can actually have practical effect. One reason for this is that the tacit purpose is itself plagued with the dominant ideology: research is assumed to be the starting point of the whole task, whereas learning has to be rejigged to bring out the ways in which it is just a form of research. *Research is left untouched*. This discourse pretends to be even-handed but enshrines the hegemony of one of the activities and the subservience of the other.

17. Coate *et al.* (2000) 'Relationships between teaching and research in England', *Higher Education Quarterly*, 55(2): 158–74; Port *et al.* (2000) *Interactions between Research, Teaching and Other Activities*. The latter report implicitly indicates the intricacy and the interconnectedness of the many aspects – financial, strategic, professional, epistemological, ontological, organizational – of the relationships between research and teaching. This crucial matter of academic life is one that we have barely begun to understand.

18. '. . . it is precisely the plurality and multi-vocality of the present day collection of the gatherings "for the sake of the pursuit of higher learning" . . . that offer the universities, old and new . . . the chance of emerging successfully from the present challenge' (Zygmunt Bauman 1997: 'Universities: old, new and different', p. 25).

19. See, for instance, the chapter on 'Research' in my (1990) book *The Idea of Higher Education*.

Chapter 12   Reasonable Universities (pp. 159–70)

1. See Cutright (ed.) (2001) *Chaos Theory and Higher Education*.

2. Although Grand Theory refuses to lie down: see Quentin Skinner (ed.) (1985) *The Return of Grand Theory in the Human Sciences*.

3. And, in turn, gives rise to the bizarre notion of 'knowledge management'; for example, Little *et al.* (2001) *Managing Knowledge*. Quite apart from the consideration that, in a democratic society the last thing one wants is that knowledge should be managed, there might also be just some acknowledgement of the irony that universities are to be places where knowledge is to be managed. Clearly, such advocates have not been reading Paul Feyerabend, whose philosophy would surely tilt any knowledge policies in the direction of the sponsorship of daring ideas, of innovation, of radicalism, of sheer elan and joy at effrontery; in short, a knowledge anarchy. See in particular Feyerabend (1978) *Against Method*, but see also his *Farewell to Reason* (1987). The whole idea of 'knowledge management' would surely have been inimical not only to Feyerabend's sense of what constitutes a free society, but also of the way in which we might develop our (human) understanding of the world around us.

4. '. . . there has been an upsurge in personal counselors, spiritual guides, spiritual advisers, and therapists. Bill Clinton made use of several spiritual advisers during his White House years but, to the best of my knowledge, no therapists. That may be because it's perfectly acceptable to utilize a coach, counselor, spiritual guide or adviser . . . But someone who visits a therapist is still assumed to have a "problem"' (Robert Reich 2000: *The Future of Success*, pp. 180–1).

5. 'Sydney has one opera house, one Arts centre, one zoo, one harbour, but two philosophy departments. The reason for this abundance is not any overwhelming demand for philosophy among the antipodes but the fact that philosophy has party lines, that different parties don't always get on with each other' (Paul Feyerabend 1982: *Science in a Free Society*, p. 154). But, as if in confirmation of the thesis of this chapter, intellectual hostilities need not last for ever: '. . . on the day I arrived in Sydney, 1 March 2000, the Departments of "General" and "Traditional and Modern" Philosophy at the University of Sydney were reunited as a single Department of Philosophy after 27 years of divorce' (Simon Critchley 2001: *Continental Philosophy*, p. xv).

6. 'In general, intellectuals are opposed to murder and bloodshed. Many of them, but by no means all, reject violence, preach tolerance, and praise argument as

the only acceptable means of settling controversies. Yet their actions can be as destructive as those of their more brutal contemporaries' (Paul Feyerabend [1999] 2001: *Conquest of Abundance*, p. 5).

7. Unlike ideologies, which assume that they have a final hold on the way things are in the world, ide*o*logies, to use a Rortian expression, are 'ironic'. For Rorty, the ironist: (1) 'has radical and continuing doubts about the final vocabulary she currently uses'; (2) 'realizes that arguments phrased in her present vocabulary can neither underwrite nor dissolve these doubts'; (3) '...does not think that her vocabulary is closer to reality than others ... [such ironists are] always aware of the contingency and fragility of their final vocabularies, and thus of their selves' (Richard Rorty 1989: *Contingency, Irony and Solidarity*, pp. 73–4). If I have a concern about Rorty's position, it is just that I do not see how it offers a lever for moving matters forward; all it can offer is the hope of better things, not the momentum for bringing them about. Indeed, Rorty (1999) himself seems almost to admit as much: '... we can, in politics, substitute *hope* for the sort of knowledge that philosophers have usually tried to attain' (p. 24).

8. For a recent philosophical account of tolerance that imparts to the notion a substantive moral and social content, see Hans Oberdiek (2001) *Tolerance: Between Forbearance and Acceptance.*

9. Op. cit., note 1.

10. See my (2000) book on *Realizing the University in an Age of Supercomplexity.*

11. Partly, I have in mind here Rorty's philosophy: op.cit., note 7.

12. See chapter 11.

13. A striking exception is Chris Duke's (2002) *Managing the Learning University.*

14. A point that some university principals have clearly yet to glean: 'One intranet facility reserves its "URGENT – ALL" channel for the Vice-Chancellor who alone can use it and uses only this mode for all intranet communications, significant or trivial as they may be' (Duke 2002: 135).

15. Cf. G. Bearn (2000) 'The university of beauty', in P. Dhillon and P. Standish (eds) *Lyotard: Just Education.*

16. For Basil Bernstein (1996: 135), '... a language of description is a translation device whereby one language is transformed into another'. However, the sense I give here to the phrase ('language of description') is entirely the opposite: the four languages of higher education that I identify are distinct, are untranslatable one to another and are even incommensurable in some respects. Indeed, this parallelism of the languages of the university's situation heightens the complexities that beset the university and extends beyond all reason.

17. George Myerson (1994: 147) talks of the 'imaginative energies' that processes of dialogic rationalism can provide.

Prospects (pp. 172–80)

1. For example, Readings (1997) *The University in Ruins*; Howard Dickman (ed.) (1993) *The Imperilled Academy*; and Simon Wortham (1999) *Rethinking the University*, who opens his account by indicating that his aim is to 'develop key critical debates in the humanities ... in the context of the legitimation crisis widely felt to be facing academic institutions' (p. 1).

   As an indication that a more positive point of view is still possible, see the recent volume by Richard Taylor, Jean Barr and Tom Steele (2002) *For a Radical Higher Education.*

2. It should be acknowledged that the two camps do not behave as if they have anything in common. Indeed, for the most part, they go out of their way to distance themselves from each other and attack each other whenever they get the chance. See, for example, Darryl Gless and Barbara Herrnstein Smith's (1992) collection and Duke Maskell and Ian Robinson's (2001) *The New Idea of a University*, both of which defend 'liberal' views of the university against the 'neo-liberal' attacks. That the new ideas of the university, for all their problematicity, may have *some* virtue on their side, does not seem to appear to some of our 'liberal' critics.

3. See Margaret S. Archer (2000) *Being Human: The Problem of Agency*, which does much to recover the idea of being human from its contemporary difficulties, not in any 'given' way, but 'because what we are is forged between our potential species' powers and our encounters with the world' (p. 317).

4. I owe the key proposition in this sentence – that the idea of recovery looks forward as well as backwards – to Denise Batchelor, PhD student at the Institute of Education, University of London.

5. For a telling example, trenchantly analysed, see Michael Shattock's (2001) report for the University of Cambridge, England, on the installation of a financial system in that University (available from the website of the University's Reporter).

6. 'Such enactments of freedom are the principal occasions of the erotic relationships between teacher and student that Socrates . . . celebrate[s] and that Plato unfortunately tried to capture in a theory of human nature and of the liberal arts curriculum. But love is notoriously unthcorizable' (Richard Rorty 1999: *Philosophy and Social Hope*, p. 125). bell hooks implies much the same thing in a chapter on 'Eros, eroticism, and the pedagogical process' in her *Teaching to Transgress* (1994). All I would add is that, if Eros is a suitable concept for university life, we might prepare ourselves to interpret in the most generous way the ideas of teacher and student and observe their incarnation in different relationships on campus, even in the most surprising places.

Bibliography

This bibliography includes a few references that offer further relevant reading.

Alexander, H.A. (1997) Rationality and redemption: ideology, indoctrination, and learning communities, in *Philosophy of Education Yearbook 1996.* Urbana, IL: Philosophy of Education Society.

Althusser, L. (1969) *For Marx.* Harmondsworth: Penguin.

Althusser, L. (1971) Ideology and ideological state apparatus, in *Lenin and Philosophy and other Essays.* New York: Monthly Review Press.

Archer, M.S. (2000) *Being Human: The Problem of Agency.* Cambridge: Cambridge University Press.

Aronowitz, S. and Giroux, H. (1986) *Education under Siege: The Conservative, Liberal and Radical Debate over Schooling.* London: Routledge.

Ashenden, S. and Owen, D. (eds) (1999) *Foucault versus Habermas: Recasting the Dialogue between Genealogy and Critical Theory.* London: Sage.

Barnett, R. (1990) *The Idea of Higher Education.* Buckingham: Open University Press.

Barnett, R. (1992) *Improving Higher Education: Total Quality Care.* Buckingham: Open University Press.

Barnett, R. (2000) *Realizing the University in an Age of Supercomplexity.* Buckingham: Open University Press.

Barnett, R. and Griffin, A. (eds) (1997) *The End of Knowledge in Higher Education.* London: Cassell.

Bauer, M. and Little, B. (1999) Academic responses to quality reforms in higher education: England and Sweden compared, in M. Henkel and B. Little (eds), *Changing Relationships between Higher Education and the State.* London: Jessica Kingsley.

Bauman, Z. (1997) Universities: old, new and different, in A. Smith and F. Webster (eds), *The Postmodern University? Contested Visions of Higher Education in Society.* Buckingham: Open University Press.

Bauman, Z. (2000) *Liquid Modernity.* Cambridge: Polity Press.

Bearn, G. (2000) The university of beauty, in P. Dhillon and P. Standish (eds), *Lyotard: Just Education.* London: Routledge.

Becher, T. (1989) *Academic Tribes and Territories.* Buckingham: Open University Press.

Becher, T. and Kogan, M. (1992) *Process and Structure in Higher Education.* London: Routledge.

Becher, T. and Trowler, P. (2001) *Academic Tribes and Territories*, 2nd edn. Buckingham: Open University Press.

Beck, U. (1992) *Risk Society*. London: Sage.

Beck, U. and Beck-Gernsheim, E. (2001) *Individualization: Institutionalized Individualism and its Social and Political Consequences*. London: Sage.

Beck, U., Giddens, A. and Lash, S. (1995) *Reflexive Modernization: Politics, Tradition and Aesthetics in the Modern Social Order*. Cambridge: Polity Press.

Bell, D. (2000) *The End of Ideology*, new edition. Cambridge, MA: Harvard University.

Bell, V. (ed.) (1999) *Performativity and Belonging*. London: Sage.

Bennett, N., Dunne, E. and Carre, C. (2000) *Skills Development in Higher Education and Employment*. Buckingham: Open University Press.

Berlin, I. ([1969] 1979) *Four Essays on Liberty*. Oxford: Oxford University.

Berlin, I. (2000) *The Power of Ideas*. London: Chatto & Windus.

Bernstein, B. (1996) *Pedagogy, Symbolic Control and Identity: Theory, Research and Critique*. London: Taylor & Francis.

Bernstein, R.J. (1991) *The New Constellation*. Cambridge: Polity Press.

Bertelsen, E. (1998) The real transformation: the marketisation of higher education, *Social Dynamics*, 24(2): 130–58.

Bérubé, M. and Nelson, C. (eds) (1995) *Higher Education Under Fire: Politics, Economics and the Crisis of the Humanities*. New York: Routledge.

Blake, N. (1995) Truth, identity and community in the University, *Curriculum Studies*, October, pp. 263–81.

Blake, N., Smeyers, P., Smith, R. and Standish, P. (1998a) *Thinking Again: Education after Postmodernism*. Westport, CT: Bergin & Harvey.

Blake, N., Smith, R. and Standish, P. (1998b) *The Universities We Need: Higher Education after Dearing*. London: Kogan Page.

Bloom, A. (1987) *The Closing of the American Mind*. London: Penguin.

Bourdieu, P. (1990a) *Homo Academicus*. Cambridge: Polity Press.

Bourdieu, P. (1990b) *In Other Words*. Cambridge: Polity Press.

Bourdieu, P. (1998) *Practical Reason*. Cambridge: Polity Press.

Bourdieu, P. (1999a) *Pascalian Meditations*. Cambridge: Polity Press.

Bourdieu, P. (1999b) Scattered remarks, *European Journal of Social Policy*, 2(3): 334–40.

Boyer, E. (1990) *Scholarship Reconsidered: Priorities of the Professoriate*. Princeton, NJ: Carnegie.

Brennan, J. (1999) Evaluation of higher education in Europe, in M. Henkel and B. Little (eds) *Changing Relationships between Higher Education and the State*. London: Jessica Kingsley.

Brew, A. (1999) Research and teaching: changing relationships in a changing context, *Studies in Higher Education*, 2(3): 291–302.

Brew, A. (2001) *The Nature of Research: Inquiry in Academic Contexts*. London: Routledge/Falmer.

Brew, A. and Boud, D. (1995) Teaching and research: establishing the vital link with learning, *Studies in Higher Education*, 24(3): 291–302.

Brown, R. (1999) 'Diversity in Higher Education: Has it Been and Gone?', Professorial Lecture, Goldsmiths College, University of London. (Mimeo.) Southampton Institute.

Burrell, G. (1997) *Pandemonium: Towards a Retro-Organization Theory*. London: Sage.

Caplow, T. and McGee, A. (2001) *The Academic Marketplace*. New Brunswick, NJ: Transaction.

Castells, M. (1997) *The Rise of the Network Society*. Oxford: Blackwell.

Castells, M. (1999) Flows, networks, and identities: a critical theory of the informational society, in M. Castells, R. Flecha, P. Freire, H.A. *et al. Critical Education in the New Information Age.* Lanham, MD: Rowman & Littlefield.

Castells, M., Flecha, R., Freire, P. *et al.* (1999) *Critical Education in the New Information Age.* Lanham, MD: Rowman & Littlefield.

Centre for Contemporary Cultural Studies (1978) *On Ideology.* London: Hutchinson.

Chambers, E. (ed.) (2001) *Contemporary Themes in Humanities Higher Education.* Dordrecht: Kluwer.

Churchill, Sir W. (1963) *Great War Speeches.* London: Corgi.

Cilliers, P. (1998) *Complexity and Postmodernism.* London: Routledge.

Clark, B.R. (1998) *Creating Entrepreneurial Universities: Organizational Pathways of Transformation.* Oxford: Pergamon Press.

Coate, K., Williams, G. and Barnett, R. (2000) Relationships between teaching and research in England, *Higher Education Quarterly,* 55(2): 158–74.

Cole, J.R., Barber, E.G. and Graubard, S.R. (1994) *The Research University in a Time of Discontent.* London: Johns Hopkins University Press.

Collier, G. (1982) Ideological influences in higher education, *Studies in Higher Education,* 7(1): 13–20.

Collins, R. (2000) *The Sociology of Philosophies: A Global Theory of Intellectual Change.* Cambridge, MA: Harvard University Press.

Cornford, F.M. ([1908] 1998) *Microcosmographia Academia,* in G. Johnson, *University Politics: F.M. Cornford's Cambridge and his Advice to the Young Academic Politician.* Cambridge: Cambridge University Press.

Crisp, R. and Slote, M. (eds) (2000) *Virtue Ethics.* Oxford: Oxford University Press.

Critchley, S. (2001) *Continental Philosophy: A Very Short Introduction.* Oxford: Oxford University Press.

Currie, J. and Newson, J. (eds) (1998) *Universities and Globalization: Critical Perspectives.* London: Sage.

Cutright, M. (2001) *Chaos Theory and Higher Education: Leadership, Planning and Policy.* New York: Peter Lang.

Daniel, J. (1998) *Mega-Universities and Knowledge Media: Technology Strategies for Higher Education.* London: Kogan Page.

de Certeau, M. (1988) *The Practice of Everyday Life.* Berkeley, CA: University of California Press.

Deertz, S. (1994) The new politics of the workplace: ideology and other unobtrusive controls, in H.W. Simons and M. Billig (eds) *After Postmodernism: Reconstructing Ideology Critique.* London: Sage.

Delanty, G. (2001) *Challenging Knowledge: The University in the Knowledge Society.* Buckingham: Open University Press.

Delanty, G. (2002) Meaning and social transformations: ideology in a post-ideological age, in Z. Laidi, P. Mandaville and A. Williams (eds) *Varieties of Meaning in International Relations.* London: Routledge.

Derrida, J. (1992) Mochlos; or, the conflict of the faculties, in R. Rand (ed.) *Logomachia: The Conflict of the Faculties.* London: University of Nebraska.

Dhillon, P. and Standish, P. (eds) (2000) *Lyotard: Just Education.* London: Routledge.

Dickman, H. (ed.) (1993) *The Imperilled Academy.* London: Transaction.

Dickson, D. (1988) *The New Politics of Science.* London: University of Chicago Press.

Di Napoli, R., Polezzi, L. and King, A. (eds) (2001) *Reflections on Modern Languages and the Humanities.* London: CILT.

Downie, R.S. (1990) Professions and professionalism, *Journal of Philosophy of Education*, 24(2): 147–60.

Duke, C. (2002) *Managing the Learning University*. Buckingham: Open University Press.

Eagleton, T. (1982) *Criticism and Ideology*. London: Verso.

Eagleton, T. (1991) *Ideology: An Introduction*. London: Verso.

Eagleton, T. (2000) *The Idea of Culture*. Oxford: Blackwell.

Edmonds, D. and Eidinow, J. (2001) *Wittgenstein's Poker: The Story of a Ten-Minute Argument between Two Great Philosophers*. London: Faber & Faber.

Elton, L. (2001) Research and teaching: conditions for a positive link, *Teaching in Higher Education*, 6(1): 43–56.

Eve, R.A., Horsfall, S. and Lee, M.E. (1997) *Chaos, Complexity and Sociology: Myths, Models and Theories*. London: Sage.

Fallows, S. and Steven, C. (eds) (2000) *Integrating Key Skills in Higher Education: Employability, Transferable Skills and Learning for Life*. London: Kogan Page.

Feenberg, A. and Hannay, A. (1995) *Technology and the Politics of Knowledge*. Bloomington, IN: Indiana University Press.

Feyerabend, P. (1978) *Against Method*. London: Verso.

Feyerabend, P. (1982) *Science in a Free Society*. London: Verso.

Feyerabend, P. (1987) *Farewell to Reason*. London: Verso.

Feyerabend, P. ([1999] 2001) *Conquest of Abundance: A Tale of Abstraction versus the Richness of Being*. Chicago, IL: University of Chicago Press.

Finkielkraut, A. (2001) *In the Name of Humanity*. London: Pimlico.

Fisher, S. (1994) *Stress in Academic Life: The Mental Assembly Line*. Buckingham: Open University Press.

Foucault, M. (1974) *The Archaeology of Knowledge*. London: Tavistock.

Foucault, M. (1980) *Power/Knowledge: Selected Interviews and Other Writings, 1972–1977*. Hemel Hempstead: Harvester Wheatsheaf.

Foucault, M. (1984) *The Foucault Reader* (edited by P. Rabinow). Harmondsworth: Penguin.

Franklin, J. (ed.) (1998) *The Politics of Risk Society*. Cambridge: Polity Press.

Fukuyama, F. (1992) *The End of History and the Last Man*. London: Penguin.

Fukuyama, F. (1995) *Trust: The Social Virtues and the Creation of Prosperity*. London: Penguin.

Fuller, S. (1993) *Philosophy of Science and its Discontents*. New York: Guilford Press.

Fuller, S. (2000) *The Governance of Science*. Buckingham: Open University Press.

Fulton, O. (1996) Which academic profession are you in?, in R. Cuthbert (ed.) *Working in Higher Education*. Buckingham: Open University Press.

Gadamer, H.-G. (1985) *Truth and Method*. London: Sheed & Ward.

Galbraith, J.K. (1969) *The New Industrial State*. London: Penguin.

Gellner, E. (1964) *Thought and Change*. London: Weidenfeld & Nicolson.

Gellner, E. (1987) *Culture, Identity and Politics*. Cambridge: Cambridge University Press.

Gellner, E. (1991a) *Spectacles and Predicaments*. Cambridge: Cambridge University Press.

Gellner, E. (1991b) *Plough, Sword and Book: The Structure of Human History*. London: Paladin.

Gellner, E. (1992) *Reason and Culture*. Oxford: Blackwell.

Geuss, R. (1981) *The Idea of a Critical Theory*. Cambridge: Cambridge University Press.

Gibbons, M., Limoges, C., Nowotny, H. *et al.* (1994) *The New Production of Knowledge: The Dynamics of Science and Research in Contemporary Societies*. London: Sage.

Giddens, A. (1995) *Modernity and Self-Identity: Self and Society in the Late Modern Age.* Cambridge: Polity Press.

Giddens, A. (1999) *Runaway World: How Globalization is Reshaping Our Lives.* London: Profile.

Giroux, H.A. (2001a) Critical education or training: beyond the commodification of higher education, in H. Giroux and K. Myrsiades (eds) *Beyond the Corporate University: Culture and Pedagogy in the New Millennium.* Lanham, MD: Rowman & Littlefield.

Giroux, H.A. (2001b) Vocationalizing higher education: schooling and the politics of corporate culture, in H. Giroux and K. Myrsiades (eds) *Beyond the Corporate University: Culture and Pedagogy in the New Millennium.* Lanham, MD: Rowman & Littlefield.

Giroux, H. and Myrsiades, K. (eds) (2001) *Beyond the Corporate University: Culture and Pedagogy in the New Millennium.* Lanham, MD: Rowman & Littlefield.

Gless, D. and Hernstein Smith, B. (eds) (1992) *The Politics of Liberal Education.* London: Duke University Press.

Gokulsing, M. and DaCosta, C. (eds) (1997) *Usable Knowledges as the Goal of University Education.* Lampeter: Edwin Mellen.

Gokulsing, M. and DaCosta, C. (eds) (2000) *A Compact for Higher Education.* Aldershot: Ashgate.

Goldman, A.I. (1999) *Knowledge in a Social World.* Oxford: Clarendon Press.

Gorz, A. (1989) *Critique of Economic Reason.* London: Verso.

Gouldner, A.W. (1976) *The Dialectic of Ideology and Technology: The Origins, Grammar and Future of Ideology.* London: Macmillan.

Gramsci, A. (1980) *The Modern Prince and Other Writings.* New York: International Universities Press.

Gramsci, A. (1971) *Selections from the Prison Notebooks of Antonio Gramsci* (edited and translated by Q. Hoare and G. Newell Smith). London: Lawrence & Wishart.

Green, A. (1992) *Education, Globalization and the Nation State.* Basingstoke: Macmillan.

Green, L. (1999) Ideology, *in* B. Horner and T. Swiss (eds) *Studying Popular Music: Key Terms.* New York and Oxford: Oxford University Press.

Gregory, M. (2001) The perils of rationality: Nietzsche, Peirce and Education, *Educational Philosophy and Theory*, 33(1): 23–34.

Habermas, J. (1972) Technology and science as 'ideology', in *Toward a Rational Society.* London: Heinemann.

Habermas, J. (1976) *Legitimation Crisis.* London: Heinemann.

Habermas, J. (1978) *Knowledge and Human Interests.* London: Heinemann.

Habermas, J. (1979) *Communication and the Evolution of Society.* London: Heinemann.

Habermas, J. (1986) *Habermas: Autonomy and Solidarity* (edited by P. Dews). London: Verso.

Habermas, J. (1989) *The Theory of Communicative Action*, Vol. 2. Cambridge: Polity Press.

Habermas, J. (1990) *The Philosophical Discourse of Modernity.* Cambridge: Polity Press.

Habermas, J. (1991) *The Theory of Communicative Action*, Vol. 1. Cambridge: Polity Press.

Habermas, J. (1995) *Postmetaphysical Thinking.* Cambridge: Polity Press.

Habermas, J. ([1971] 1996) *Theory and Practice.* Cambridge: Polity Press.

Halpin, D. (2003) *Hope and Education: The Role of the Utopian Imagination.* London: Routledge-Falmer.

Halsey, A.H. (1992) *Decline of Donnish Dominion*. Oxford: Clarendon Press.

Harcourt, E. (ed.) (2000) *Morality, Reflection and Ideology*. Oxford: Oxford University Press.

Hardt, M. and Negri, A. (2000) *Empire*. Cambridge, MA: Harvard University Press.

Hawkes, D. (1996) *Ideology*. London: Routledge.

Held, D. (1980) *Introduction to Critical Theory: Horkheimer to Habermas*. London: Hutchinson.

Henkel, M. (2000) *Academic Identities and Policy Change in Higher Education*. London: Jessica Kingsley.

Henkel, M. and Little, B. (eds) (1999) *Changing Relationships between Higher Education and the State*. London: Jessica Kingsley.

Hollis, M. (1998) *Trust within Reason*. Cambridge: Cambridge University Press.

hooks, bel (1994) *Teaching to Transgress: Education as the Practice of Freedom*. London: Routledge.

Hoy, D.C. and McCarthy, T. (1995) *Critical Theory*. Oxford: Blackwell.

Hutton, W. (1995) *The State We're In*. London: Jonathan Cape.

Jacob, M. and Hellstrom, T. (eds) (2000) *The Future of Knowledge Production in the Academy*. Buckingham: Open University Press.

Jacoby, R. (1999) *The End of Utopia: Politics and Culture in an Age of Apathy*. New York: Basic Books.

Jahanbegloo, R. (2000) *Conversations with Isaiah Berlin*. London: Phoenix.

Jarvis, P. (2001) *Universities and Corporate Universities: The Higher Learning Industry in Global Society*. London: Kogan Page.

Jay, M. (1996) *The Dialectical Imagination: A History of the Frankfurt School and the Institute of Social Research, 1923–1950*. Berkeley, CA: University of California Press.

Jenkins, A. (2000) The relationship between teaching and research: where does geography stand and deliver?, *Journal of Geography in Higher Education*, 24(3): 325–51.

Jones, R. (1990) Educational practices and scientific knowledge: a genealogical reinterpretation of the emergence of physiology in post-revolutionary France, in S.J. Ball (ed.) *Foucault and Education: Disciplines and Knowledge*. London: Routledge.

Kant, I. (1992) *The Conflict of the Faculties*. London: University of Nebraska.

Kerr, C. (1995) *The Uses of the University*, 4th edn (with 1994 Commentaries on Past Developments and Future Prospects). Cambridge, MA: Harvard University Press.

King, B. (2002) Managing institutional change and the pressures for new approaches to teaching and learning, in F. Reeve, M. Cartwright and R. Edwards (eds) *Supporting Lifelong Learning: Vol. 2, Organizing Learning*. London: Routledge/Falmer.

Kress, G. and van Leeuwen, T. (2001) *Multimodal Discourse: The Modes and Media of Contemporary Communication*. London: Edward Arnold.

Lakatos, I. (1977) Falsification and the methodology of scientific research programmes, in I. Lakatos and A. Musgrave (eds) *Criticism and the Growth of Knowledge*. Cambridge: Cambridge University Press.

Lakatos, I. and Musgrave, A. (eds) ([1970] 1977) *Criticism and the Growth of Knowledge*. Cambridge: Cambridge University Press.

Larrain, J. (1979) *The Concept of Ideology*. London: Hutchinson.

Larrain, J. (1994) *Ideology and Cultural Identity: Modernity and the Third World Presence*. Cambridge: Polity Press.

Leach, E. (1968) *A Runaway World?* (Reith Lectures). London: BBC.

Leavis, F.R. ([1948] 1966) *The Great Tradition*. Harmondsworth: Penguin.

Leavis, F.R. (1969) *English Literature in our Time and the University*. London: Chatto & Windus.

Little, S.E., Quintas, P. and Ray, T. (eds) (2001) *Managing Knowledge*. London: Sage.

Luntley, M. (1995) *Reason, Truth and Self: The Postmodern Reconditioned*. London: Routledge.

Lyotard, J.-F. (1984) *The Postmodern Condition: A Report on Knowledge*. Manchester: Manchester University Press.

Lyotard, J.-F. (1992) Apostil on narratives, in *The Postmodern Explained to Children: Correspondence 1982–1985*. London: Turnaround.

MacIntyre, A. (1985) *After Virtue: A Study in Moral Theory*. London: Duckworth.

MacIntyre, A. (1990) *Three Rival Versions of Moral Enquiry*. London: Duckworth.

Mannheim, K. ([1936] 1976) *Ideology and Utopia*. London: Routledge & Kegan Paul.

Marcuse, H. (1972) *Eros and Civilization: A Philosophical Inquiry into Freud*. London: Ark.

Marginson, S. and Considine, S. (2000) *The Enterprise University: Power, Governance and Reinvention in Australia*. Cambridge: Cambridge University Press.

Marion, R. (1999) *The Edge of Organization: Chaos and Complexity Theories of Formal Social Systems*. London: Sage.

Marx, K. and Engels, F. (1977) *The German Ideology*. London: Lawrence & Wishart.

Maskell, D. and Robinson, A. (2001) *The New Idea of a University*. London: Haven.

Masschelein, J. (2000) Can education still be critical?, *Journal of Philosophy of Education*, 34(4): 603–16.

McCarthy, D. (1996) *Knowledge as Culture: The New Sociology of Knowledge*. Routledge: London.

McClennan, D. (1995) *Ideology*, 2nd edn. Buckingham: Open University Press.

Minogue, K. (1973) *The Concept of a University*. London: Weidenfeld & Nicolson.

Montefiore, A. (ed.) (1975) *Neutrality and Impartiality: The University and Political Commitment*. London: Cambridge University Press.

Morley, L. (2002) A comedy of manners: quality and power in higher education, in P. Trowler (ed.) *Higher Education Policy and Institutional Change: Intentions and Outcomes in Turbulent Environments*. Buckingham: Open University Press.

Morris, E. (2001) Speech by Secretary of State for Education and Skills, at London Guildhall University, 22 October (untitled). London: DFES.

Mourad, R. (1997) *Postmodern Philosophical Critique and the Pursuit of Knowledge in Higher Education*. Westport, CT: Bergin & Garvey.

Myerson, G. (1994) *Rhetoric, Reason and Society*. London: Sage.

Myerson, G. (2001) *Heidegger, Habermas and the Mobile Phone*. Duxford: Icon.

Neave, G. (1998) The evaluative state, *European Journal of Education*, 33(1): 265–84. [See also that issue of the journal for a symposium on 'The Evaluative State'.]

Newby, H. (2001) *From Solitude to Engagement: The University in the New Millennium*. (Mimeo.) Southampton.

Newman, J.H. (1976) *The Idea of a University* (edited by I.T. Ker). Oxford: Clarendon Press.

Niblett, W.R. (1974) *Universities between Two Worlds*. London: University of London Press.

Niblett, W.R. (2001) *Life, Education, Discovery: A Memoir and Selected Essays*. Bristol: Pomegranate.

Nietzsche, F. ([1887] 1988) *Beyond Good and Evil*. London: Penguin.

Nietzsche, F. ([1901] 1968) *The Will to Power*. New York: Vintage.

Nightingale, D. and Cromby, J. (1999) *Social Constructionist Psychology: A Critical Analysis of Theory and Practice*. Buckingham: Open University Press.

Nixon, J., Beattie, M., Challis, M. and Walker, M. (1998) What does it mean to be an academic? A colloquium, *Teaching in Higher Education*, 3(3): 277–98.

Nonaka, I., Umemoto, K. and Sasaki, K. (1998) Three tales of knowledge-creating companies, in G. von Krogh, J. Roos and D. Kleine (eds) *Knowing in Firms: Understanding, Managing and Measuring Knowledge*. London: Sage.

Norris, C. (1996) *Reclaiming Truth: Contribution to a Critique of Cultural Relativism*. London: Lawrence & Wishart.

Nowotny, H. (1994) *Time: The Modern and the Postmodern Experience*. Cambridge: Polity Press.

Nowotny, H., Scott, P. and Gibbons, M. (2001) *Re-Thinking Science: Knowledge and the Public in an Age of Uncertainty*. Cambridge: Polity Press.

Nussbaum, M. (1997) *Cultivating Humanity: A Classic Defense of Reform in Liberal Education*. Cambridge, MA: Harvard University Press.

Nuyen, A.T. (1995) Lyotard and Rorty on the role of the professor, in M. Peters (ed.) *Education and the Postmodern Condition*. Westport, CT: Bergin & Garvey.

Oakeshott, M. (1989) *The Voice of Liberal Learning* (edited by T. Fuller). New Haven, CT: Yale University Press.

Oberdiek, H. (2001) *Tolerance: Between Forbearance and Acceptance*. Lanham, MD: Rowman & Littlefield.

Paechter, C., Edwards, R., Harrison, R. and Twining, P. (eds) (2000a) *Learning, Space and Identity*. London: Paul Chapman.

Paechter, C., Preedy, M., Scott, D. and Soler, J. (eds) (2000b) *Knowledge, Power and Learning*. London: Paul Chapman.

Palfreyman, D. (ed.) (2001) *The Oxford Tutorial: 'Thanks, you taught me how to think'*. Oxford: OxCheps.

Peters, M. (ed.) (1995) *Education and the Postmodern Condition*. Westport, CT: Bergin & Garvey.

Peters, M. (ed.) (1999) *After the Disciplines: Disciplinarity, Culture and the Emerging Economy of Studies*. Westport, CT: Bergin & Garvey.

Phillips, M. (1996) *All Must Have Prizes*. London: Little, Brown.

Phillipson, N. (ed.) (1983) *Universities, Society and the Future*. Edinburgh: Edinburgh University Press.

Phipps, A. (2001) Busy foundries in modern languages and the humanities, in R. Di Napoli, L. Polezzi and A. King (eds) *Reflections on Modern Languages and the Humanities*. London: CILT.

Pickstone, J.V. (2000) *Ways of Knowing: A New History of Science, Technology and Medicine*. Manchester: Manchester University Press.

Pippin, R.B. (1999) *Modernism as a Philosophical Problem*. Oxford: Blackwell.

Plamenatz, J. (1970) *Ideology*. London: Macmillan.

Popper, Sir K. (1975) *Objective Knowledge*. London: Oxford University Press.

Porter, R. (2000) *Enlightenment: Britain and the Creation of the Modern World*. London: Penguin.

Preston, D.S. (2001) Managerialism and the post-enlightenment crisis of the British university, *Educational Philosophy and Theory*, 33(3&4): 343–64.

Putnam, H. (1995) *Pragmatism: An Open Question*. Cambridge, MA: Blackwell.

Putnam, R.D. (2001) *Bowling Alone: The Collapse and Revival of American Community*. New York: Touchstone.

Rapp, C. (1998) *Fleeing the Universal: The Critique of Post-Rational Criticism.* New York: State University of New York Press.

Readings, B. (1997) *The University in Ruins,* 2nd imprint. Cambridge, MA: Harvard University Press.

Reich, R.B. (2000) *The Future of Success: Work & Life in the New Economy.* London: Heinemann.

Reid, I. (1996) *Higher Education or Education for Hire?* Rockhampton: Central Queensland University.

Rescher, N. (1998) *Complexity: A Philosophical Overview.* New Brunswick, NJ: Transaction.

Robinson, F.N. (ed.) (1957) *The Works of Geoffrey Chaucer.* London: Oxford University Press.

Roderick, R. (1986) *Habermas and the Foundations of Critical Theory.* Basingstoke: Macmillan.

Rorty, R. (1980) *Philosophy and the Mirror of Nature.* Oxford: Blackwell.

Rorty, R. (1989) *Contingency, Irony and Solidarity.* Cambridge: Polity Press.

Rorty, R. (1999) *Philosophy and Social Hope.* Harmondsworth: Penguin.

Rorty, R. ([1982] 2001) *Consequences of Pragmatism.* Minneapolis, MN: University of Minnesota Press.

Rosen, M. (1996) *On Voluntary Servitude: False Consciousness and the Theory of Ideology.* Cambridge: Polity Press.

Rothblatt, S. (1997) *The Modern University and its Discontents: The Fate of Newman's Legacies in Britain and America.* Cambridge: Cambridge University Press.

Rouse, J. ([1987] 1994) *Knowledge and Power: Toward a Political Philosophy of Science.* Ithaca, NY: Cornell University Press.

Rowland, S. (1996) Relationships between teaching and research, *Teaching in Higher Education,* 1(1): 7–20.

Rowland, S. (2000) *The Enquiring University Teacher.* Buckingham: Open University Press.

Salter, B. and Tapper, T. (1994) *The State and Higher Education.* London: Woburn Press.

Salter, B. and Tapper, T. (2000) The politics of governance in higher education: the case of quality assurance, *Political Studies,* 48: 66–87.

Sartre, J.-P. (undated) *Being and Nothingness.* New York: Philosophical Library.

Schmitt, F.F. (ed.) (1994) *Socializing Epistemology: The Social Dimensions of Knowledge.* Lanham, MD: Rowman & Littlefield.

Schopenhauer, A. ([1819] 1995) *The World as Will and Idea.* London: Everyman.

Scott, P. (1995) *The Meanings of Mass Higher Education.* Buckingham: Open University Press.

Scott, P. (1997a) The crisis of knowledge and the massification of higher education, in R. Barnett and A. Griffin (eds) *The End of Knowledge in Higher Education.* London: Cassell.

Scott, P. (1997b) The postmodern university?, in A. Smith and F. Webster (eds) *The Postmodern University? Contested Visions of Higher Education in Society.* Buckingham: Open University Press.

Scott, P. (1997c) The changing role of the university in the production of new knowledge, *Tertiary Education and Management,* 3(1): 5–14.

Scott, P. (ed.) (1998a) *The Globalization of Higher Education.* Buckingham: Open University Press.

Scott, P. (1998b) Massification, internationalization and globalization, in P. Scott (ed.) *The Globalization of Higher Education.* Buckingham: Open University Press.

Scott, P. (2000) A tale of three revolutions? Science, society and the university, in P. Scott (ed.) *Higher Education Reformed.* London: Falmer Press.

Searle, J. (1995) *The Construction of Social Reality*. London: Allen Lane.

Siegel, H. (1997) *Rationality Redeemed: Further Dialogues on an Educational Ideal*. New York: Routledge.

Simons, H.W. and Billig, M. (eds) (1994) *After Postmodernism: Reconstructing Ideology Critique*. London: Sage.

Skinner, Q. (ed.) (1985) *The Return of Grand Theory in the Human Sciences*. Cambridge: Cambridge University Press.

Slaughter, S. and Leslie, L.L. (1997) *Academic Capitalism: Politics, Policies and the Entrepreneurial University*. Baltimore, MD: Johns Hopkins University Press.

Smith, A. and Webster, F. (eds) (1997) *The Postmodern University? Contested Visions of Higher Education in Society*. Buckingham: Open University Press.

Smith, H., Armstrong, M. and Brown, S. (eds) (1999) *Benchmarking and Threshold Standards in Higher Education*. London: Kogan Page.

Snow, C.P. ([1959] 1978) *The Two Cultures and a Second Look*. London: Cambridge University Press.

Squires, J. (ed.) (1994) *Principled Positions: Postmodernism and the Rediscovery of Value*. London: Lawrence & Wishart.

Stehr, N. (1994) *Knowledge Societies*. London: Sage.

Stehr, N. (2001) *The Fragility of Modern Societies: Knowledge and Risk in the Information Age*. London: Sage.

Steiner, G. (1976) *After Babel: Aspects of Language and Translation*. Oxford: Oxford University Press.

Steiner, G. (1998) *Errata: An Examined Life*. London: Weidenfeld & Nicolson.

Stone, L. (1983) Social control and intellectual excellence: Oxbridge and Edinburgh 1560–1983, in N. Phillipson (ed.) *Universities, Society and the Future*. Edinburgh: Edinburgh University Press.

Tapper, T. and Palfreyman, D. (2000) *Oxford and the Decline of the Collegiate Tradition*. London: Woburn.

Taylor, P.G. (1999) *Making Sense of Academic Life: Academics, Universities and Change*. Buckingham: Open University Press.

Taylor, R., Barr, J. and Steele, T. (2002) *For a Radical Higher Education: After Postmodernism*. Buckingham: SRHE and Open University Press.

Thompson, J.B. (1985) *Studies in the Theory of Ideology*. Cambridge: Polity Press.

Thompson, J.B. ([1988] 1996) *Ideology and Modern Culture*. Cambridge: Polity Press.

Thorne, M. (ed.) (1999) *Universities in the Future*. London: Department of Trade and Industry.

Tight, M. (ed.) (2000) *Academic Work and Life: What it is to be an Academic, and how this is Changing*. New York: Elsevier Science.

Tight, M. (2002) What does it mean to be a professor?, *Higher Education Review*, 34(2): 15–32.

Toulmin, S. (2001) *Return to Reason*. Cambridge, MA: Harvard University Press.

Tribe, J. (2002) The philosophic practitioner, *Annals of Tourism Research*, 29(2): 338–57.

Trow, M. (1992) Thoughts on the White Paper of 1991, *Higher Education Quarterly*, 46(3): 213–26.

Trowler, P. (1998) *Academics Responding to Change: New Higher Education Frameworks and Academic Cultures*. Buckingham: Open University Press.

Trowler, P. (ed.) (2002) *Higher Education Policy and Institutional Change: Intentions and Outcomes in Turbulent Environments*. Buckingham: Open University Press.

Trowler, P. and Knight, P. (2002) Exploring the implementation gap: theory and practices in change interventions, in P. Trowler (ed.) *Higher Educational Policy and Institutional Change: Intentions and Outcomes in Turbulent Environments.* Buckingham: Open University Press.

Urry, J. (1998) Contemporary transformations of time and space, in P. Scott (ed.) *The Globalization of Higher Education.* Buckingham: Open University Press.

van Dijk, T.A. (1998) *Ideology: A Multidisciplinary Approach.* London: Sage.

Velody, R. and Williams, R. (eds) (1998) *The Politics of Constructivism.* London: Sage.

Virilio, P. (1994) *The Lost Dimension.* New York: Semiotext(e).

Warner, D. and Palfreyman, D. (eds) (2001) *The State of Higher Education: Managing Change and Diversity.* Buckingham: Open University Press.

Watson, D. (2000) *Managing Strategy.* Buckingham: Open University Press.

Webster, F. (2001) The postmodern university? The loss of purpose in British universities, in S. Lax (ed.) *Access Denied in the Information Age.* London: Palgrave.

White, M. (2002) *Rivals: Conflict as the Fuel of Science.* London: Vintage.

Williams, R. (1977) *Marxism and Literature.* Oxford: Oxford University Press.

Williams, R. (1988) *Key Words: A Vocabulary of Culture and Society.* London: Fontana.

Williams, R. (1989) *Resources of Hope: Culture, Democracy, Socialism.* London: Verso.

Winter, R. (1995) The University of Life, plc, in J. Smyth (ed.) *Academic Work.* Buckingham: Open University Press.

Wittgenstein, L. ([1953] 1978) *Philosophical Investigations.* Oxford: Blackwell.

Wolff, R.P. (1997) *The Ideal of the University.* New Brunswick, NJ: Transaction.

Wortham, S. (1999) *Rethinking the University: Leverage and Deconstruction.* Manchester: Manchester University Press.

Young, R. (1989) *A Critical Theory of Education: Habermas and our Children's Future.* Hemel Hempstead: Harvester Wheatsheaf.

Zizek, S. (1999) *The Sublime Object of Ideology,* 8th imprint. London: New Left Books.

Reports

ACU (2001) *Engagement as a Core Value for the University: A Consultation Document.* London: Association of Commonwealth Universities.

CVCP (1997) evidence to Dearing 8/4.

J.M. Consulting *et al.* (2000) *Interactions Between Research, Teaching and Other Activities.* Report to the Higher Education Funding Council for England and Wales as part of the Fundamental Review of Research Policy and Funding. Bristol: J.M. Consulting Ltd.

NCIHE (1997) *Universities in a Learning Society.* Report of the National Committee of Inquiry (the Dearing Report). London: HMSO.

QAA (2000) *History.* Subject Benchmark Statements. Gloucester: Quality Assurance Agency.

Newspaper articles

Baty, P. (2001) Russell elite go for jugular of ailing QAA, *Times Higher Education Supplement,* 21 September, p. 1.

Boseley, S. (2002) Scandal of scientists who take money for papers ghostwritten by drug companies, *The Guardian,* 7 February, p. 4.

Leon, P. (2000) Risk is now an option, *Times Higher Education Supplement*, 12 May, p. 37.

Maslen, G. (2000) Global group [Universitas 21] is close to deal with multinational, *Times Higher Education Supplement*, 12 May, p. 13 (cf. Universitas 21 – see under websites below).

Scott, P. (2002) High wire (Not only has ideology been ostracised, but ideas seem to be out of fashion), *The Guardian – Education Supplement*, 5 March, p. 12.

Vasagar, J. (2001) Rise of the wealthy Oxford scientists, *The Guardian*, 21 April, p. 7.

Websites

Foresight programme: http://www.foresight.gov.uk/

Review of University management and governance issues arising out of the CAPAS project: a report prepared for the Audit Committee and the Board of Scrutiny of University of Cambridge, England, by Professor Michael Shattock: http://www.admin.cam.ac.uk/reporter/2001–02/weekly/5861/5

The Observatory on borderless higher education: http://www.obhe.ac.uk/news

Universitas 21: http://www.universitas.edu.au

Author Index

Subject Index

Page numbers in bold indicate key references.

The Society for Research into Higher Education

The Society for Research into Higher Education (SRHE), an international body, exists to stimulate and coordinate research into all aspects of higher eduction. It aims to improve the quality of higher education through the encouragement of debate and publication on issues of policy, on the organization and management of higher education institutions, and on the curriculum, teaching and learning methods.

The Society is entirely independent and receives no subsidies, although individual events often receive sponsorship from business or industry. The Society is financed through corporate and individual subscriptions and has members from many parts of the world. It is an NGO of UNESCO.

Under the imprint *SRHE & Open University Press*, the Society is a specialist publisher of research, having over 80 titles in print. In addition to *SRHE News*, the Society's newsletter, the Society publishes three journals: *Studies in Higher Education* (three issues a year), *Higher Education Quarterly* and *Research into Higher Education Abstracts* (three issues a year).

The Society runs frequent conferences, consultations, seminars and other events. The annual conference in December is organized at and with a higher education institution. There are a growing number of networks which focus on particular areas of interest, including:

Access	Learning Environment
Assessment	Legal Education
Consultants	Managing Innovation
Curriculum Development	New Technology for Learning
Eastern European	Postgraduate Issues
Educational Development Research	Quantitative Studies
FE/HE	Student Development
Funding	Vocational Qualifications
Graduate Employment	

Benefits to members

Individual

- The opportunity to participate in the Society's networks
- Reduced rates for the annual conferences
- Free copies of *Research into Higher Education Abstracts*

- Reduced rates for *Studies in Higher Education*
- Reduced rates for *Higher Education Quarterly*
- Free copy of *Register of Members' Research Interests* – includes valuable reference material on research being pursued by the Society's members
- Free copy of occasional in-house publications, e.g. *The Thirtieth Anniversary Seminars Presented by the Vice-Presidents*
- Free copies of *SRHE News* which informs members of the Society's activities and provides a calendar of events, with additional material provided in regular mailings
- A 35 per cent discount on all SRHE/Open University Press books
- The opportunity for you to apply for the annual research grants
- Inclusion of your research in the *Register of Members' Research Interests*

Corporate

- Reduced rates for the annual conferences
- The opportunity for members of the Institution to attend SRHE's network events at reduced rates
- Free copies of *Research into Higher Education Abstracts*
- Free copies of *Studies in Higher Education*
- Free copies of *Register of Members' Research Interests* – includes valuable reference material on research being pursued by the Society's members
- Free copy of occasional in-house publications
- Free copies of *SRHE News*
- A 35 per cent discount on all SRHE/Open University Press books
- The opportunity for members of the Institution to submit applications for the Society's research grants
- The opportunity to work with the Society and co-host conferences
- The opportunity to include in the *Register of Members' Research Interests* your Institution's research into aspects of higher education

Membership details: SRHE, 76 Portland Place, London W1B 1NT, UK Tel: 020 7637 2766. Fax: 020 7637 2781. email: srhe@mailbox.ulcc.ac.uk world wide web: http://www.srhe.ac.uk./srhe/
Catalogue: SRHE & Open University Press, Celtic Court, 22 Ballmoor, Buckingham MK18 1XW. Tel: 01280 823388. Fax: 01280 823233. email: enquiries@openup.co.uk

REALIZING THE UNIVERSITY
in an age of supercomplexity

Ronald Barnett

The University has lost its way. The world needs the university more than ever but for new reasons. If we are to clarify its new role in the world, we need to find a new vocabulary and a new sense of purpose.

The university is faced with *supercomplexity*, in which our very frames of understanding, action and self-identity are all continually challenged. In such a world, the university has explicitly to take on a dual role: firstly, of compounding super-complexity, so making the world ever more challenging; and secondly, of enabling us to live effectively in this chaotic world. Internally, too, the university has to become a new kind of organization, adept at fulfilling this dual role. The university has to live by the uncertainty principle: it has to generate uncertainty, to help us live with uncertainty, and even to revel in our uncertainty.

Ronald Barnett offers nothing less than a fundamental reworking of the way in which we understand the modern university. *Realizing the University* is essential reading for all those concerned about the future of higher education.

Contents

224pp   0 335 20248 9 (Paperback)   0 335 20249 7 (Hardback)

MANAGING THE LEARNING UNIVERSITY

Chris Duke

This book debunks prevailing modern management theories and fashions as applied to higher education. At the same time it provides practical guidance for a clear and easily understood set of principles as to how universities and colleges can be re-energized and their staff mobilized to be effective in meeting the growing and changing needs of the global knowledge society. It is anchored in knowledge of management and organizational theory and in the literature about higher education which is critiqued from a clear theoretical perspective based on and tested through long experience of university management and leadership.

Chris Duke offers challenging advice for managers in tertiary and higher education – from self-managing knowledge workers who may feel themselves to be the new academic proletariat, through to institutional heads, some of whose attempts to manage using strategic planning, management-by-objectives and other techniques seriously unravel because they fail to benefit from the talents and networks which make up the rich 'underlife' of the institution. Loss of institutional memory and failure to tap tacit know-how and mobilize commitment through genuine consultation and shared participatory management inhibits organizational learning and generates apathy – or drives staff dedication and creativity into oppositional channels.

Managing the Learning University indicates how higher education institutions can link and network their internal energies with external opportunities and partners to be successful and dynamic learning organizations. It points the way to enabling an enterprising and valued university to thrive in hard times, and to be a community where it is actually a pleasure to work.

Contents

176pp   0 335 20765 0 (Paperback)   0 335 20766 9 (Hardback)

ACADEMIC TRIBES AND TERRITORIES
INTELLECTUAL ENQUIRY AND THE CULTURES OF DISCIPLINES
Second Edition

Tony Becher and Paul R. Trowler

Acclaim for the first edition of *Academic Tribes and Territories:*

Becher's insistence upon in-depth analysis of the extant literature while reporting his own sustained research doubled the thickness of the material to be covered . . . Academic Tribes and Territories is a superb addition to the literature on higher education . . . There is here an education to be had.

Higher Education

Becher's landmark work. The higher education community – both practitioners and educational researchers – need to assimilate and to heed the message of this important and insightful book.

Journal of Higher Education

. . . a bold approach to a theory of academic relations . . . The result is a debt to him [Becher] for all students of higher education.

The Times Educational Supplement

. . . a classic in its field . . . The book is readily accessible to any member of the academic profession, but it also adds significantly to a specialist understanding of the internal life of higher education institutions in Britain and North America. I confidently predict that it will appear prominently on citation indices for many years.

Studies in Higher Education

How do academics perceive themselves and colleagues in their own disciplines, and how do they rate those in other subjects? How closely related are their intellectual tasks and their ways of organizing their professional lives? What are the interconnections between academic cultures and the nature of disciplines? *Academic Tribes and Territories* maps academic knowledge and explores the diverse characteristics of those who inhabit and cultivate it.

This second edition provides a thorough update to Tony Becher's classic text, first published in 1989, and incorporates research findings and new theoretical perspectives. Fundamental changes in the nature of higher education and in the academic's role are reviewed and their significance for academic cultures is assessed. This edition moves beyond the first edition's focus on elite universities and the research role to examine academic cultures in lower status institutions internationally and to place a new emphasis on issues of gender and ethnicity. This second edition successfully renews a classic in the field of higher education.

Contents
Landscapes, tribal territories and academic cultures – Points of departure – Academic disciplines – Overlaps, boundaries and specialisms – Aspects of community life – Patterns of communication – Academic careers – The wider context – Implications for theory and practice – Appendix: Data for the initial study – Bibliography – Index – The Society for Research into Higher Education.

c.256pp   0 335 20627 1 (Paperback)   0 335 20628 X (Hardback)